SHIPWRECKS
OF THE
CUNARD LINE

SHIPWRECKS
OF THE
CUNARD LINE

SAM WARWICK AND MIKE ROUSSEL

The
History
Press

Harry Harding.

Harry Harding
(21 September 1920 – 21 June 2011)

The authors dedicate this book to the memory of Harry Harding who was a survivor from the sinking of the *Lancastria* in June 1940.

Harry Harding was determined during his lifetime to ensure that the memory of those that lost their lives in this terrible disaster will never be forgotten.

To that end Harry Harding was very keen to share his personal experiences of that fateful day for inclusion in this book.

Sam Warwick & Mike Roussel

First published 2012

This edition first published in 2018

The History Press
The Mill, Brimscombe Port
Stroud, Gloucestershire, GL5 2QG
www.thehistorypress.co.uk

British Library Cataloguing in Publication Data.
A catalogue record for this book is available from the British Library.

ISBN 978 0 7509 8538 3
Typesetting and origination by The History Press
Printed in India by Thomson Press

CONTENTS

~ ACKNOWLEDGEMENTS ~

Sam Warwick

EVER SINCE MY discovery of a small broken piece of crested Cunard china on a dive to the *Aurania* in 1996, I have talked of writing a book on Cunard shipwrecks. When I first started my research all those years ago one of the first people I corresponded with was John Chatterton, who had recently dived to the *Lusitania*, and I would like to thank him for writing the foreword. It was not until I met Mike Roussel in 2009 that this publication started to become a reality. Without Mike's experience, encouragement and wisdom this book might never have been written.

A considerable number of people have contributed knowledge, time and content for this book. However, first and foremost I want to give special thanks to the underwater photographers whose stunning images have brought the pages of the book to life. In particular I would like to thank my friend Catherine de Lara, who has contributed fantastic images for four of the wrecks (*Malta*, *Alaunia*, *Ascania* and *Campania*). I am very grateful to Leigh Bishop of Deep Image for sharing some of his highly regarded *Lusitania* photographs. My thanks go to Bradley Sheard for allowing me to use his beautiful image of the *Oregon*, along with Tim White for his pictures of the wreck. Thank you to Barry McGill for the *Carinthia* photographs and allowing me to reproduce extracts from his dive report. Only one diver has taken photographs of the *Carpathia* and I give special thanks to Ric Waring for sharing them and his recollections of the dive. I am grateful to all the other divers who have provided their photographs: Cliff Vachon (*Curlew*), Dave Riordan (*Folia*), Hervé Sévère (*Thracia*), Paul Mee (*Flavia*), Ian Derrick and Tom Forwood (*Aurania*). My thanks go to Gregg Bemis, owner of the *Lusitania*, for providing his unique underwater photograph. I would like to thank Dianne Strong for her and Ron Strong's unique photographs of *Caribia* (ex-*Caronia*) taken in 1974, and also her generosity and contribution to the *Caribia* story. In addition to taking photographs in Guam of *Scotia* and *Caribia*, my good friend Stanley Haviland has provided help in many other ways. Thank you to another special friend, Steve Metcalfe, for additional *Malta* photos. A warm thank you goes out to Timmy Carey, not just for his *Folia* photos, but for sharing his great knowledge of the wrecks in southern Ireland, especially the *Lusitania* and *Feltria*. Finally, thank you to Tim Cashman for allowing me to publish stills from his video footage of the *Andania*.

Further to the underwater photographers and videographers named above, I would like to thank all the other divers who have helped me in so many ways, especially with the wrecks that I have not dived personally. First of all I would like to thank the rest of my very good friends in the '4/5ths Technical' team from the *Ascania* 2006 expedition and other diving adventures: Johno de Lara, Mick 'Mad Dog' Cullen and the late Phil Waddington, who sadly passed away before this book could be completed. A very special thank you goes to Stewart Andrews for all his help and contributions regarding the deep wrecks in Irish waters. Another diver from Ireland I would like to thank is Eoin McGarry.

I would like to express my sincere gratitude to Paul Edwards for all his contributions and help regarding the wrecks of *Scotia* and *Caribia* in Guam. Andrew Trent deserves a special thank you for assistance with the *Lusitania*. Herb Kassmann has provided valuable information on the *Oregon* wreck and also let me use material from his excellent book. I also thank Evelyn Dudas for her help with the *Oregon*. Two *Carpathia* divers that have helped me in numerous ways are Helmuth Biechl and Zaid Al-obaidi. I am very grateful to Mark Dixon of the Dark Star technical dive team for sharing information about the deep wrecks in the Northern Approaches. Two other diving friends that I would like to acknowledge are Alan English and Mike Whitworth. My thanks to Dr Geoff Vernon for the recent *Aurania* artefact photo.

The following dive boat captains and operators deserve my thanks: Ben Slater of Land's End Diving (*Malta*), Mark Blyth of Dive Bunker (*Campania*), Mike Keane of Sussex Shipwrecks and Dave Ronnan of Dive 125 (*Alaunia*), Steve Bielenda (Long Island) and Will Naden (Guam). Finally, a very special thank you to Rick Stanley of Ocean Quest for making the *Ascania* expedition so much fun and a great success.

Numerous maritime historians, both amateur and professional, have helped in many ways, which have included providing photographs of ships and artefacts.

So thank you to: Brian Hawley, David Barron, Eric Sauder, John Langley, Michel Perrin, Rich Turnwald, Stewart Wilson, Ian Lawler and Ian Boyle.

I would like to express my further gratitude to the following people who have provided images: Captain Lacey, John Hudson, Yasuma Ogawa, Petr Stach, Martin Dean of ADUS and Philip Robertson of Historic Scotland. My thanks also to Claudia Jew of Mariners Museum.

Thank you to the following people who have provided personal stories and memorabilia, all of whom have relatives with connections to the ships in this book: John Humphreys, Elizabeth O'Reilly, Ian McAllister and Patrick Lynch.

Both Mike and I are extremely grateful to the maritime artists who have provided artwork for this book. Firstly to Robert Lloyd (www.robertlloyd.co.uk) for his cover painting of the *Malta* and other works contained within the book. Thank you to Stuart Williamson (website.lineone.net/~stu_williamson) for his amazing underwater renderings of the wrecks of *Carpathia* and *Lusitania*. Finally, thank you to Simon Fisher (www.simonfishermaritime.com) for his wonderful line drawing of the *Thracia*.

My thanks go to Chris Frame for introducing me to The History Press and to Amy Rigg and her colleagues there for embracing the concept of this book.

The following people also deserve credit for assistance: Ian Gledhill, Owen Griffin, Stephen Nash-Williams and Stephen Payne. I would also like to thank my colleagues at Odin Technology for supporting this endeavour and giving me the most valuable gift of time.

I would like to thank the following members of my family: my father Commodore Ron Warwick, for assistance in researching the material for this book and providing advice and guidance since the project's inception; my stepmother Kim Warwick for all her encouragement and support. Sincere thanks to my mother Karen for instilling in me an insatiable appetite for books and reading since an early age. I am grateful to my sister Rebecca for all her help reviewing the manuscript.

Last, but by no means least, the biggest thank you of all goes to my wife Hilary and daughter Beth.

Mike Roussel

IT HAS BEEN a great pleasure working with my co-author Sam Warwick and learning about the fascinating world of sports and technical diving. I thank all the divers that have contributed their knowledge and expertise to the book.

I am deeply indebted to Commodore Ron Warwick OBE for his advice and support from his extensive knowledge and experience as a master mariner, and also both Commodore Warwick and Kim Warwick for their hospitality during the time Sam and I worked together on the book in Somerset.

It was the raising of the *Mary Rose* that first captured my interest in shipwrecks and then the discovery of the *Titanic* that led to a deeper interest in the subject. By the 1990s I had moved to Hampshire and became deeply interested in the maritime history of Southampton, and this led to writing two books on the subject.

I am indebted to the advice and support for my research from the staff of the Hampshire County Library Service, Southampton Archives and the Southampton Maritime Museum. My thanks also go to all the ex-mariners who sailed in and out of Southampton and were keen to enlighten me to what it was like working on the Cunarders. They include: Pat Royl, John Fahy, Geoffrey Le Marquand, Barbara Pedan, Gordon Brown, Jim Taylor, John Merry, Gus Shanahan, Robbie Peck and Geoff Bradley.

My grateful and sincere thanks go to Bert Moody, Mick Lindsay, Mark Hirst, archivist at the Lancastria Association, Charles and James Hutton, Area 10 RNA, Nick Messinger, Tim Gedge and Derek and Adrian Harding for their support with photographs.

Finally, I must thank my wife Kay for her constant support and for putting up with me disappearing into my study for many hours at a time.

ABOUT THE AUTHORS

SAM WARWICK FIRST learned to dive with the British Sub-Aqua Club in his home country of England in the early 1990s and is a certified diving instructor and technical diver. Sam has logged over 1,000 dives around the world and is passionate about exploring and researching shipwrecks. He has dived many of the wrecks in this book personally. Sam has always had a personal interest in Cunard history due to family connections with the line, since both his father and grandfather were Cunard Line commodores.

He has written two other books with Mike Roussel: *Shipwrecks of the P&O Line*, and *The Union-Castle Line - Sailing Like Clockwork*.

MIKE ROUSSEL HAS always had a deep interest in history and historical studies, influenced by an inspirational history teacher who challenged him to engage in his own historical investigations. This experience led him later as a teacher to aim to develop challenging historical projects with his classes, including the development of oral history, investigating local history projects, which brought history to life for the pupils.

Mike has further developed his research studies interest into local history, and also the historical development of transport on land, sea and air.

After moving to Hampshire in the 1990s, he had the opportunity to research the maritime history of Southampton, and this resulted in *The Story of Southampton Docks*. Such was his interest that he continued his research to write a second book, *Southampton – Maritime City: From Ocean Liners to Cruise Ships*, which charts the development of the ocean liner from the nineteenth century to the cruise ships of today.

— FOREWORD —

BY JOHN CHATTERTON

SEVERAL YEARS AGO, my wife and I sailed aboard the Cunard liner *Queen Mary 2*, from New York to Rio de Janeiro. I was privileged to receive a tour of the ship by Commodore Ron Warwick. The *QM2* is a thoroughly modern super liner, with a state-of-the-art wheelhouse, propulsion and infrastructure. Of course, the ship offered all the luxuries you might expect from a five-star hotel, like spas, shopping, gyms, salons, pools and such. At the same time, I was able to watch the evening news on television in my suite, keep up with my email, and access the internet on my laptop. I was on vacation. It was fun, and it was safe.

But my experience aboard the *QM2* is so radically different from that of the ocean travellers of the late eighteenth and early nineteenth century, it is hard to even compare the two. Cunard and its competitors made ocean travel available, affordable, and modern. For the first hundred years or so, the passengers of Cunard wanted to travel the oceans to build new lives, to seek out new business and to reunite with family. Ocean travel to them was an inconvenient and even dangerous necessity. Cunard wanted to make ocean travel what it actually is today, and they did.

With all that Cunard did for ocean travel, there were inherent dangers, and infamous tragedies. Inclement weather, mechanical failures and acts of war all took a toll. The possibility of a vessel sinking from one of these causes was unlikely, but it was still a very real possibility. For the vessels unlucky enough to end up on the bottom, their career of ferrying passengers and cargo was abruptly over. However, with the invention of scuba diving technology shortly after the Second World War, some of these shipwrecks began second careers as destinations for underwater explorers.

What is it about shipwreck diving that attracts divers? If you ask a dozen different divers, you might get a dozen different answers. For me, I love the personal challenges. Divers need to know human physiology and decompression theory. We need to know our equipment, and how it operates. If it can fail, it will, so what is the plan when it does? What can be learned about the wreck we might be diving or looking for? If the wreck has been visited by divers before, what information have they brought back? How was the ship constructed? What are the dimensions? How deep is the water? What sort of drawings, photos, paintings or imagery is available for divers to study prior to diving? This helps us navigate the wreck, as well as set and accomplish any goals.

In many cases, executing these dives requires a certain level of physical stamina. Divers need to be fit, but they also need to possess mental toughness and discipline to survive. Venturing into the interior of a wreck, with more dark than light, requires a certain degree of skill, insight and courage. It is a moment of truth, and shipwrecks do not tolerate fools well. Deeper, more difficult wrecks are even more demanding.

With greater access to information and improved diving technologies, capable divers have been able to go deeper. This means we have been able to access shipwrecks that were previously beyond our reach. Air-breathing scuba divers were effectively limited to little more than 60m (200ft) of water. Now, technical divers using rebreathers and employing varying mixtures of helium, nitrogen and oxygen are able to access shipwrecks down to 120m (400ft) and beyond. Rebreather divers are diving on deeper wrecks and staying down longer.

Early in my wreck diving career, I enjoyed diving the wreck of the *Oregon*, off Long Island in New York. As I developed as a diver, I acquired more skills and looked for greater challenges. I was fortunate to join a British group in Kinsale, Ireland, where we made the first technical diving expedition to the wreck of the *Lusitania*. Today, deeper and more remote shipwrecks, like the *Carpathia*, tempt me. The Cunard wrecks are woven into pretty much every aspect of my personal dive history.

Shipwreck diving is a lot of hard work. It requires a significant allocation of resources; time, money, and energy are all going to be required. It often evolves from an avocation into a lifestyle. Wreck divers have to be passionate about what they do, or they would have already given up.

Sam Warwick is an accomplished and passionate diver, whose father helped to make Cunard what it is today. Mike Roussel is a dedicated researcher. The teaming of these two authors brings significant enthusiasm, attention to detail and affection for these wrecks and their history to the reader in a unique way. I expect divers and non-divers alike to be inspired by the story of Cunard, as told by these authors, through these shipwrecks.

~ INTRODUCTION ~

Here on the ocean floor is the only independence. Here I am free.
– Jules Verne (1828–1905), 20,000 *Leagues Under the Sea*

THE CUNARD LINE was founded in 1840 and its ships are still sailing the world's oceans to this day, making Cunard one of the oldest shipping companies in existence. During a period spanning nearly two centuries Cunard has owned and managed over 300 ships. Many of these fine vessels have become well-known names of the regular North Atlantic service such as *Lusitania*, *Mauretania*, *Queen Mary*, *Queen Elizabeth 2* and *Queen Mary 2*. Cunard also sailed to other destinations and was not just confined to passenger services. The history of the Cunard Line is well documented and many books have been published that recount the line's rich heritage and celebrate the diverse range of vessels during their time in service. However, the final fate of these ships is often little more than a footnote, with the ship being declared either scrapped or wrecked. Once a ship has been scrapped that really is the end of the story, with maybe just a few artefacts and mementos preserved in museums and private collections for posterity. But when a ship is lost at sea it becomes a shipwreck and that is when a whole new chapter begins. The aim of this book is to continue the story.

The Cunard Line has proudly maintained an exemplary safety record and has never lost a human life at sea through any fault of the company during peacetime. But the ships themselves have not always been so fortunate and no ship is ever unsinkable, as the *Titanic* so dramatically proved. A number of Cunard vessels were lost in the nineteenth century through adverse weather, navigational error and plain bad luck. By far the biggest single cause of losses in the twentieth century has been through acts of war. In the First World War alone over twenty ships were deliberately sunk through enemy action. Further ships were lost in the Second World War, including the *Lancastria*, along with thousands of lives. As recently as 1982 the container ship *Atlantic Conveyor* was sunk by missiles in the Falklands conflict.

Some shipwrecks gain notoriety after their loss and become well known to the public at large through media such as books, documentaries and even Hollywood movies. Obvious examples are the White Star Liner *Titanic* and Cunard's own *Lusitania*, which was controversially torpedoed in the midst of the First World War. However, there are thousands more sunken shipwrecks all over the world that are being explored on a regular basis by recreational scuba divers, and some of these are Cunard vessels.

Shipwrecks of the Cunard Line includes all ships that at some point in their lifespan have been owned by Cunard. The diveable Cunard wrecks span a period that is almost as long and diverse as the company's history itself, taking us from the loss of the *Curlew* in 1856 to the *Caribia* (ex-*Caronia*) in 1974. Although the majority of the losses are concentrated in the waters of the British Isles, some are as remote as the *Ascania* in Newfoundland and *Scotia* off Guam in the Pacific. Some are in shallow depths, diveable by all levels of diver, such as the *Malta* off the coast of Cornwall, England. Others are deep, technical dives, reachable by a select few divers, such as the famous *Titanic* rescue ship *Carpathia*, 158m down (518ft) and 260 miles out in the Atlantic.

Divers explore wrecks for all sorts of different reasons. For some it is the excitement of recovering a special artefact, such as a brass porthole or crest-bearing crockery. Others may be interested in the diverse range of marine life for which wrecks make an excellent habitat. Many like to record their dives with underwater cameras and video. For most, just the excitement of being underwater and seeing a part of history revealed is the reward.

As diving equipment and methods evolve, new wreck discoveries continue to be made, many in deeper waters further from shore. Technical divers are now routinely making dives to depths in excess of 100m (328ft) and locating new wrecks such as the *Flavia* off the northern coast of Ireland. However, there remain more than fifty Cunard shipwrecks that have still not been found or lie in waters too deep for scuba divers. In 1895 the *Java* simply went missing en route from San Francisco to Queenstown and was never heard of again. The *Andania* (2) lies in water over 2 miles deep after being torpedoed in the Second World War. These and other ships are described in the final chapter.

Once settled on the seabed, shipwrecks are by no means static structures and are in a continual state of decay and collapse. Eventually nothing recognisable will remain and many of the images shown in the pages that follow will not be there for future generations to experience. It is hoped that non-diving readers will enjoy learning about the new era of these ships beneath the waves. Maybe some will be tempted to consider taking up diving and explore shipwrecks for themselves. For those that already dive, maybe their dives will become a little more rewarding through knowing the past history of the ships. The wrecks in the last chapter could serve as inspiration for making new diving discoveries. Appendix A contains more information on the main wrecks and is intended to assist qualified divers in their dive planning.

Please see the companion website for the book, www.cunardshipwrecks.com, for video clips of dives to some of the wrecks and other resources relating to the shipwrecks in this book.

~ INTRODUCTION ~
TO THE SECOND EDITION

THE YEAR 2015 marked the 175th anniversary of the formation of the Cunard Line and the historic July 1840 maiden transatlantic crossing of the *Britannia* from Britain to America. Cunard celebrated the occasion with numerous special events throughout the year, one of which was the meeting of the three Queen liners in Liverpool on 25 May; *Queen Victoria*, *Queen Elizabeth* and the flagship *Queen Mary 2*. Earlier the same month *Queen Victoria* had sailed on a special voyage to Ireland in order to commemorate the centenary of the sinking of the *Lusitania*, which was torpedoed off Old Head of Kinsale on 7 May 1915. The international diving community also paid tribute to the liner's loss by laying a plaque at the wreck site. The *Lusitania* was the first of over twenty Cunard vessels to be lost during the course of the First World War and many of the other centenaries have been similarly acknowledged.

Since the first publication of *Shipwrecks of the Cunard Line* in 2012 further information has come to light on Cunard's long history and the many vessels of the fleet. Two ships previously believed to have ended their careers by shipwreck are now known to have had different fates; the *Caledonia* was scrapped in 1860 and the *Hibernia* was decommissioned in 1865 after many years sailing as *Velasco*

for the Spanish Navy. These ships have both been removed from the Other Losses chapter, along with the five First World War vessels managed by Cunard Line and two chartered vessels, *Vandyck* and *Vestris*. This has made way for eight new shipwrecks whose fates had previously been recorded as either unknown or scrapped. One such example of the latter is the *Albania* (2) which was sunk by British aircraft in the Second World War while being employed as the Italian hospital ship *California*.

Some of the diving information has been updated to reflect changes to the wrecks in recent years, such as the *Folia*, from which the distinctive anti-aircraft gun has been raised from the seabed and placed on permanent display overlooking the sea in the town of Ardmore. As deep-water underwater survey technology continues to evolve, new wrecks are being discovered such as the *Transylvania*, located in 2011 at a depth of 630m (2,067ft).

The Cunard Line fleet list in Appendix B has been extensively revised to reflect the latest known information. The authors would like to acknowledge the excellent *Cunard Line: A Fleet History* by Peter Newall (2012), which has been an invaluable resource for the revised edition of *Shipwrecks of the Cunard Line*.

Authors' Note

One of the challenges when researching Cunard history is the amount of ships with similar names and the reuse of the same name multiple times. The convention adopted by many and employed in this book, where appropriate, is to place a numeric suffix in brackets after the name. For example, the first ship to be called *Andania* in 1913 is *Andania* (1) and the later vessel constructed in 1922 is *Andania* (2).

This book has entailed many years of research that has included travelling around the world to dive many of the wrecks in person. For wrecks not dived by the author, first-hand accounts from other divers have been sought where possible. Every effort has been made to ensure the accuracy of both the history and wrecks described within these pages. However, the authors would welcome any feedback from readers who have any new or updated information.

Disclaimer

The activity of recreational scuba diving, and in particular wreck diving, requires specialised training and instruction through study, education and in-water teaching. This book does not purport to offer any kind of substitute for seeking professional instruction through the established professional training agencies. The diving techniques and practices recounted are presented in their historical context and do not constitute, advocate or promote any given approach. It should also be noted that scuba diving is a constantly evolving pursuit and as such the equipment, technique and best practices adapt accordingly.

I

~ CUNARD LINE ~

THE BRITISH AND North American Royal Mail Steam Packet Company was formed in 1839 and formally incorporated in May 1840. The company very soon became known more simply as the Cunard Line, after the company founder Samuel Cunard. The original objective of the company was to establish a regular steamship service for transporting mail across the Atlantic Ocean from Great Britain to North America. The first ship built specifically for this purpose was the 1,150-ton wooden paddle steamer *Britannia*. Despite surviving periods of intense competition from other shipping lines and in more recent decades air travel, the Cunard Line remains as the only company to regularly cross the North Atlantic with their 150,000-ton liner *Queen Mary 2*. The ships of the modern-day Cunard fleet still carry the name of the company founder proudly on their sides and sport the same distinctive red and black funnel.

Samuel Cunard

Samuel Cunard was born in Halifax, Nova Scotia, on 21 November 1787. He was the great-great-grandson of Thones Kunders, a German Quaker who had immigrated to Germantown, Philadelphia, in 1683. Samuel was the second son of Abraham Cunard, a master carpenter who relocated to Halifax in 1783. After completing school, Samuel served an apprenticeship for a shipping agent in Boston. By this time he was already demonstrating a strong set of business skills and went into partnership with his father to form the shipping company A. Cunard & Son in 1812. The first vessel purchased by the company was a small sailing ship called the *Margaret*, which operated on the coastal trade between Halifax and nearby ports. A second ship *Nancy* soon followed and was captained by Samuel's younger brother, William Cunard. Later, in 1823, William was travelling as a passenger on board *Wyton* when the vessel was lost off Cape North, Cape Breton. Sadly William was drowned and this was a cruel reminder to Cunard of the inherent risks associated with sea travel. They were risks that the young Cunard was already all too well aware, as evidenced by his appointment as a commissioner of the lighthouses in 1816.

In 1813 the Cunards purchased their first full-rigged sailing ship at auction, the *White Oak*, which became the first Cunard ship to cross the Atlantic on the London trade. Other Cunard vessels sailed regularly to the Caribbean, importing spirits, brown sugar and coffee from ports such as those in Jamaica and Trinidad.

In 1815 A. Cunard & Son secured their first official contract with the Royal Mail carrying monthly mails between Halifax and Bermuda. In 1816 this was extended to include Boston. The company continued to expand and purchase additional sailing ships and it also operated other businesses, including coal, logging, whaling and an ironworks. At the end of the decade Abraham Cunard retired and Samuel took over the business. In 1824 he renamed the company Samuel Cunard & Company, which was later shortened to S. Cunard & Company. By the end of the decade more than forty-five sailing ships were registered to Samuel Cunard. In 1825, with his typical eye for business, Samuel Cunard saw that there was a need for real tea to satisfy the population of Nova Scotia, many of whom were of English extraction. He sailed to London and made a successful approach to the East India Company to secure the exclusive agency rights in Halifax.

Cunard's first significant involvement in steam-powered ships began in 1825 when he purchased stock in the newly

Sir Samuel Cunard (1787–1865), founder of the Cunard Line.

The first ship to be built for the Cunard Line was the *Britannia* in 1840, shown here conducting builders' trials on the Clyde. *(Courtesy of Robert Lloyd)*

formed Québec and Halifax Steam Navigation Company. This resulted in the construction of the 1,370-ton *Royal William* in 1831. Although originally intended for service between Québec and the Atlantic colonies, the ship was not a commercial success. The owners decided to send the *Royal William* to Europe in order to be sold. In doing so the ship became one of the first vessels to cross the Atlantic Ocean almost entirely under steam power. By 1838 several other vessels made the crossing by steam, including *Sirius*, *Great Western* and *Liverpool*. This convinced Samuel Cunard that: 'Steamers, properly built and manned, might start and arrive at their destinations with the punctuality of railway trains on land.'

British and North American Royal Mail Steam Packet Company

In November 1838 the British Government invited tenders for a North Atlantic mail service from Liverpool to Halifax and Boston. Samuel Cunard was unable to secure any financial backing locally so in January 1839 he travelled to England to present his plans to the Admiralty. Cunard had actually missed the official deadline for submission but was able to make use of his extensive connections to ensure his proposal was given consideration. This demonstrated Cunard's confidence as at this stage he had neither financial backing nor a builder for the ships. However, the Admiralty were suitably impressed and on 4 May a formal

contract was signed between the Lords of the Admiralty and Cunard. The seven-year contract was worth £55,000 per annum and mandated a fortnightly mail service between Liverpool and Halifax for eight months of the year, reduced to once a month in winter.

Cunard's proposal was based on a service that would be maintained by three identical ships and the next step was for him to find a suitable shipbuilder. The secretary of the East India Company introduced him to Robert Napier of Glasgow, who had already constructed a steamship for his own company. Cunard's requirement was simple: 'I want a plain and comfortable boat, with not the least unnecessary expense for show.' Napier was keen to be a partner in the venture but felt strongly that Cunard would need slightly larger ships than those envisaged and that a fourth ship should be added. Consequently additional investors were sought in order to raise further funding and Napier introduced Cunard to three other Scots: James Donaldson, George Burns and David MacIver. This resulted in the founding of the British and North American Royal Mail Steam Packet Company, with a capital of £270,000. Cunard was the biggest investor with a stake of £55,000 for 20 per cent of the business, which soon became known more simply as the 'Cunard Line'. Due to the larger ships and the additional vessel, the company were able to renegotiate the terms of the contract with the government. This resulted in an increased annual fee of £60,000 on the condition that the service was extended to include Boston, and a new contract was signed on 4 July 1839.

The Boston 'Loving Cup' that was presented to Samuel Cunard on *Britannia*'s first call to Boston in 1840. This is now traditionally carried on the Cunard Line flagship and is currently on *QM2*. *(Warwick Family Collection)*

The final order was placed for four steamers of similar design to be named *Britannia*, *Acadia*, *Caledonia* and *Columbia*. The names of the vessels were chosen to reflect the development of Cunard, and were in reference to Great Britain, Nova Scotia, Scotland and America. Cunard also required an additional ship to operate as a feeder service between Pictou and Québec for the mail travelling overland from Halifax to Pictou. The Burns Line steamer *Unicorn* was purchased for this purpose and sailed on 15 May 1840 under the command of Captain Walter Douglas. Among the twenty-seven passengers was one of Cunard's sons, Samuel Cunard Jr.

Not long afterwards the *Britannia* was completed and placed under the command of Captain Henry Woodruff RN. The ship left Liverpool on 4 July 1840 for her maiden voyage with sixty-three passengers on board, including Samuel Cunard and his daughter Ann. At a speed of 8½–9 knots, the crossing to Halifax took twelve days ten hours, arriving at 2 a.m. on 17 July. Owing to the arrival in the early hours, the welcome celebrations were somewhat subdued and by 9 a.m. *Britannia* had already sailed for Boston. When the ship arrived in Boston later the next day the reception was much more extravagant and three days later the local residents celebrated 'Cunard Festival Day'. At a special dinner Samuel Cunard was presented with a large ornate commemorative silver vase engraved with a picture of *Britannia*. This later became known as the 'Loving Cup' and has remained with the company to this day, and for many years it was displayed on the *Queen Elizabeth 2* outside the nightclub. The cup was later transferred to *Queen Mary 2* when the new ship took over the modern-day transatlantic service in 2004.

The *Acadia* was the next vessel to sail on 4 August the same year, followed by *Caledonia* on 19 September. Finally, *Columbia* departed on 5 January 1841 for a winter Atlantic crossing. It soon became clear that the company had underestimated their operating costs and once again were able to renegotiate the terms of the Admiralty contract. This time the remuneration was increased to £81,000 on the condition that a fifth vessel was added to the fleet and the *Hibernia* entered service in April 1843. The new ship proved essential because a few months later Cunard Line suffered their first loss when the *Columbia* grounded in thick fog off Cape Sable. A sister ship to the *Hibernia*, *Cambria*, was swiftly ordered and launched in 1845. In 1846 the mail contract was extended to New York and inaugurated by *Hibernia* in 1857, thus starting Cunard Line's long association with the port.

With the success of the transatlantic service, other lines soon started to compete on the route, building bigger, faster and more elaborate ships. Unfortunately this was often at the expense of safety and many ships and lives were lost. One of Cunard's biggest rivals was the Collins Line, but they suffered a bitter blow when the *Arctic* collided with another vessel in fog off Newfoundland in 1854 and sank. Most of the 383 people on board lost their lives, including Collins' wife, son and daughter. When another Collins ship, the *Pacific*, disappeared without trace on a voyage from Liverpool to New York in 1856 the company struggled to recover and was wound up in 1858.

In contrast, Samuel Cunard always insisted to his captains that they put safety before speed: 'Your ship is loaded, take her; speed is nothing, follow your own road, deliver her safe, bring her back safe. Safety is all that is required.' The line soon started to earn a deserved reputation for excellent safety, reliability and seamanship. Cunard set, and continues to maintain, very high standards for their British captains, only trusting commands to those with many years of practical experience. In 1842 the author Charles Dickens sailed on *Britannia* and wrote an account of his voyage. Although Dickens and his fellow passengers found the rough Atlantic crossing somewhat of an ordeal they were full of praise for the ship's captain, presenting him with an inscribed silver service:

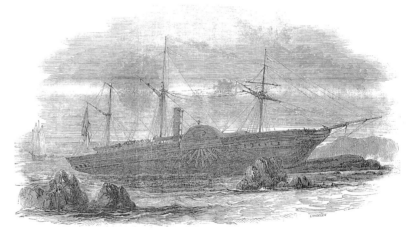

WRECK OF THE COLUMBIA STEAM-SHIP.

The *Columbia* was the first Cunard ship to be wrecked when it grounded in 1843 off Cape Sable, Nova Scotia, in fog. No lives were lost and all the mail was saved. *(Courtesy of Nova Scotia Archives)*

Presented to Captain John Hewitt of the *Britannia* Steamship, by the passengers aboard that vessel in a voyage from Liverpool to Boston, in the month of January 1842, as a slight acknowledgement of his great ability and skill, under circumstances of much difficulty and danger, and as a public token of their lasting gratitude.

Building on their early success, the Cunard Line began to expand and build new vessels for the fleet. In 1852 a new service was established between Liverpool and Mediterranean ports. A few years later this resulted in the formation of a new company by Cunard, Burns and MacIver specifically for this purpose, the British and Foreign Steam Navigation Company. The year 1852 also saw the introduction of Cunard's first iron-hulled screw-propelled ships, *Andes* and *Alps*. Screw propulsion was not a new technology, having first been introduced on the *Archimedes* for the Ship Propeller Company in 1839. However, the delayed adoption by Cunard was typical of Samuel Cunard's conservative approach to new concepts, which was to adopt change only once already tried and tested by others. Sometimes this caused conflict with his business partners as George Burns had wanted to adopt screws in favour of the paddlewheel much sooner.

Crimean War and Increased Competition

The 1850s started to see a growing demand for passenger trade on the North Atlantic, which was driven by immigrants from Europe seeking new opportunities in America, with an estimated 3 million people emigrating that decade alone. Unfortunately it was in 1854 that Cunard's ships were called up by the British Admiralty to provide support in the Crimean War and eleven of the vessels were diverted from the Atlantic. Most of the ships were involved in transporting troops, horses and supplies to the battle zone, and two served as hospital ships. Luckily none of the ships were lost and the efficiency demonstrated by Cunard was greatly appreciated by the government. This would have surely contributed to Samuel Cunard being granted a baronetcy by Queen Victoria in 1859, thereafter becoming Sir Samuel Cunard. He was awarded the privilege of having his own coat of arms for which he adopted the motto 'By Perseverance'.

With the Crimean War over, Cunard started to concentrate more on the immigrant trade and building ships with accommodation specifically designed for steerage passengers travelling on a minimal budget. In 1862 the *China* (2,529 tons) became the first iron-screw steamer to service the Atlantic and carry the mails. This required a special dispensation from the British Government since the original contract stipulated that paddle steamers were to be used. Also in 1862, Cunard built their last paddle steamer, the 3,871-ton *Scotia*. With increasing competition on the North Atlantic came the demand for faster crossings. When a ship made a record-breaking westbound crossing it was awarded the unofficial accolade of the 'Blue Riband'. This really captured the

imagination of the public and certainly gave the current holder a marketing advantage. The first Cunard vessel to attain the Blue Riband was the *Columbia* in 1841, with an average speed of 9.78 knots. The *Scotia* took the record in 1863 with a speed of 14.46 knots and held the award for the next nine years.

Samuel Cunard retired from a successful and profitable shipping business in 1863 at the age of seventy-five and his son Edward took over as the senior partner in the Cunard Line. Sir Samuel's last Atlantic voyage was on the *Scotia* in 1864 and he died the following year on 28 April, aged seventy-seven. Unfortunately, Edward's tenure with Cunard was a brief one, he himself passing away in 1869 at just fifty-four years of age, when the mantle was passed to his younger brother William.

Over the next two decades the amount of competition Cunard had on the North Atlantic increased dramatically, with new lines from the United Kingdom, Europe and America being founded. One of these companies was the Inman Line (1850), who took over the mail contract for the Liverpool–Boston route in 1867. However, that same year Cunard managed to get a new contract operating a weekly service to New York via Queenstown for a subsidy of £80,000. It was also at this time that the postmaster general took over the administration of mail contracts from the Admiralty.

Cunard Steamship Company Limited

The most significant competitor to Cunard to appear in this period was the White Star Line, which was originally founded in 1845. In 1871 White Star commenced a service between Liverpool and New York with a fleet of ships that had newer compound engines and superior standards of passenger accommodation. Although Cunard fought back by lengthening existing ships (such as the *Damascus*) and building bigger ones they still proved slower than White Star liners such as the *Adriatic*, which took the Blue Riband away from the *Scotia* in 1872.

The Cunard owners decided that in the face of the White Star competition there was no alternative but to establish a public company. Therefore in 1878 the assets of the founders, or their heirs, in the British and North American Royal Mail Steam Packet Company and in the British and Foreign Steam Navigation Company were transferred to the new Cunard Steamship Company Ltd. The Cunard prospectus simply stated: 'The growing wants of the Company's transatlantic trade demand the acquisition of additional steam ships of great size and power, involving a cost for construction which may best be met by a large public company.'

The new influx of capital made it possible for Cunard to embark on a new shipbuilding programme immediately and in November 1881 the first transatlantic steel Cunarder, the 7,392-ton *Servia*, came into service. This was also the first time that Cunard had built a ship with electric lighting. The *Servia* attracted considerable public attention, receiving many favourable comments

The Cunard Line logo has been revised many times over the years and is often seen on the china recovered from wrecks. *(Warwick Family Collection)*

about the luxury of her first-class accommodation for 480. She also had room for 750 passengers in steerage, which was critical to any steamship line's success. The *Servia* was an outstanding Cunard ship but she only followed existing trends, consistent with the company's evolutionary approach to change.

In 1885 Cunard's new ships brought further rewards when the *Etruria* reclaimed the Blue Riband with a record crossing of just over six days at an average speed of 18.73 knots. It was also around this time that Cunard purchased the *Oregon* from the struggling Guion Line. The *Oregon* was an outstanding ship and itself a Blue Riband holder. Not all the new ships were quite so successful: the *Aurania* (1) suffered a mishap on her maiden voyage to New York when there was an engine room explosion in mid-Atlantic. No one was hurt and the ship completed the journey under sail. Although the ship was out of service for nearly a year, she subsequently proved to be a worthy addition to the fleet until being eventually sold in 1905. Sadly, the *Oregon*'s service with Cunard was short-lived as in 1886 she sank in the approaches to New York following a collision with an unknown sailing vessel in fog. All passengers and crew were rescued by a passing steamer, with no lives lost. A few years later the *Malta* (1866, 2,132 tons) of the Mediterranean service was wrecked off Land's End. Again there was no loss of life and this preserved Cunard Line's distinguished reputation.

Towards the close of the century Cunard started to face intense competition from the Inman Line and specifically their vessels *City of New York* and *City of Paris*. In response Cunard commissioned their most exceptional vessels to date and in 1893 the 12,950-ton twin-screw *Campania* and *Lucania* entered service. The ships had twin sets of five-cylinder triple-expansion engines and were also the first Cunarders to completely dispense with the use of sail. They were also the most luxurious ships built to date and had accommodation for

600 first-class, 400 second-class and 1,000 steerage passengers with a crew of 400. Both vessels were fast and reliable and both became Blue Riband holders, with the *Lucania* proving fractionally faster, making her best crossing in 1894 at a speed of 21.81 knots. The *Campania* completed 250 round voyages and was eventually sold for breaking up in 1914. But she had a temporary reprieve when the Admiralty purchased her for conversion to an aircraft carrier. In 1918 the ship was wrecked in the Firth of Forth when its moorings broke in a storm. The *Lucania* was laid up in 1909 and following a fire was sold for scrap.

The first vessels to be built in the new century were the *Ivernia* (1) (13,800 tons) and *Saxonia* (1) (13,963 tons) in 1900. Although they were the largest Cunard ships to date and very popular, they were not quite fast enough to compete with the German-owned *Kaiser Wilhelm der Grosse*, which had taken the Blue Riband from the *Lucania* in 1898.

In 1902 the American John Pierpont Morgan founded the International Mercantile Marine Company and soon started buying up British shipping lines, including White Star, Dominion and Leyland. There was a very real threat that Cunard could be next, therefore giving the American company a monopoly on the Atlantic. Cunard appealed to the British Government for support and they eventually agreed a loan to assist in funding the construction of new superior ships. This was on the condition that they were built to Admiralty specification in case their services were ever required for wartime service. The new rebuilding period culminated in the 1907 construction of the massive *Lusitania* (31,550 tons) and *Mauretania* (1) (31,938 tons), built respectively by John Brown in Glasgow and Swan Hunter in Newcastle. These quadruple-screw ships instantly surpassed all existing Atlantic tonnage in terms of size, speed, accommodation and luxury. The *Lusitania* took the Blue Riband in October 1907 with the first ever crossing of less than five days and a speed of 23.99 knots. The *Mauretania* (1) took the record in September 1909 with a crossing speed that averaged 26.06 knots and retained the Blue Riband for the next twenty years. The *Lusitania*'s career reached a cruel and premature end in 1915 when the ship was torpedoed by the German submarine *U-20*. However, the *Mauretania* (1) got through the war unharmed and had a long prosperous career, eventually being sold for scrap in 1935.

The first two decades of the twentieth century were a very busy time for Cunard. In 1911 and 1912 the *Franconia* (1) and *Laconia* were introduced for the Boston service. The company also made a number of key acquisitions, the first of which was of three ships from the Thomson Line for a new Canadian service to Québec and Montréal. Three additional vessels were also purpose built for the route: *Andania* (1), *Alaunia* (1) and *Aurania* (2). In 1912 Cunard purchased all shares in the Anchor Line and in 1916 they acquired Canadian Northern Steamships Ltd. The last major new build before the war intervened was the *Aquitania*, which entered service in 1914. At 45,647 tons, this was the largest liner built by Cunard so far, but not quite as fast as *Lusitania* and *Mauretania* (1). The *Aquitania* was registered in Southampton and was the last Cunard ship to be built with four funnels. She was to prove a very robust and successful ship, surviving both world wars and crossing the Atlantic 475 times before finally being retired in 1950.

The War Years

The *Aquitania* only had time to make three transatlantic round voyages before the First World War intervened and she was requisitioned for use as a troop transport and hospital ship. Although *Aquitania* survived the war, many Cunard ships were not so fortunate. A staggering twenty-two ships were lost during this period, mostly due to enemy mines and torpedoes. By far the worst disaster occurred on 7 May 1915, when the *Lusitania* was lost along with over a thousand lives. After the war Cunard received over £7 million in compensation for a total lost tonnage of 220,440. For a while this meant that only a skeleton service could be operated on the Atlantic and liners from other companies had to be chartered. A comprehensive rebuilding programme soon commenced and a record order for thirteen new ships was placed.

Over the course of the next decade the new builds gradually came into service, the first being the modest 12,767-ton *Albania* (2) in 1921. After the war Britain had been ceded the German liner *Imperator* (1913, 52,226 tons) by the Treaty of Versailles. In 1921 this was renamed *Berengaria* and provided many years of useful service complementing the *Mauretania* (1) and *Aquitania* on the transatlantic route. Changes to the American immigration laws considerably reduced the need for steerage accommodation and this was replaced by an increasing and lucrative tourist trade. The 1920s also saw a growing demand for cruising and in 1923 the *Laconia* became the first ship to complete a full world cruise, circumnavigating the globe with calls to twenty-two different ports. Just

as a new era was dawning another one came to a close when the last member of the Cunard family left the company.

In 1930 the keel was laid down at John Brown's shipyard for a new 80,000-ton vessel with the yard number 534. However, a year later work ground to a halt due to the onset of the Depression and the incomplete hull gathered rust. Cunard appealed to the government for financial aid to complete it along with another sister ship. This was agreed under the proviso that Cunard merged with the ailing White Star Line and the new company became the Cunard White Star Line. Number 534 was finally completed in 1936 and the 80,774-ton vessel was christened *Queen Mary*. Just a few months after the maiden voyage *Queen Mary* took the Blue Riband back for Cunard with a crossing speed of 30.14 knots in just over four days. Meanwhile, work was well under way on constructing *Queen Mary*'s sister ship when the Second World War intervened. The vessel was rapidly completed and the *Queen Elizabeth* sailed secretly to safety in New York. For the duration of the war the two Queens served as troopships, where their speed and ability to carry up to 15,000 troops at a time made them ideal for this role.

Although Cunard only lost nine ships in the Second World War the death toll was considerably higher. The most tragic loss was the *Lancastria* in 1940, with around 4,000 lives. During the war Cunard managed nearly forty ships for the Ministry of War Transport, one of which was the *Cuba* (1923, 11,337 tons), seized as a war prize and previously owned by the Compagnie Générale Transatlantique.

The *Aquitania* survived both world wars. It is shown here operating as a hospital ship. *(Mick Lindsay Collection)*

At the end of the war both Queens were fully refurbished and settled into a weekly transatlantic service. The *Queen Elizabeth*'s final statistics were 83,673 tons with a length of 314.2m (1,031ft), which made her the largest passenger ship that had ever been built. The first-class service offered by the *Queen Mary* and *Queen Elizabeth* became legendary and gave a well-needed boost to Cunard's finances. Eventually this meant that Cunard could buy out the remaining shares in White Star and by 1949 the name reverted back to the Cunard Steamship Company Ltd. A variety of new ships were built and one of the most popular proved to be the 34,183-ton *Caronia* (2), or 'Green Goddess' as she was affectionately called.

End of an Era

The transatlantic trade faced a new threat in the 1950s when air travel started to offer passengers an alternative. By the end of the decade more passengers were crossing the Atlantic by air than by sea, and the Queens were no longer financially viable. Consequently both ships were sold in the 1960s, with the *Queen Mary* becoming a hotel in Long Beach, California. The *Queen Elizabeth* sailed to Hong Kong, where she was renamed *Seawise University* and underwent conversion to a floating university. However, the plans came to a premature end when the vessel caught fire and sank before the work was complete.

Cunard still believed there was a market for transatlantic travel and conceived a new ship that could alternate between Atlantic crossings in the summer and cruising in the winter. The *Queen Elizabeth 2* (*QE2*) entered service in 1969 under the command of Commodore W.E. Warwick. Although slightly smaller than her predecessors at 65,863 tons (final tonnage 70,732 tons), the *QE2* was still capable of service speeds in excess of 30 knots. At this time there were only two other ships remaining in the Cunard passenger fleet, which were *Carmania* (3) and *Franconia* (3).

In order to offset the dwindling passenger trade Cunard increased their involvement with cargo vessels. In 1965 the Atlantic Container Line (ACL) was formed as a container shipping consortium, with the partners that included Cunard Line, CGT French Line, Holland America Line and several others. Cunard built two ships for ACL, *Atlantic Conveyor* and *Atlantic Causeway*. Cunard also had interests in Associated Container Transportation (ACT).

Ownership Changes

On 24 August 1971 the Cunard Steamship Company was purchased by Trafalgar House Investments, which marked the end of Cunard as an independent company. However, the new owners did not waste any time introducing new tonnage to the fleet. The *Cunard Adventurer* and *Cunard Ambassador* were introduced in 1972, primarily aimed at the Caribbean cruise market. Not long afterwards they were joined by the popular *Cunard Countess* and *Cunard Princess*, sister ships both of

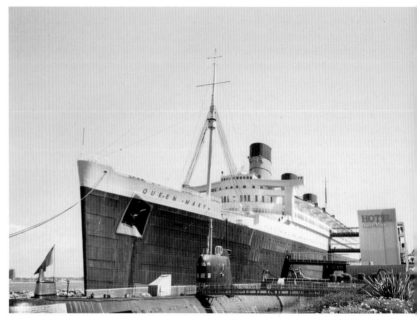

The *Queen Mary* is now retired permanently in Long Beach, California, and towers over the Russian Scorpion submarine. *(Sam Warwick)*

The *Queen Elizabeth 2* sails up the Solent to Southampton one last time, before departing on her farewell voyage to Dubai in November 2008. *(Sam Warwick)*

17,495 tons. In the 1980s the top-end luxury cruise ships *Sagafjord* and *Vistafjord* were purchased from Norwegian Cruise Lines. *Vistafjord* was later renamed as *Caronia* (3). In 1986 Cunard purchased *Sea Goddess I* and *Sea Goddess II*, which were small vessels of 4,333 tons and served the top-end luxury market.

When the Falklands War broke out in 1982 Cunard ships were called upon once again and the *QE2* was requisitioned, along with both of Cunard's ACL ships. Sadly, the *Atlantic Conveyor* was sunk by enemy action with the loss of twelve lives. After the war *Cunard Countess* was chartered by the Ministry of Defence to reposition troops and take families to visit the final resting place of their lost relatives.

In 1996 Trafalgar House was acquired by the Norwegian conglomerate Kværner, who were keen to sell off the Cunard Line. Finally a buyer was found and Cunard was sold to the American-owned Carnival Corporation in 1998.

Carnival immediately announced exciting plans to build a new true transatlantic liner to take over from the ageing *QE2*. In 2004 the 150,000-ton *Queen Mary 2* (*QM2*) entered service under the command of Commodore R.W. Warwick, son of the *QE2*'s first captain. The *QE2* was sold to the hotel division of the Nakheel development corporation in 2008 and now faces an uncertain future in Dubai. During a career of forty years, *QE2* had sailed nearly 6 million miles, carried 2.5 million passengers and made over 800 transatlantic crossings.

The dwindling Cunard fleet was expanded in 2007 with the 90,000-ton cruise ship *Queen Victoria*. Another similar ship, the *Queen Elizabeth* (92,000 tons), entered service in 2010. The Cunard Line of the current day is small with just three vessels, but the ships are young and modern. Most importantly, the Cunard name still continues to reign supreme on the North Atlantic and Samuel Cunard's legacy sails on into the new millennium.

Cunard Line's newest transatlantic liner the *Queen Mary 2*, anchored in Tortola, December 2005. *(Sam Warwick)*

2

~ WRECK DIVING ~

THIS CHAPTER IS primarily intended to provide an overview of scuba diving and in particular wreck diving to the non-diving reader. For a diver to be able to explore shipwrecks like the ones that follow there are two essential requirements: a means to accurately locate the site of the wreck and proficiency in scuba diving. Most wreck dives also require specialised skills in the discipline of wreck diving itself. Diving is a sport where once one has mastered the essential skills there are many areas for further specialisation and training. Wreck diving is not for everyone and diving conditions vary tremendously in different parts of the world. For example, diving a shallow warm water wreck like the *Curlew* in Bermuda in excellent visibility could not be more different than diving the *Campania* in the cold murky waters of the Firth of Forth in Scotland.

Locating Sunken Shipwrecks

These days the majority of recreational divers do not have to concern themselves too much with how to find wrecks to dive. This is because they will typically be booking on commercial dive-boat charters destined for the locations of well-known and popular wrecks, such as the *Oregon* and *Alaunia*. Someone else has already done the hard work discovering the wreck, and using modern navigation equipment such as Global Positioning System (GPS) the skipper can readily locate the wreck's exact position. However, there are still plenty of wrecks out there waiting to be discovered and it also helps to get an appreciation of how they are first located.

For years some of the best allies for the diver seeking new wrecks to dive have been fishermen. For commercial fishing boats shipwrecks represent an underwater hazard that can entangle nets and cause expensive equipment to be lost. As such, skippers will often keep their own personal record of which positions to avoid. The wreck of the *Carpathia* was marked on a fisherman's chart as an obstruction long before the wreck's identity was established. Wrecks often attract large quantities of fish so this makes them a popular destination

for recreational anglers. On the south coast of England it is common to find both dive boats and fishing boats positioned above the same wreck on a busy summer weekend.

The period and the manner in which a ship was sunk have a big influence on how easy it will be to locate the wreck. Wrecks of ships that run aground are often easiest to locate since specific landmarks can be readily identified and there can be additional witnesses on land. When the *Malta* ran aground off Cape Cornwall in 1889 contemporary photographs clearly pinpointed the exact location on the Cornish coast. The downside to ships lost in this manner is that being in shallow water in exposed areas they often break up and disperse very quickly, leaving little to discover underwater. Another Cornish wreck, the *Balbec*, broke up in just a few metres of water and there is nothing visible to dive today. For vessels that are lost offshore having visible landmarks that are recorded in contemporary accounts helps narrow down the potential search area. For example, when the *Lusitania* was torpedoed in broad daylight many witnesses could clearly see the southern coast of Ireland and the Old Head of Kinsale.

A lot will depend on survivor's accounts and especially those of the captain and deck officers. This is where the era of the vessel's loss becomes significant due to advances in navigational technology over the centuries. Prior to the twentieth century the primary means of calculating a ship's position was using the stars and dead reckoning. This could result in errors, especially during periods of poor visibility and bad weather, often becoming a contributing factor in the loss of the ship itself. In recent times electronic navigation systems mean a ship's position is always known to within a few metres. For ships that were sunk by enemy action, such as by U-boats, the commander would normally record the co-ordinates in his log, many of which are available in historic archives.

Most maritime nations have a department responsible for producing navigational charts. One of the essential requirements for a chart is to show any underwater obstructions that could form a hazard to shipping. Hydrographic surveys are carried out to establish the depth and profile of the seabed and wrecks are frequently identified. The hydrographers then make sure that any such shipwrecks are marked on the chart with a special symbol. In some cases

A typical dive-charter boat used for locating and diving shipwrecks in the British Isles. Note the lift on the back for getting divers out of the water. (Catherine de Lara)

certain wrecks are declared as 'Historic' and these will also be clearly marked on charts with an exclusion zone. The *Campania* and *Lusitania* are good examples.

Ultimately, locating any wreck requires a degree of effort and the amount of research needed will depend on many different factors. Other sources available include: libraries, maritime museums, contemporary newspaper accounts, archive records, etc.

Research will normally result in an approximate position of the wreck somewhere out in the ocean and the final stage is to pinpoint the exact co-ordinates. This is an area where again modern technology has made the process easier. Depth sounders that show the profile of the seabed are one of the best tools. While conducting a search in the area the wreck will often 'come up' on the sounder above the profile of the surrounding seabed. Prior to sounders a boat might trail a grapple in the hope of snagging something on the wreck. Other tools include magnetometers and side-scan sonar.

Finally, a positive identification of the wreck needs to be made in order to identify the ship conclusively. This is normally the stage at which divers would first enter the water and dive on the wreck. For deep wrecks a Remote Operated Vehicle (ROV) is often used, or in some cases essential, such as the *Laconia* (1), which is in a depth in excess of 400m (1,312ft). There are many ways of identifying a wreck, but undoubtedly one of the best and most desired by divers is to locate the ship's bell. Other distinguishing features like the builder's plate are ideal and artefacts from the wreck such as china with a shipping company crest also help. However, there are frequent cases of wrecks being wrongly identified, especially around the British Isles where there are so many. Unfortunately, because a lot of artefact recoveries end up in private collections few clues remain on the seabed for future divers. Many wrecks are discovered that never get named and remain forever anonymous.

The knowledge of a shipwreck's location does not automatically grant the finder the right to recover artefacts and in some cases diving may be prohibited entirely. Wreck ownership and salvage rights are a complex subject often embroiled in bureaucracy and red tape, of which the *Lusitania* is a classic example. The main influencing factors are normally the ship's historical importance and the value of the cargo. In some countries there is a blanket ban on all artefact recoveries from ships over a certain age.

Scuba Diving

Diving can be undertaken as a commercial profession or as a recreational hobby, and the equipment and techniques vary accordingly. Recreational diving is also referred to as 'sport diving' and is the main scope of the diving within this book. The word 'scuba' originated as the acronym 'SCUBA', which stands for Self-Contained Underwater Breathing Apparatus. A scuba diver does not require any form of physical tether to the surface and can swim throughout the water column without restriction. Nearly all sport diving employs the use of scuba equipment.

Broadly speaking, the depth limit for mainstream recreational diving is considered to be around 30–40m (100–130ft). However, advances in equipment, procedures and training have seen the emergence of 'technical diving', which pushes the depth boundaries to well in excess of 100m (330ft). Examples of technical dives on Cunard wrecks include the *Lusitania* at 93m (305ft) and *Carpathia* at 153m (502ft).

Sport diving was first popularised in the late 1950s and early 1960s, following the development of the aqualung in 1943 by Jacques-Yves Cousteau and Emile Gagnan. In 1953 Cousteau co-authored the acclaimed book *The Silent World* with Frédéric Dumas, which was made into an Academy Award-winning documentary three years later. Around the same time period, German diving couple Hans and Lotte Hass started to publish books, films and television shows

Stanley Haviland searches for remains of the *Caribia* (ex-*Caronia*) in the clear warm waters of Guam. He is diving with a minimal open-circuit scuba set. (Sam Warwick)

dedicated to exploring the underwater world. This triggered a growing interest in diving from the general public and soon some of the first training agencies were formed. The British Sub-Aqua Club (BSAC) was formed in England in 1953 and remains the governing body for the sport in the United Kingdom. The first commercial scuba-diving training organisation was the Professional Association of Diving Instructors (PADI), which was formed in America in 1966. PADI has gone on to become the biggest diver training agency in the world and typically issues close to 1 million individual dive certifications each year. In the last two decades a number of specialised agencies have appeared dedicated to technical diving.

Scuba Equipment

Equipment is an integral part of scuba diving and the core component required to go diving is the breathing apparatus itself. The most common type of scuba set is known as 'open circuit' and consists of a diving regulator connected to one or more pressurised gas cylinders strapped to the diver's back. The regulator delivers the gas at ambient pressure to the diver through a demand valve in the diver's mouth. The exhaust gases are exhaled directly into the water. Note the use of the word 'gas' instead of 'air'. Although most sport diving is carried out using compressed air, alternative breathing mixtures are becoming more common, as we will see later.

The alternate scuba system to open circuit is the rebreather. Rebreathers have been in use by the armed forces for over a century, but are now becoming commonplace in recreational diving, primarily amongst technical divers. The biggest advantage afforded by a rebreather is more efficient use of gas. Unlike open circuit, where all exhaust gases are wasted, the rebreather removes the carbon dioxide from exhaled air and replaces it with oxygen. Since the normal air we breathe contains 21 per cent oxygen and we exhale air with 16 per cent oxygen, only a small amount needs to be replenished. This means that far less gas needs to be carried by the diver and is therefore a major benefit for deep dives.

An essential accessory of both open-circuit and rebreather scuba sets is the pressure gauge. This allows the diver to monitor their remaining gas supply throughout the dive and ensure there is adequate reserve for contingencies.

The fundamental skill that must be attained by all divers is that of neutral buoyancy. This is a state where the diver can remain stationary in the water at any given depth without sinking deeper or floating to the surface. Any air spaces or compressible materials, such as those in some types of dive suits, will shrink as the diver descends, reducing the amount of water displaced and making the diver negatively buoyant. This needs to be offset by some kind of buoyancy compensation device (BCD). This is typically in the form of an inflatable bladder or wing, most commonly part of the scuba-diving harness. As the diver descends gas can be injected, thereby offsetting the negative buoyancy. When the diver ascends the expanding air needs to be vented.

Above Catherine de Lara preparing for a dive on the *Ascania* using open-circuit twin cylinders. She is also wearing a drysuit and neoprene hood required for the cold conditions. The gauge hanging down to the right shows the gas pressure in the cylinders. *(Sam Warwick)*

Left Johno de Lara prepares for a dive on the *Campania* using a closed-circuit rebreather. The item hanging above the crotch is a rolled up Surface Marker Buoy (SMB) attached to a reel of line. *(Sam Warwick)*

Right The author on a dive-boat lift, after a mixed-gas dive off the south coast of England. *(Aldo Bimbato)*

Even in warm water environments a diver normally requires some form of thermal protection since water conducts body heat away twenty-five times faster than air. There are many different types of diving suit, but they broadly fall into two main categories of wetsuit and drysuit. As the name suggests, a wetsuit remains wet and the water trapped inside the suit aids the insulation properties of the suit itself. With a drysuit the suit is sealed at the neck and wrists and the diver remains completely dry (theoretically!). Thermal undergarments are worn under the suit to provide whatever degree of insulation is required by the diving conditions. Diving on the *Scotia* in Guam would not need anything more than a thin wetsuit, but drysuits are commonplace for dives in temperate climates.

Other basic equipment includes a mask and fins. A cutting device of some description is carried. A torch is essential in low visibility, serves as a useful signalling device and restores natural colours, which are filtered out as depth increases. A watch or other timing device is essential for keeping track of the dive's duration.

The activity of scuba diving is one that entails an inherent degree of risk and the biggest concerns that need to be addressed are due to changes in air pressure and the effects of breathing pressurised gas. As a diver descends nitrogen is absorbed into the bloodstream. The deeper the diver goes and the longer they stay the more nitrogen is absorbed. When the diver starts their ascent the nitrogen will start to be released. If this is not done in a controlled manner then bubbles can form in the bloodstream causing a condition called decompression sickness or 'the bends'. In extreme cases this can result in paralysis or even death. Long and/or deep dives may require the diver to make a series of stops during the ascent to allow the nitrogen to diffuse. The stops are commonly referred to as decompression (or just 'deco') stops. Most entry-level diving is 'non-stop' diving, meaning that dives are planned such that there is no need to make any scheduled decompression stops during the ascent. In order to plan dives for any given depth and time decompression schedules are used. Traditionally these are in the form of printed or computer-generated tables. However, now most divers carry a 'dive computer' on their wrist or instrument console that calculates the non-stop time and any decompression requirements on the fly.

As a diver descends deeper, the nitrogen content in regular compressed air becomes narcotic. The onset of this is generally around the 30m (98ft) mark and the effects are very similar to those induced by alcohol. The deeper the diver goes the worse it becomes, such that judgement can become severely impaired. This is one of the reasons why most sport divers do not dive deep and why the mainstream agencies do not advocate deeper diving. Different divers have differing tolerances to narcosis and it can also be affected by the prevailing diving conditions such as visibility, current and temperature. At depths beyond 55m (180ft) oxygen itself becomes toxic and any dives beyond these depths on air become incredibly risky.

Once considered to be purely in the realms of technical diving, the use of a gas termed Enriched Air Nitrox (EAN, or just nitrox) is now becoming

A Remote Operated Vehicle (ROV) used for unmanned survey of wrecks. This one was used on the expedition to the *Lusitania* wreck in 2008. Live video is transmitted direct to the operator on the surface via the umbilical cable. (© *Timmy Carey*)

mainstream. Nitrox is air with an increased oxygen content, typically 32 per cent or 36 per cent. By reducing the amount of nitrogen in the breathing mixture and replacing it with oxygen divers can spend longer at a given depth before incurring any decompression penalties. Nitrox does not reduce the effects of narcosis and does not allow divers to go deeper.

Technical Diving

As already mentioned above, the main driver for technical diving is to facilitate dives that go beyond the traditional limits of scuba and compressed air. This is primarily achieved by the use of gas mixtures other than air to offset the problems outlined above that are caused by breathing nitrogen and oxygen at depth.

The technical diving gas mixture most commonly used is trimix. This is where a percentage of the nitrogen in air is replaced with helium. Helium is inert and does not have any narcotic effects. The use of increasingly higher percentages of helium means that dives well in excess of 100m (330ft) can be made. However, since oxygen still represents a problem for dives deeper than 55m (180ft), the oxygen content has to be reduced. This is not a problem to the diver at depth since the human body can function so long as a minimum partial pressure of .16 bar absolute is maintained. However, a mixture low in oxygen content represents a problem at shallower depths. This can be overcome by using what is known as a travel gas, which is typically a nitrox mix in a separate cylinder that the diver breathes until switching to trimix 'back gas' at a deeper depth.

Any trimix dive that does not require use of a travel gas is referred to as 'normoxic' and has a lower limit of 18 per cent oxygen in the gas mixture. Sixty metres (197ft) is the maximum depth for a normoxic trimix dive.

In addition to using helium mixtures for depth, technical divers use oxygen-rich mixtures for decompression. For the final, shallow decompression stops from 6m (20ft) to the surface 100 per cent pure oxygen is often used. This allows the nitrogen and helium to be flushed out of the system sooner, meaning less time spent in the water decompressing.

Divers using drysuits normally have to inject a small amount of gas into their suits during the descent to relieve any squeeze caused by increased pressure. This is normally fed from a hose connected to their back gas or a separate suit-inflation cylinder. Helium is a very thin gas with poor insulation properties so trimix divers will often use argon for suit inflation instead.

Technical divers using open-circuit scuba will always dive with double 'twin' cylinders, which are normally connected via an isolation manifold in the centre. The valve can completely isolate one cylinder in the event of a serious equipment failure. For deep dives beyond the normoxic range, the use of open circuit becomes increasingly challenging as more and more gas needs to be carried due to the increased pressure. Helium is also a very expensive gas to purchase and there is a huge amount of waste with open circuit. Consequently, this is an area where rebreathers really start to come into their own and are now very much preferred for deep technical dives.

Wreck Diving

Diving on most wrecks introduces additional challenges and considerations for the diver. Diving on deep wrecks requires a combination of the technical-diving techniques and wreck-diving disciplines. There are, however, wrecks that can be safely explored by recreational divers without the need for additional specialised training. A good example is the *Curlew* in Bermuda. Being such an old wreck, it is very flat and broken, and in many ways diving the wreck itself is no different to the coral reef and rocks that surround it.

A lot of wrecks, especially the ones in this book, are in parts of the world where the water is tidal and/or subject to strong currents. For wrecks in tidal waters, such as the British Isles, all dives must be carried out during a period of slack water. This is normally at the point when the tide turns and will occur four times within a given twenty-four-hour period. The length of the slack water period varies depending on the location, the time of the year and the phase of the moon. This is often referred to as the slack water window and is typically around thirty to forty-five minutes.

Wrecks can present a number of hazards to the unwary diver and one of the biggest is entanglement. This can be caused by fishing line and netting that is frequently snagged by commercial fishing boats and anglers. There is also often loose line and cables from the wreckage itself. In low-visibility conditions a diver can inadvertently enter the wreck and become disoriented or even lost.

There are many factors that determine how much of a vessel will survive underwater and for how long. The circumstances surrounding the loss of the ship are a significant factor, and in many cases are violent, involving torpedoes and explosions. Once on the seabed wrecks start to deteriorate and collapse very quickly, being constantly ravaged by weather and tides. Eventually they all become little more than piles of rubble on the seabed.

Wreck divers need to learn how to navigate around a wreck and recognise distinctive features as often it is desirable for them to return to the start point of the dive, where typically their boat is anchored or a shot line has been dropped. In low-visibility conditions, or if exploring a wreck for the first time, sometimes divers will 'reel off' from the shot. This means attaching a spool of thin line to the anchor and gradually reeling it out as they explore the wreck, taking care to secure the line at various points so that it doesn't float up and become a hazard. At the end of the dive the diver simply reels back in to retrace their route.

Some wrecks present the diver with the opportunity to penetrate the wreck and explore the interiors. For many wrecks, especially those in low visibility, the diver may elect to lay a guide line. The interiors of wrecks are generally very silted up and it doesn't take much to stir up the sediment and to lose sight of the exit route and all sense of direction. Most of the Cunard wrecks featured in this book are in advanced state of collapse and there are few opportunities to explore far inside. There are, however, wrecks of liners such as the Italian Line's *Andrea Doria*, which is famed for explorations deep into the ship's deep dark interiors.

Many wreck divers are interested in locating and recovering artefacts. Some of these, such as portholes, can be extremely heavy and cannot be simply carried to the surface. The way divers raise heavy items is through the use of lift bags, which can be likened to large underwater balloons. The bag is attached to the object using ropes and clips then inflated from one of the diver's gas cylinders. Once sufficient gas has been blown in, the artefact will be carried to the surface.

Shipwrecks are home to all manner of marine life, most of which is harmless to the diver if treated with respect. Conger eels are very common on wrecks in the British Isles. Although they look menacing, they will leave divers alone unless severely provoked. Lobsters and crabs are also fond of dwelling on wrecks.

It is easy to get carried away exploring an interesting wreck or digging out an elusive artefact, so wreck divers also need to be very diligent in monitoring their depth and time. Gas consumption can also vary through overexertion caused by swimming around the wreck, especially in current, or trying to prise away stubborn objects.

3

~ SHIPWRECKS ~

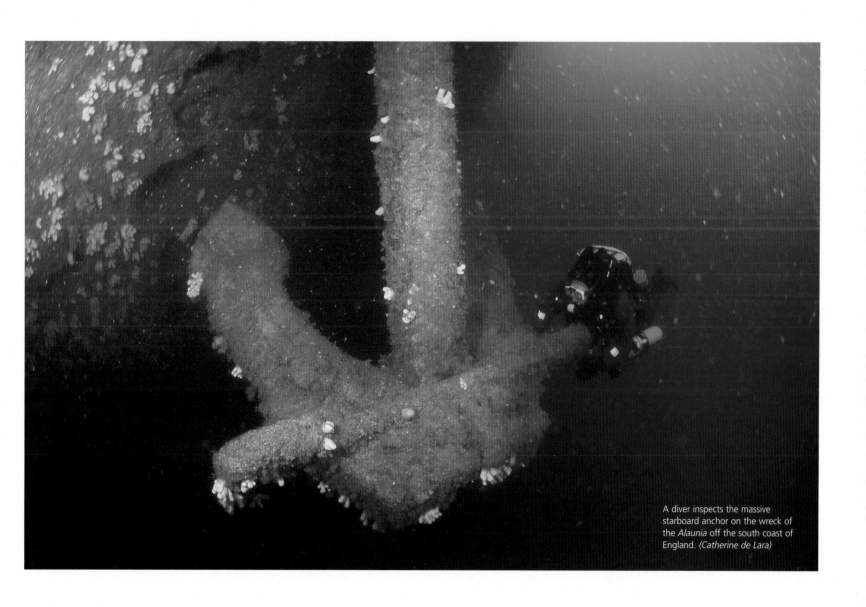

A diver inspects the massive
starboard anchor on the wreck of
the *Alaunia* off the south coast of
England. *(Catherine de Lara)*

Curlew

1853–1856, Bermuda

THE *CURLEW WAS* a single-screw iron steamship built in 1853 at the Denny's Shipyard, Dumbarton. The ship was 528 tons, 55.5m (182ft) in length, with a beam of 6.7m (22ft). She was barquentine rigged with three masts and a poop deck.

Up until 1833 the mail packet service from Falmouth, England, terminated at Halifax, Canada. In order to continue the service onward to Bermuda, Samuel Cunard was awarded a contract by the British Admiralty to provide a monthly mail service between Halifax and Bermuda. Later, in November 1850, Cunard introduced a further steamship service from New York to St Thomas, which called at Bermuda en route. The New York service did not prove particularly successful and a new direct Halifax–Bermuda–St Thomas itinerary was inaugurated by the *Curlew* in July 1854.

Samuel Cunard was disappointed in the quality of the hotel accommodation that was available in Bermuda at the time, wanting only the best for his passengers. Consequently, he threatened to withdraw his ships from calling there and in response Bermuda's first luxury hotel, the Hamilton Hotel, was built. The Bermuda service ran successfully over the next two years until the *Curlew* left Halifax on 14 March 1856 for her final fateful voyage to Bermuda under the command of Captain Hunter.

Two days into her journey the vessel ran into rough seas, causing the captain to remain up all night in command of the vessel. He retired exhausted to his cabin to get some much-needed sleep. Not long after, on the morning of 18 March, Captain Hunter was awakened to find that the *Curlew* had gone aground on the northern reefs of Bermuda and his cabin was filling with water. There were problems launching the lifeboats and two were severely damaged in the process; a third drifted away empty. Eventually a fourth boat was launched successfully and the crew rowed ashore to get help while the officers stayed on board. Two naval vessels were swiftly dispatched and rescued the remaining men from the rapidly sinking vessel. Seven of the nine mail bags carried by *Curlew* were also saved.

The *New York Times* reported on the loss of the *Curlew* on 31 March 1856, at which time they believed that all the mail had been lost:

> We learn by the arrival of the bark *Messenger Bird*, at Provincetown, (Cape Cod, Mass.) that the Cunard steamer *Curlew*, from Halifax to Bermuda, ran ashore on the North Breaker, off Bermuda, at 4 o'clock on the morning of the 18th inst., and sank in three minutes. The mails were lost, but the crew were saved. She lies with decks under water, and is broken in two. Assistance had been sent to her, but the sea ran so high they could not save anything.

The residents of Bermuda were sympathetic to Captain Hunter and the loss of his ship, and the mayor presented him with an address:

> The unfortunate loss of the Royal Mail steam packet *Curlew*, under your command, on the coast of these Islands, on the morning of the 18th inst, and

Above There are hundreds of wrecks in the waters surrounding Bermuda, a selection of which are commemorated on this first day cover of 1986. Left to right with year wrecked: HMS *Pallas* (1783), *Warwick* (1619), *Curlew* (1856), *Early Riser* (1876) and *Constellation* (1943).

Left The *Curlew* was built in 1853 and was wrecked off the north coast of Bermuda in 1856.

the distress of mind, in consequence, it has caused you, have very naturally called forth the sympathy of the inhabitants of this town on your behalf – assured as we are that the disaster was purely the result of accident, (to which we need scarcely say all are liable) your abilities as a navigator having been fully established from the circumstance of your commanding; at different periods, one or other of the mail steamers on this station for upwards of eighty voyages. The untoward event which has elicited this letter we sincerely hope will be looked upon by those more immediately concerned, in the same light that it is regarded by us, and that you will not be in the remotest degree prejudiced or injured by the sad occurrence.

A letter that was carried by the *Curlew* on her final voyage was sold at auction with Christie's, London, in 1999 for £1,380. The letter was postmarked 13 February 1856 and was reported to have had a small amount of water damage.

Curlew Wreck

The island of Bermuda was first discovered in 1505 and has been a British territory since 1612. It is located in the North Atlantic Ocean and the nearest point of land is the east coast of the United States, which is over 600 miles away. In addition to the main island itself there are over 360 islands in total, covering an area of 20 square miles. Bermuda is on the eastern tip of the notorious Bermuda Triangle, which is legendary for the number of ships and aircraft that have disappeared without trace. The whole area is surrounded by shallow coral reefs.

Due to its location, history and treacherous reefs, Bermuda has been a magnet for shipwrecks over the centuries and at least 400 ships are known to have been wrecked there. One of the first and most famous was the *Sea Venture* in 1609, which was carrying urgent supplies to settlers in the early colony of Virginia in America. It is believed that the story of the wreck and the ensuing ordeals of the survivors influenced Shakespeare's play *The Tempest*. One of the more recent wrecks was that of the four-mast schooner *Constellation*, which went aground on the western reef in 1942. This became the inspiration for the Peter Benchley novel *The Deep*, which was later made into a motion picture.

With clear warm waters and an abundance of wrecks at shallow depths, Bermuda has become a popular diving destination. Many of the wrecks are classified as Historic Wrecks by the Bermuda Government. These are subdivided into two categories of Open Wrecks and Restricted Wrecks. Recreational divers are permitted to dive on Open Wrecks as long as they do not interfere with the site in any way, but Restricted Wrecks are strictly off limits. The *Sea Venture* is a good example of a Restricted Wreck, but the *Curlew* is one of thirty-eight (as of 2007) Open Wrecks.

The *Curlew* lies on the north edge of the reef, 1 mile east of North Rock. The wreck was first discovered by the renowned marine explorer, diver and

The wreck of the *Curlew* is firmly embedded in the coral reef. *(Clifton Vachon)*

The wreck is covered in over 150 years of marine growth so individual features are hard to distinguish. *(Clifton Vachon)*

A dive on the *Curlew* is like being in an aquarium. The fish on the left is a blue tang and to the right is a smooth trunkfish. *(Clifton Vachon)*

treasure hunter Teddy Tucker, who has located over 100 shipwrecks in Bermuda, including the treasure ship *San Pedro*. Tucker salvaged some of the *Curlew's* brass fittings and recovered various artefacts. Close by and to the east of the *Curlew* is the wreck of the *Cristobal Colon*. This was a Spanish luxury liner built in 1923 and lost on 25 October 1936. At 19,833 tons and with a length of 152m (500ft) the *Cristobal Colon* is the largest shipwreck in Bermuda.

The *Curlew* is an easy shallow dive that is suitable for divers of all levels. The maximum depth is 10m (35ft), the visibility often in excess of 12m (40ft) and there is little current. Access to the wreck site is by boat. Not much remains of the small sailing steamer today, which has been steadily pounded by Atlantic breakers for over 150 years. However, there are still enough small sections of the hull and deck plating to get a feeling for this old and historic wreck. There are some parts of the wreck which stand a little over 1m (3ft) proud of the coral seabed, but it is difficult to identify their original purpose with any degree of certainty.

The real attraction of a dive on the *Curlew* is the abundance of colourful marine life and sea creatures that have made the wreck their new home. Attached to the coral and metal plates divers will see brain coral, sea whips and sea fans. The fish include grouper, hog fish and trumpet fish.

Over a century after the loss of the *Curlew* Bermuda remains a popular destination for visiting cruise ships and was often on the itineraries for Cunard's own *Caronia* and *QE2*. During their brief stays on the island some passengers elect to take part in organised diving excursions to the many popular wrecks.

Scotia

1862–1904, Guam

THE *SCOTIA* (1) was an iron paddle steamer of 3,871 tons, with a length of 115.6m (379ft) and beam of 14.6m (48ft). The ship was built for Cunard by Robert Napier & Sons, Glasgow, and launched 25 June 1861. *Scotia* had two funnels and two masts that were rigged for sail, as was common in those days, to be used along with her steam engine. Two side-lever engines powered the paddlewheels, providing a service speed of 14 knots. The paddlewheels themselves were 12m (40ft) in diameter, making them the largest in use on the transatlantic route at the time, with the exception of the *Great Eastern* a few years previously. A walkway bridge with railings connected both paddlewheels, but at that time the ship's steering wheel was normally situated at the stern. As ship construction evolved it became more common for the steering wheel to be placed on a dedicated navigation bridge towards the forward end of the vessel. There was passenger accommodation for 275 cabin-class passengers, but the *Scotia* was designed so that she could be fitted out to carry up to 1,500 troops in times of war. Approximately 1,400 tons of cargo and 1,800 tons of coal could be carried.

The *Scotia* was the last paddle steamer built for Cunard, and was described as 'the finest, fastest and strongest ship of her day'. An extract from the *Illustrated London News*, on 22 March 1862, stated:

> This vessel, the second largest mercantile steamer in the world, was built by Messrs. Napier and Sons, of Glasgow (under the orders of Messrs. Burns, of that city), for the Cunard or British and North American Royal Mail Steam-packet Company. She was launched in June last; and on the 5th inst. She made her trial-trip on the Clyde, a highly satisfactory one, notwithstanding the unpropitious state of the weather. The distances were performed under the following conditions: Against a strong flood tide, and also against a double-reefed topsail breeze of wind, from the Cloch to Cumbrae Light in 59 minutes; after passing the Little Cumbrae, the Scotia was brought round with great ease, and performed the upward run between the Cumbrae and Cloch Lights, but on this occasion with wind and tide in her favour, in 49 minutes – mean time, 54 minutes.

The *Glasgow Daily Herald* also reported that: 'Stupendous as the Scotia is, the lines of beauty have been so well worked out in the preparation of her model that her appearance is singularly graceful.'

The cabins for the passengers were on the main deck and were said to be '9ft in height; and, coupled with the excellent system of ventilation introduced into all the Cunard liners, we need scarcely say that they are alike pleasant, airy, and healthful'. Crew accommodation was provided in the forecastle for the seamen and firemen; amidships was the accommodation for officers and engineers, with the galley and cooks' quarters situated behind, while aft, on each side of the wheel, were the cabins of the senior officers. The main dining room had long tables with revolving chairs and padded seats that were bolted to the floor. The dining and public rooms were described as luxurious and she was thought of as a 'floating hotel'. There were side windows and skylights that gave ample light in fair weather.

The *Scotia* made its maiden voyage from Liverpool to New York on 19 May 1862 under the command of Captain Judkins, commodore of the Cunard fleet, previous captain of the *Persia*, from whom the *Scotia* took the westbound and eastbound records in 1863. The westbound record voyage was gained in July 1863 in eight days, three hours, at an average speed of 14.46 knots, and the eastbound in December 1863 in eight days, five hours, forty-two minutes, at an average speed of 14 knots.

The *Scotia* was popular with the American passengers, but failed to come up to the Cunard drive for efficiency to ensure greater profits on the North Atlantic trade. This was mainly due to the inefficiency of the paddlewheels, especially when the vessel was fully laden with fuel and cargo, causing the ship to use up to 164 tons of coal a day. The *Scotia* made her last transatlantic voyage in 1874 and was then laid up.

In 1878 *Scotia* was sold to the Telegraph Construction & Maintenance Co. and was converted at Laird Bros, Birkenhead, to become a twin-screw cable steamer, when her tonnage was increased to 4,667 tons and of one of her funnels was removed. She commenced laying cables between England and Spain and also from Gibraltar to India.

In 1896 the *Scotia* was sailing approximately 60 miles off Eddystone when there was an explosion in her cable anti-fouling paint store, which caused serious damage to the ship's bow. During the construction of *Scotia* Cunard introduced safety improvements that included seven watertight compartments, a reinforced forward bulkhead and buoyancy chambers. These probably saved the vessel since she managed to remain afloat and reach port, where repairs were swiftly carried out.

In 1903 the *Scotia* was again sold, this time to the Pacific Cable Co. where she was used as a repair ship in the Pacific and based at Guam.

On 11 March 1904 the *Scotia* was wrecked on Spanish Rock, Catalan Bank, near Guam. It was a fairly calm sea and clear day when the *Scotia* approached

Right, from top

Scotia, the last Cunard Line paddle steamer, entered service for Cunard in 1862. *(Courtesy of Paul D. Edwards)*

Homeward Bound, Samuel Walters' painting of the paddle steamer *Scotia* heading for port in 1863.

Close up of the *Scotia*'s ornate paddle box on the original Robert Napier builders' model.

The *Scotia* was sold to the Telegraph Construction & Maintenance Co. in 1878 for use as a cable-layer. After conversion to screw propulsion and having one funnel removed the ship is barely recognisable as *Scotia*. (The Mariners' Museum, Newport News, VA)

Guam on Friday, 11 March. She was observed by the chief mate of the US Navy's collier *Justin*, the Guam station ship approaching from a westward direction at 6.10 a.m.

As they approached the harbour Captain Rushton and the *Scotia*'s chief mate, J.H. Richardson, identified what they thought was the port channel marker indicating the reef at the southernmost point of Catalan Bay. Captain Rushton set the course of the steamer to pass the buoy on the portside, which for vessels entering the harbour was a safe, although narrow, deep-water passage.

By 6.45 a.m. the chief mate on the *Justin* noted in the log that the steamer appeared to be stranded on Catalan Bank. This was confirmed when she hoisted flags 'NA', indicating that she was 'aground, wanting assistance'. The *Justin* launched a boat immediately and prepared to raise steam to go to the assistance of the *Scotia*. However, they were later informed that further assistance was not required.

The weather was fine and clear with a moderate breeze, but by 9 a.m. it was confirmed that the *Scotia* was hard on the reef near Spanish Rock.

A steam launch from the *Scotia* arrived at 9.40 a.m. alongside the *Justin*, towing boats that contained the captain's wife and the chief mate's wife and child, complete with their personal belongings.

The weather in the afternoon remained clear, although still with a moderate breeze, and the ship prepared to attempt to clear the reef. All personal belongings were taken ashore and it was reported that no further assistance was required. The ship was supplied with fresh water, but it was later reported by the master that the *Scotia* was fast on the rocks and was unlikely to be moved.

A cable was sent to the *Shipping Gazette* and Lloyd's List on 11 March stating that the cable ship *Scotia* was stranded on Spanish Rocks 'with water nearly up to decks and will probably be total wreck'.

By 12 March the Salvage Association in London received a more positive telegram from the Lloyd's correspondent in Guam, stating that the *Scotia* was 'in an upright position exposed northerly swell, fore and aft holds full of the water, cable tanks undamaged and not likely to break up if the weather holds good'. Although the damage below water could not be checked it was not thought to be serious.

The Lloyd's correspondent considered that there was a 'Fair prospect of salvage if the weather holds good'. The cable steamer *Patrol* was sent from Singapore on 16 March to recover the cable on board the *Scotia*, but the weather started to deteriorate and the Lloyd's representative in Guam sent a message on 17 March: 'Blowing a northerly gale, heavy seas vessel is bumping heavily.' This was followed by a cable sent the next day by the Lloyd's representative: 'Abandoned: all aboard saved and landed here. Blowing and northerly gale. Main engine adrift. Bunker coal on fire. Afraid must become a total wreck.' On 25 March the cable received in London dated 24 March from the Lloyd's correspondent in Guam stated that: 'Scotia broken in two, afterpart sunk.'

An investigation on the loss of the *Scotia* was conducted by the acting naval governor of Guam, Lt Raymond P. Stone, which revealed some disturbing facts. This concerned the buoy near Spanish Rock, and how the master of the *Justin* had been warned of its dangerous condition and possibility of sinking, thus putting vessels approaching the harbour in grave danger. The master was told to investigate and rectify.

On 9 March Lt Stone had written to the master of the *Justin* expressing his concern about the buoy near Spanish Rock at the entrance to the harbour, which was reported to be 'In a sinking or sunken condition'. The naval governor

View of Apra Harbor, Guam. The wreck of the *Scotia* is just outside the breakwater behind the vessel at anchor. The *Caribia* (ex-*Caronia*) was wrecked in the harbour entrance seventy years later. (Sam Warwick)

Diver Paul Edwards exploring the wreck of the *Scotia* in the 1980s. The top of a boiler can be seen to the left of the photograph. *(Andy Fikus, The Mariners' Museum, Newport News, VA)*

The ribs of the *Scotia* like a 'peeled artichoke'. *(Andy Fikus, The Mariners' Museum, Newport News, VA)*

When the author dived the *Scotia* site in April 2011 most of the wreck was covered with shifting sand. *(Stanley Haviland)*

This piece of wreckage could be part of the *Scotia*'s double-bottom hull. The edge of the Glass Breakwater is to the right of the picture. *(Stanley Haviland)*

also commented that a vessel leaving the harbour had recently marked the buoy with a wooden log.

The master of the *Justin* was asked specifically: 'Please have this matter investigated as soon as possible, and rectify it, using such yard craft as may be advisable and necessary. Report steps taken.' He also advised that the cable ship *Scotia* was due to arrive around 12 March to work on the submarine cable, and for the *Justin* to be available to help the *Scotia* in any way possible through consultation with the superintendent of the cable company and the master of the *Scotia*. However, in the event it is strange that as the *Scotia* approached the harbour no warning was given to the vessel on the direction of the course she was taking, nor that any arrangements had been put in place for a pilot to be on board to see the vessel safely into port.

Scotia Wreck

The wreck of the *Scotia* remained untouched on the reef outside Apra Harbor until attracting the attention of Japanese salvors six years later in 1910. In order to salvage the engine the team used explosives extensively on the wreck, resulting in it being flattened from amidships forward.

In 1944 construction commenced on building the Glass Breakwater around the Apra Harbor and this was eventually completed in 1946. This resulted in part of the breakwater being literally built on top of the bow section of the wreck, hiding it forever. What remained became a popular dive among local Guam divers in the 1970s and 1980s.

Being outside the breakwater, the wreck site is in an area of excellent visibility, often in excess of 30m (98ft). The downside of this location is that the area can be subject to very strong tidal currents so diving is better timed to coincide with periods of slack water. The best time of year to dive is in the monsoon season between May and November when the seas are normally calmest. It used to be possible to access the wreck as a shore dive directly from the breakwater but in recent years the US Navy has closed the access road. Thus use of a boat for diving is now essential. The wreck is in a maximum depth of 14m (46ft), meaning long bottom times are possible with no decompression obligations to worry about. Large pelagic fish can often be seen in this area.

The following description of the wreck is based on information provided by Paul Edwards, who dived the wreck extensively between 1978 and 1986:

> The remnants were lying flat on the bottom, like a peeled artichoke with the iron riveting construction still evident. The Glass Breakwater covers part of the bow, and from there leading aft on the ship, there was a large maybe 30m (98ft) in length section of the double bottom still visible lying on the sand bottom of the bank which she struck. The machinery space, crank shaft and boiler remnants were readily apparent and heavily overgrown with coral. The port side of counter stern was visible and partially intact.

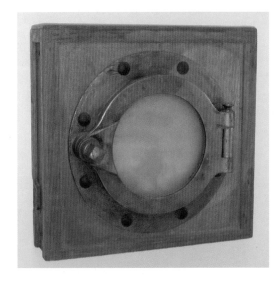

Brass porthole recovered from the wreck in the 1980s. *(Courtesy of Paul D. Edwards)*

During this period the wreck would often yield artefacts, particularly after recent storms. Some of the items discovered included a brass dolphin stick barometer gimbal and a glass torpedo bottle. Several portholes were also uncovered in an area near the boilers. These were secured with eight to ten countersunk rivets. A bronze 12mm thick plate with ornate scroll work with 1–2m exposed was observed firmly embedded in iron and coral.

Unfortunately, very little visible evidence of this once famous paddle steamer remains to be seen today and nature seems to have reclaimed *Scotia* as her own. What was once a coral seabed scattered with interesting old iron wreckage has now become covered in a mass of dense shifting sand. Guam is in a part of the Pacific that is subject to violent typhoons and storms, which can have a dramatic effect on both man-made and natural structures. The last major typhoon was super typhoon Pongsana in 2002 that actually destroyed the tip of the breakwater. It is perfectly feasible therefore that large sand masses moved around in storms could cover the wreck. It is further possible that the erection of the breakwater itself has contributed to changes in the dynamic of the seabed. This probably accounts for why most local divers and dive operators have either never heard of the *Scotia* wreck or have little interest in visiting the site. The positive side to this is that the remnants of *Scotia* will stay preserved for now and may eventually reveal themselves one day to visiting divers.

On a dive in April 2011 some broken sections of wreckage were observed near the breakwater, which appeared to be part of the *Scotia*'s double bottom under the cable storage tanks. A short distance out across the sand there were also some isolated fragments of hull plating, lying flat on the seabed. Some other small sections of wreckage found in the general area could very well be the remnants from a container ship and barge that grounded on the breakwater in the 1980s.

Malta

1865–1889, England

THE *MALTA* WAS an iron passenger cargo vessel of 2,132 tons, with a length of 92.3m (303ft) and beam of 11.9m (39ft). The steam-powered geared oscillating engine drove a single-screw propeller, giving a service speed of 10 knots. There was a single funnel and two masts, which were also rigged for sail. The bow was adorned with a magnificent golden female figurehead. *Malta* was built by J. & G. Thomson, Glasgow, launched on 19 October 1865, and entered service in December 1865. There was accommodation for forty first-class passengers, of a standard that was considered quite luxurious for the time, 535 third-class passengers and a crew complement of forty. She had two sister ships: *Aleppo* (1865) and *Tarifa* (1865).

In 1840 the first Cunard Line ships were wooden paddle steamers. Over the next twenty-five years the transatlantic trade began to expand and became more and more profitable for the shipping companies. With the increasing trade came a greater demand for vessels to be built for faster speed, greater cargo and passenger capacity, thus the construction of the ships began to change. At first the wooden paddle steamers were replaced by ships with iron hulls and the paddlewheels were replaced by single-screw propellers. Later the iron hulls and superstructure were changed to steel construction with twin screws, and later still, moving into the twentieth century, quadruple screws.

The *Malta*'s first transatlantic crossing was from Liverpool to New York, but thereafter her main route was to be the Liverpool to Boston service. From 1873 the ship also spent some time on the Mediterranean routes. During a major refit in 1879 *Malta* was fitted with 212hp compound engines, built by J. Jack & Co. of Liverpool. The compound engine is a steam engine that uses the steam more than once through operating the cylinders at different pressure levels. This was found to improve the ship's efficiency in speed or reduced operating costs through using less coal.

The *Malta* had been sailing regularly on the Mediterranean service for six years when, on 14 October 1889, the ship left Liverpool for the final time, bound for Genoa and Venice, calling at Falmouth. *Malta* was carrying a full complement of passengers and 2,000 tons of general cargo, which included: 633 tons of copper ingots, iron, tin plate and pig iron, 160 tons of herrings, 720 tons of sugar, various textiles, wine, beer and spirits. The next day she ran aground in poor visibility under the cliffs of Kenidjack Castle, approximately half a mile from Cape Cornwall, off Land's End. Fortunately, all the passengers and crew were safely rescued.

The *Falmouth Packet and Cornwall Advertiser* reported the wreck on 19 October 1889 with the headline 'Wreck of a Cunard Steamer':

Late on Tuesday evening the Cunard steamship '*Malta*' an iron screw steamship of 2,244 tons register, built at Glasgow in 1865, while proceeding from Liverpool to Falmouth, en route for the Mediterranean, ran ashore at Cape Cornwall, a very dangerous part of the coast. At the time the ship struck there was a dense fog, but otherwise the weather was fine. The captain and officers acted with much celerity and calmness, and thus prevented anything like a panic among the eighteen passengers, every one of whom was landed safely. The work of rescuing the crew was then commenced, and they were all landed in perfect safety. Telegrams were at once sent to Messrs C.C. Fox & Co. at Falmouth, the local agents of the company, who promptly sent two tugs to tow the '*Malta*' off, but they only succeeded in dragging her off the rocks, her stern settling down in deep water. The latest particulars to hand shew that she will very quickly become a total wreck. The decks are all smashed in, the cargo is coming to the surface, considerable wreckage is coming ashore, and salvors are busy all along the coast. The rock on which the '*Malta*' came to grief is not very far from the scene of the wreck of the '*Asia*' about two months ago. The cliff there is lofty and terribly steep, and the passengers could not possibly have got ashore had the sea been at all rough. None of the passengers' luggage was saved. One lady is said to have left £700 in a drawer on board, while others of the passengers had many valuables among their baggage.

On Wednesday a party of Sennen Cove fishermen put off to salve, securing a considerable quantity of goods, baggage, etc. On their return the sea struck the boat and turned it over, John Roberts, a fisherman of Sennen Cove unfortunately being drowned. According to most accounts, when the *Malta* grounded, a scene of great confusion ensued, but only with the crew. Orders were given which were not obeyed; things that were required could not be found; and there was general disorder, arising probably from the fact that the crew were a scratch crew, and many of them did not have any previous

One of the *Malta*'s two identical sister ships, the *Aleppo*. The other ship was the *Tarifa*. (*Eric Sauder Collection*)

knowledge of the vessel and the officers. An idea of the confusion which existed may be imagined from the fact that it was an hour and three-quarters before the first boat was launched. Rockets were sent up from the ship as a signal to the coastguard, and some St. Just people who happened to be in the neighbourhood at the time quickly spread the news.

The RNLI (Royal National Lifeboat Institution) awarded its thanks on vellum to local St Just miners Edward and William Roberts for their help in landing the passengers from the *Malta*. A financial reward of £5 was also given to two other men who had risked their own lives to save six men from the boat that capsized.

The *Falmouth Packet and Cornwall Advertiser* account also published the personal view of a reader, who commented:

> The matter ought not lightly to be passed over. The ship struck on a well known rock apparently through incompetency to take correct soundings. Even the passengers seem to have seen the land, which the look-out men failed to do. Who is responsible for sending this ship to sea with a 'scratch' crew, which surely means a crew of men totally unfit for their work? The Cunard have always been a company noted for the care they have taken to secure the safety of their passengers. If the account before us today be anywhere near the truth, the ship has been sacrificed, the passengers lives endangered, and their baggage lost, owing to the *Malta* having been sent to sea under conditions best calculated to bring about the disaster which followed.

An official Board of Trade inquiry into the cause of the stranding of the vessel was held in Liverpool between 31 October and 2 November 1889. It was established that when the *Malta* departed from Liverpool under the command of Captain Richard Lavis the ship was in good order and condition. The detailed sequence of events leading up to the loss was recorded in the report:

> The courses were given by the standard compass on the saloon deck aft, and she was steered by the steering compass in the wheelhouse. She took her departure off the South Stack about 8.55 p.m., when about 3 miles abeam, there being then a moderate breeze, the weather clear, and the wind. S.W. The master set a course S.W. ½ S., which was equal to S.W., correct magnetic. At 8.10 a.m. on the 15th he altered the course to S. by W., and continued that course to 4.43 p.m. At that time it still continued a moderate breeze, and the weather was overcast, but they could see never less than a mile. They were going at full speed, which was nine knots, and the master considered that in such weather he was justified in going that speed. At 5.50 p.m. the master altered his course to S.S.W. This was done he said to make allowance for the tide, and to put her further out. At 5.57 he put her S.W. by. S. ½ S. to ensure her being kept further off the land. There were no whistles or fog horns going. Up to this point they had not sounded; but a little after 7 p.m. not seeing any

The *Malta* foundering off Cape Cornwall, near Land's End. *(Bert Moody Collection)*

> lights, he prepared to take a cast of the lead, and had seen that the lead was ready, and had given orders to slow, but before he could do so he heard a noise on the port quarter, upon which the master sung out 'Hard-a-port,' and went back to the bridge, but the ship struck about 100 yards from the cliffs, and just then the look-out man reported 'Land ahead.' Orders were immediately given to get out the boats. The passengers were all landed by 8.30 p.m. The crew remained till midnight, when they were ordered into the boats. They remained by the ship till 8.30 a.m. on the 16th, when the master who was the last to leave the ship, and those who had remained on board with him, got into the boats and went ashore. No life was lost, but all efforts to move the ship were fruitless, and the vessel soon filled and became a total wreck.

The court learned that although the errors to the compasses had been recorded on deviation cards and sent to the ship, 'The master preferred to use his own deviations, which he had made on previous voyages, and these differed three degrees from the deviation cards'. Key factors in the case were also that 'Safe and proper alterations were not made in the course from time to time thereafter,

Having safely landed all passengers and crew, the *Malta* starts to break up on the harsh Cornish coast. *(Courtesy of Robert Lloyd)*

The treacherous Cornish waters over the wreck of the *Malta* have changed little in 100 years. *(Catherine de Lara)*

The location of a porthole, long ago removed by a brass-seeking diver. *(Catherine de Lara)*

nor was due and proper allowance made for tide', and that 'The lead should have been used, having ran his distance, and not having seen the lights'. This led the inquiry to conclude that 'the casualty was caused by the master not having made due allowance for tide, and probably from having applied an incorrect deviation, and the neglect of the lead'. The lights that Captain Lavis should have seen were at Trevose Head and Godrevy Island, and it was through not seeing those lights that he ordered a reduction in speed and for the leadsman to take sounding. It was all too late because at that time the *Malta* ran aground.

The contemporary newspaper account praised the conduct of the captain and officers but was highly critical of the 'scratch crew' when they reported that 'great confusion ensued, but only with the crew'. This was not something that was commented on in the inquiry, most probably since it did not contribute directly to the loss of the vessel, only the aftermath, the report having stated 'a good and proper look-out seemed to have been kept'.

Captain Richard A. Lavis was born in Plymouth in 1839 and joined Cunard in 1856 at the age of seventeen. He worked his way up through the ranks, becoming chief officer of the *Stromboli* in 1874. Lavis was eventually promoted to master (Certificate #20087) and his first command was the *Balbec* in 1883. He then went on to command *Atlas*, *Aleppo* and *Malta*. The court took into consideration Captain Lavis' previous excellent safety record and endorsements from Cunard, and they suspended his master's certificate for three months. Cunard themselves did not take such a lenient view and as a direct consequence of the loss of the *Malta* he was dismissed from the company.

Ribs from the iron hull angle out across a rock and sand seabed. (Catherine de Lara)

Below, left to right

Ribs reach up through the kelp forest into the Atlantic swells. (Catherine de Lara)

An anemone, the same distinctive red colour as the Cunard funnel. (Steve Metcalfe)

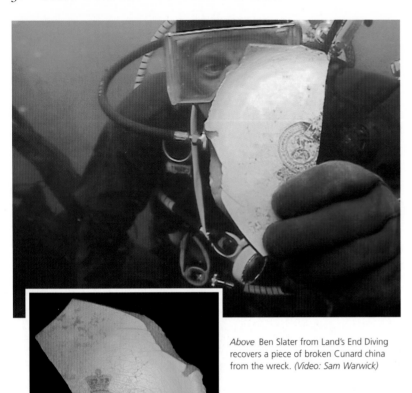

Above Ben Slater from Land's End Diving recovers a piece of broken Cunard china from the wreck. *(Video: Sam Warwick)*

Left Despite over 100 years underwater the Cunard lion logo is still clearly defined.

Another vessel was wrecked close by in similar conditions in 1937. The Italian steamer *Aida Lauro* (4,538 tons) bound from West Africa to Hull ran ashore and broke her back just 150m away from the wreck of the *Malta* on 1 July 1937.

Malta Wreck

The *Malta* lies in shallow water off the western end of Cornwall, not far from Land's End and surrounded by spectacular coastline. When approaching the area by boat it is not hard to imagine the challenges faced in order to rescue the passengers and crew so close to perilous cliffs. With a maximum depth of just 15m (50ft), the dive can be made by divers of all levels and does not require any

special equipment considerations. The main difficulties encountered are likely to be strong swells rolling in off the Atlantic, so the site is best dived during extended periods of calm weather. This is also an area of the UK coast that is seldom visited by commercial dive-boat operators. Although close to the shore, the dive should not be attempted without a boat.

Due to the shallow depth of the wreck, kelp grows abundantly across the site. This coverage can be so dense in the summer that the wreck cannot be seen at all. Therefore diving in the winter months is better as the kelp dies back a bit, although the water temperature is much cooler. Even diving in March the water is typically around 8°C (46°F). The wreck lies roughly east–west, with the bow pointing in towards the cliffs. It is fairly flat, with the highest points standing little more than 2m (7ft) proud.

There is still a significant amount of wreckage to explore and is quite easy to spend over an hour investigating the wreck and rummaging for any remaining elusive Cunard artefacts. The *Malta* has been extensively dived since the popularisation of sport diving in the UK in the 1970s. It made easy pickings for divers, who located much Cunard silver and china bearing the Cunard crest. Despite the abundance of items removed from the wreck little has been officially declared to the Receiver of Wreck. Droit number A/3323 reads: '2 x portholes, 1 x silver coffee pot, 1 x grill, 1 x dead-eye.'

The wreck has been somewhat overlooked in recent years and it is possible there may be a few artefacts remaining as the weather and tides shift around the site. On a dive in March 2005 the author found a couple of pieces of broken china with the Cunard lion clearly shown in bright red. On diving the wreck again the following June the kelp was too thick to navigate the site. The only way to get to the seabed was to cut away sections of the kelp forest with an axe. Divers always carry a knife and/or a line-cutting device, but sometimes the prevailing conditions call for something extra!

Despite the amount of wreckage in the area it is hard to make out the overall shape of the ship. However, various distinctive features are still evident, such as fair-leads and mooring bollards. Random pieces of pipe are often encountered and the occasional obscure brass fixture fused into the wreckage. Looking up to the surface, the ribs of the ship's frame can be seen along with waving fronds of kelp silhouetted against the clear Atlantic seas. The occasional flat fish might be seen and sea urchins can be found nestled amongst the wreckage and boulders.

The *Malta* is rated number ninety-five in Kendall McDonald's top 100 UK wreck dives. In a time when divers are looking to explore deeper, more challenging and intact wrecks, a site such as the *Malta* often gets overlooked and forgotten. But every wreck dive and underwater experience offers something special and the *Malta* is no exception. This is a ship that was built in 1865, the year in which Samuel Cunard himself died. Who could have imagined that nearly 150 years later vessels the size of the 150,000-ton *Queen Mary 2* would be crossing the Atlantic Ocean following the same route as the *Malta*, still bearing the name of their company's founder?

Oregon

1883–1886, USA

The steamship *Oregon* of the Cunard Line sailed between New York and Liverpool, via Queenstown.

THE *OREGON* WAS built by John Elder & Co. at the Fairfield Yard, Glasgow, for the Guion Line and launched on 23 June 1883. The iron vessel was 7,375 tons, 152.8m (501ft) in length with a beam of 16.5m (54ft). The ship had two funnels and was powered by three compound engines driving a single screw, giving a service speed of 18 knots. There were also four masts that were rigged for sail. The extensive passenger accommodation was for 340 first class, 92 intermediate (second class) and a further 1,000 in steerage.

The *Oregon* left Liverpool on 6 October 1883 for her maiden voyage under the command of Captain James Price, who was also commodore of the Guion fleet. On the maiden voyage there was no attempt to gain any transatlantic records. However, she still made the westbound voyage in a respectable seven days, eight hours and thirty-three minutes, the current record being held by another Guion Line ship *Alaska* (six days, twenty-three hours, forty-eight minutes).

It was not until her third transatlantic voyage that any records were broken. After *Oregon* had left Queenstown on 13 April 1884 she had completed the transatlantic crossing before she ran into fog on the Newfoundland Banks, and then encountered ice that caused her to take a more southerly route than usual. She passed Sandy Hook during the afternoon of 19 April, but then ran aground on a shoal in the Gedney Channel. However, she was safely floated off on the rising tide and then continued on to complete her voyage to New York. Even so, the overall time for the crossing was six days, ten hours and ten minutes, at an average speed of 18.56 knots. This took the Blue Riband from the *Alaska*, with a crossing that was thirteen hours, thirty-eight minutes faster. The *Oregon* also took the eastern record away from the *Alaska*, and was for a time the fastest transatlantic liner in the world for both the east and west transatlantic crossings.

At that time *Oregon* became known as the 'Greyhound of the Atlantic', which was one of the reasons that Cunard was interested in her. Cunard ordered two vessels of their own from the builder of the *Oregon*, John Elder & Co., with the instruction that they wanted the two builds to be faster than the *Oregon* to be able to compete with the Guion Line. These vessels were the last two Cunarders fitted with auxiliary sails, and were to become transatlantic record breakers. They were the *Umbria* (7,718 tons), who commenced her maiden voyage on 1 November 1884, and the *Etruria* (7,718 tons), whose maiden voyage was on 25 April 1885. Both were built for speed and ran at a service speed of 19 knots, 1 knot faster than the *Oregon*.

In 1884 the Guion Line was having financial difficulties and *Oregon* was sold to the Cunard Line in May that year. *Oregon* made her last transatlantic voyage for Guion from Liverpool, leaving on 10 May to New York, calling at Queenstown. The *Oregon* made her first eastbound record crossing for Cunard in July 1884 in six days, twelve hours and fifty-four minutes, at an average speed of 18.18 knots, and bettered that in September 1884, also on an eastbound crossing when she achieved the record in six days, eleven hours and nine minutes, at an average speed of 18.39 knots. In August 1885 the record was taken away from her by the *Etruria*. With the *Etruria* and *Umbria* joining the *Oregon*, Cunard Line had the world's three fastest transatlantic vessels in their fleet.

Shortly after the *Oregon* set her last record she was requisitioned by the British Government for war service and fitted out as an AMC (Armed Merchant Cruiser) should a conflict with Russia start. This was not to happen and all the requisitioned ships were returned to their owners, with the exception of the *Oregon*, which was kept back for naval manoeuvres. This was to assess how well the commercial ships would work in their naval role if they needed to be requisitioned for war service.

On 6 March 1886 *Oregon* left Liverpool for New York, calling at Queenstown to embark more passengers and mail. She was under the command of Captain Philip Cottier for what was to be her last voyage, with 186 first-class, 66 second-class and 389 steerage-class passengers, and officers and crew numbering 255.

As the *Oregon* was heading towards New York on the night of 14 March she was struck on her port side by a sailing schooner, which was thought to be the *Charles H. Morse*, approximately 18 miles off Fire Island, Long Island. The collision resulted in the *Oregon* being badly holed below the waterline, causing the ship to start sinking. All the passengers were taken off by the schooner *Fannie A. Gorham* and local pilot boat *Phantom*. The crew took to the lifeboats.

The NGL (North German Lloyd) liner *Fulda* arrived at the scene at about noon and all the passengers and crew were transferred.

Various theories were put forward as to which vessel *Oregon* had collided with and since it disappeared without trace there were even initial suggestions that the *Oregon* may have hit an underwater obstruction. But the fact that the fully laden coal schooner *Charles H. Morse* had disappeared in the area near the route that the *Oregon* would have taken led to thinking that the vessel was involved in the collision. Later wreckage thought to be from the *Charles H. Morse* was found in the area, which seemed to confirm the theory that she was the cause of the sinking of the *Oregon*.

The *Oregon* was struck on the port side, near to Mr and Mrs Hurst who occupied stateroom number fifty-four. This was an outside cabin and just abaft of the point at which the bow of the schooner ploughed through the iron side of the *Oregon*. Mrs Hurst described the event for the *New York Times*:

> I had passed a sleepless night and was looking through the deadlight into the almost impenetrable darkness. I could see the twinkling of a few stars away out where sea and sky seemed to meet. My husband awoke just then, and I spoke to him without turning my head. Suddenly the stars were shut out from view by some passing object. Then a brilliant red light shot by my cabin window, and I was calling my husbands attention to it when there was a terrible crash at the vessel's side, close to our stateroom. It was so severe as to nearly throw me off my feet, and it made the vessel shiver and tremble in a frightfully suggestive manner.

One of the last passengers to leave the stricken vessel was Mr I.C. Hopkins, who described his version of events for *The World*:

> I was seasick all the way over, and did not once have my clothes off. At 3.30am on Sunday I left my wife in our stateroom and went out on deck. It was a beautiful night, and I thought I had never before found air so clear or the stars so bright. I believe I was the only passenger up. It was a little after 4 o'clock when I went down with the steward in the galley and showed him how to make me some milk toast. I was eating it when there came a crash against our port side that made the ship quiver, and then there was the rattling of falling objects. There was a second and third shock, lighter than the first. Less than ten minutes thereafter everybody was ordered up on deck. There was no panic whatever, although all were more or less excited. Men came up half dressed, children turned out in bare feet, and many of the women appeared in their night clothes.

Mr Hopkins said that although some passengers went below to put on more clothes, others remained on deck. However, as it started to become light some steamers were seen passing the stricken ship and despite signal rockets they continued on their way. Mr Hopkins stated that after two hours of waiting

THE SUNKEN STEAMSHIP "OREGON."—VESSELS OF THE MERRITT WRECKING COMPANY PICKING UP MAIL-POUCHES, BAGGAGE, ETC., FROM THE WRECK.

Early hard-hat diver salvaging mail and cargo from the wreck of the *Oregon*.

a ship was sighted on the horizon, signal rockets were sent up and the vessel responded, making her way over to the *Oregon*.

The New York tabloid *The World* reported the loss on 15 March 1886 with the headline 'THE OREGON LOST, Sunk off Long Island by an unknown schooner. The 845 persons on board all taken off safely':

> A Pilot Boat and a coaster luckily nearby, and all are brought to the city by the German steamer Fulda – The schooner lost with all on board, it is believed – Incidents of the narrow escape – The vessel sunk in sixty feet of water – Three holes in the Oregon's side – She fills slowly and goes down head first, leaving twenty feet of her topmasts above water – Captain Cottier the last to leave the vessel – One of the officers rows ashore and sends the story of the wreck to New York – Suicide of a clergyman on board.
>
> The mighty Cunard steamer Oregon with 846 souls on board, was struck by an unknown deep laden three-masted schooner at 3.45 o'clock yesterday morning, while preceeding under a full head of steam twenty-five miles

southeast of Watch Hill, which is near Center Moriches, Long Island. Three holes were stove in the Oregon's side, one almost twenty feet square and the others smaller in dimension. The vessels drifted apart, and in the darkness the people on board the Oregon heard the despairing cries of the crew on the schooner as she settled and sank.

Further first-hand accounts followed, starting with a report from Third Officer Taylor about the moment the *Oregon* was struck:

I was below sorting the mails when I felt the shock. The first officer was in charge and was standing on the bridge at the time. The schooner was standing inshore on the port tack, and struck the Oregon in compartment 3, directly under the bridge, making a large hole in her. The hole was under water beneath the dining saloon. We tried to stop the hole, and stuffed seven beds and a number of pillows in the hole, but it did not stop the water to any large amount. Then we got out the boats and tried to save the crew of the schooner, but she sank so quickly that no trace of any of her men could be found, and we saw nothing more of them during the time we remained by the ship, which was until 11.30 o'clock this morning. Indeed the schooner went down so quickly that they were unable to get her name or even communicate with any of her crew.

The Pilot-boat #11 was sighted at 5 o'clock when the work of transferring our passengers commenced. The Oregon carried ten boats, all of which were brought into use.

The officer commends the conduct of the passengers, who did not appear at all excited and even helped in launching the boats:

The ladies were transferred first and then we commenced with the rest of the passengers and the crew of 205. Four hundred people were placed on the pilot-boat and the remainder on the schooner Fannie A. Gorham, which was sighted later. Captain Cottier remained on the ship until all were taken off. After they were all transferred we went back on board the vessel and saved all the mail we could. We succeeded in getting about one hundred bags out of about six hundred. The passengers saved none of their baggage and the crew none of their clothes or effects.

The senior officer in charge at the time was Chief Officer William Mathews, the master being below in his cabin. Mathews described getting ready for his four o'clock watch and stated that although there was a fourth officer with him on the bridge and two other lookouts, the first indication they had that another craft was nearby was when a bright light showed off the port bow, which quickly darkened; this was the usual signal that a pilot boat was near. There was no time to change course before the collision.

A comprehensive Board of Trade inquiry was held into the loss of the *Oregon* in Liverpool the following month. Thirty-four witnesses were called and two depositions were received from New York, and fourteen questions were raised for discussion. One of the key points, and one that some witness accounts differed on, was regarding the weather conditions on the night of the collision. Since the *Oregon* was travelling at her full speed of 18 knots, poor visibility would have demanded that the speed be reduced. If the visibility was good then the issue became whether or not a 'good and proper lookout was kept'. Most accounts agreed that red and green navigation lights had been seen on another vessel and that the vessel was a three-mast schooner. However, the opinions of officers and crew differed on whether the lights could have been seen sooner. The officers stated the visibility was excellent, but the ordinary seamen believed there was a haze over the water. The court accepted the officers' opinions which then raised the issue of the lookout, the conclusion being that 'there was not a good and proper lookout on board, the blame for which must rest with the chief officer'. However, the court showed leniency and Chief Officer Mathews did not have his master's certificate stamped, stating that: 'He had been negligent but not so culpably negligent that the court felt bound to visit him with any further punishment than that involved in the modified censure passed upon him.'

The inquiry also raised the issue of whether anything more could have been done to save the vessel and why the watertight doors did not prevent the vessel from sinking. They found that Captain Cottier was fully justified in all the actions he took to try to save his ship. It was concluded that the vessel might not have filled with water so quickly had there not been an issue with closing the watertight bulkhead door between No.3 hold and the coal bunker. These doors closed horizontally and the chief engineer stated his belief that the door had got blocked with coal dust or some other such debris. The inquiry suggested that vertically closing doors should be considered in the future.

Oregon Wreck

Early Salvage

Upon hearing that the *Oregon* had been lost, Cunard's New York agent Vernon Brown promptly arranged for an inspection to be carried out of the wreck site.

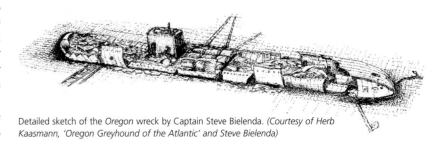

Detailed sketch of the *Oregon* wreck by Captain Steve Bielenda. *(Courtesy of Herb Kaasmann, 'Oregon Greyhound of the Atlantic' and Steve Bielenda)*

He contracted the services of the Merritt Wrecking Co. and the wrecking steamer *Rescue* was duly dispatched. The crew returned two days later and the *New York Times* reported that 'They found the Oregon lying at the bottom of the sea in 22 fathoms of water, with her three masts standing. Two of the masts are visible above the surface, about 15 feet of the mainmast being in sight.'

Since the wreck presented a major navigation hazard in the busy approaches to New York a red gas-lit buoy was placed 500ft south of the wreck. This was later replaced by lightship *LV-20*, which was moored there permanently for the next six months. By that time many ships' captains had found the lightship to be a useful aid to navigation and they petitioned congress to have a permanent one instated, but this did not materialise.

Within days of the sinking the salvage company sent hard-hat divers down to the wreck to perform a detailed inspection and commence recovery of the *Oregon*'s cargo, baggage and as many of the 598 mail bags as possible. The *Rescue* was joined by the Merritt salvage schooner *Edwin Post* and the operations were personally overseen by Captain Isaac Merritt himself. The first ten days were hampered by rough seas and only half a day of work was completed in this time. By the middle of April some progress had been made and Cunard's agent was able to forward a report to the company's headquarters in England. This included a statement from one of the divers who:

… found that the vessel had broken in two between hatches Nos. 2 and 3. The after part of the hull had been twisted out of line from the forward part, showing that the vessel had probably sheered over as she went down and had

Diver Evelyn Dudas next to one of the large capstan winches. *(Tim White)*

then broken. About 25 feet aft of the break and in line with the fore part of the bridge was found the hole which caused the vessel to sink. It was covered with canvas, which had been secured by two cords running under the keel, and five cords which had been attached to the rail. The canvas was cut away, and a break 6 feet long and 3½ feet wide was found.

It had originally been hoped that there may be a chance of raising the *Oregon*, but the survey concluded that this was not possible.

No records exist today of the salvage effort so one can only speculate as to what might have been recovered. However, the cargo manifest can give some clues to the sort of items found in the holds:

905 tons of fine goods, including laces, satin and silks
200 tons of china and earthenware
320 tons of fruit
265 tons of sundries, partly wires
145 tons of plate, rubber and steel

The cargo was valued at £205,049. To this can be added all of the personal effects of the wealthy first-class passengers and the high-quality fixtures and adornments of the vessel itself.

Early Dives
The first scuba diver to visit the wreck of the *Oregon* was Al Boehm in the late 1950s, using the services of a local fishing boat called the *Jess-Li IV*. This was big news amongst the embryonic east coast dive community and the wreck

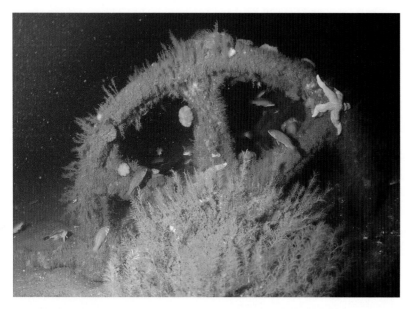
Part of the *Oregon*'s crow's nest, lying on the seabed next to the wreck. *(Tim White)*

soon became a popular destination for the newly formed Oceanographic Historic Research Society (OHRS). In 1960 the OHRS surveyed the wreck with a team of twenty divers who salvaged Cunard and Guion china, proving the wreck's identity beyond any doubt. During this period the first underwater photographs were taken by local diving legend Mike deCamp. The pictures showed a vast amount of crockery and artefacts scattered across the wreck. These early dives also helped to establish the wreck's reputation for being a prolific source of large lobsters.

The *Oregon* has since become one of the most popular and regularly dived wrecks off the north-east American coast.

On 14 March 1986 divers aboard the *R.V. Wahoo* skippered by Captain Steve Bielenda, himself a veteran *Oregon* diver, celebrated the hundredth anniversary of the ship's sinking. Thirty-five divers took part, many of whom were well-known names in the east coast diving scene. Limited edition, numbered, copper wall plaques were issued to commemorate the historic dive.

Harvey Leonard

Pioneering New York diver and dive shop owner Harvey Leonard deserves a special mention and the *Oregon* was known to be his favourite wreck in the area. Harvey recovered his fair share of artefacts, but it was definitely the lobsters that were the main attraction for him and he had a well-earned reputation for bagging plenty of the big ones.

On one occasion Harvey embarked on an Atlantic crossing on board a much newer and larger Cunard liner, the *Queen Elizabeth 2*. He took with him many items of china and glassware that had been recovered from dives to the *Oregon*. The captain on that voyage happened to be the author's father, Ron Warwick. On learning of Harvey's unique collection the captain invited him to the captain's cabin, where the historic dinnerware was laid out on the dining table in recreation of a scene from a bygone era. The captain and Harvey remained good friends from then on.

Sadly Harvey lost his life on a dive to the *Oregon* in July 1998 at the age of sixty. It is a poignant reminder of the inherent risks entailed in pursuit of an adventurous activity such as wreck diving.

Wreck Today

The *Oregon* is located 15 miles off the east coast of Long Island in an area known locally as Wreck Valley due to the abundance of sunken vessels. Despite having steadily deteriorated during more than a century below the waters of the Atlantic there is a lot to see of this famous ocean liner. The *Oregon* lies at depth of 40m (130ft), with the bow pointing due north and the shallowest part being the engines at 25m (85ft). With a length of nearly 160m (525ft), it takes several dives to cover all of the wreck. The starboard side is higher than the port side, where the wreckage slopes down into the seabed. Much of the hull plating has fallen away to the sides and is perforated with holes that once housed portholes.

The bow is the most intact and recognisable part of the original hull, although it lies rolled over on the starboard side for the first 23m (75ft) or so. The bow still takes on the sleek narrow appearance of a Blue Riband winner. There are several large winches near the bow along with other parts of deck gear. After the bow the wreck becomes very flat and broken. This is also the area of the forward holds, where cargo and luggage was stowed.

The next main feature is the bank of boilers featuring nine identical coal-fired boilers in three rows of three. Described by diver David Rosenthal: 'They are like little cottages with alleys between them. You can go here, then make left and then a right, swimming between them.' There are a lot of scattered firebricks in this area. Immediately behind the boilers are the remains of *Oregon*'s giant compound steam engine standing upright high above the wreck. There are three distinct pistons and it is possible to swim through the piston arms.

Aft of the engine the wreck again starts to flatten out into an area that was once part of the promenade deck. Somewhere under here must be the remains of the prop shaft. Finally the diver will arrive at the stern, where there is one of the most distinctive and photogenic parts of the wreck, the huge steering quadrant that was used to control the rudder. The large single iron propeller is still in place below the rudder and two of the propeller blades are prominent.

The *Oregon* can be dived at any state of the tide but currents can be very strong at times. The standard practice among divers in this part of the world is to anchor or 'tie-in' to the wreck. This means it is imperative to return to the anchor line at the end of the dive. If the current is running then a jon line can be used to make any decompression stops more comfortable.

Visibility can vary considerably, being anything from a metre (3ft) to 30m (100ft), but the average tends to be around 9m (30ft). The east coast diving

The top of the engine is covered in marine life and is the shallowest part of the wreck. *(Tim White)*

The massive steering quadrant on the *Oregon* wreck dwarves the diver in the foreground. *(© 2012 Bradley Sheard)*

season typically runs from April until November with water temperatures varying from 7°C (45°F) to 16°C (60°F).

The *Oregon* has become a haven for marine life. In addition to the large lobsters already described, divers are likely to see: ling, cod, hake, ocean pout, blackfish, stone crabs and rays. Much of the wreck itself is covered with a variety of colourful plumose anemones. Sharks have also been known to appear in the shallower depths.

Artefacts

By far the largest item to be raised in recent times was the *Oregon*'s spare Trotman anchor, which had a length of 4m (13ft) and weighed over 3 tons. A Trotman anchor is based on the standard Admiralty pattern but has a swivelling crown and unusually shaped flukes. The anchor lay undiscovered on the seabed near the bow of the wreck for many years until it was recognised by diver Pat Rooney during a routine tie-in. Rooney was a veteran of the *Oregon* having made over 1,000 dives to the wreck. On 12 July 2008 Rooney organised two boats with a team of more than twenty people to make the recovery. Divers from the *Lockness* dive boat shackled secure lifting cables to the anchor on the seabed, which was then winched aboard the fishing vessel *Susan H.* The anchor was successfully brought ashore and is currently on proud display outside a Long Island dive shop.

The range of items recovered from the *Oregon* over the years is nothing short of astounding. Some of the earlier navigational items raised were the binnacle, compass and helm stand. The helm itself got lost on its journey to the surface and has never been relocated. One unique aspect of *Oregon* artefacts is that the ship still carried a significant amount of Guion Line chinaware in addition to the newer Cunard Line crockery. The range of finds includes: portholes, bottles, silver, crystal, china, plates, cups, jars, chamber pots, all manner of brass fixtures and fittings, deck prisms, vases, dead eyes, watches and statues. Even porcelain toilets have been brought up!

Even after fifty years of diving amazing discoveries are still made, albeit at a much slower rate. Also divers are now concentrating on finding the smaller items, such as jewellery, silver cutlery, officers' buttons and coins.

Amazingly the most prized possession for any wreck diver, the *Oregon*'s bell, has never knowingly been found.

Iberia

One of the other numerous wrecks in the area worthy of a special mention is the *Iberia*, which was a small freighter of 1,388 tons built in 1881. Although the ship has a name ending in the traditional Cunard 'ia', the *Iberia* belonged to a French company called Cyprien Fabre. However, its loss was caused by a collision with the Cunard ship *Umbria* on 10 November 1888, two and a half years after the *Oregon* went down. The *Umbria* was damaged but was able to make it safely to New York where repairs were carried out.

Both Guion Line and Cunard Line china is found on the wreck of the *Oregon*. *(Eric Sauder Collection)*

 # *Feltria*

1891–1917, Ireland

THE *FELTRIA* WAS a passenger/cargo ship built in 1891 as the *Avoca* for the British India Steam Navigation Co. The ship was constructed by William Denny & Bros of Dumbarton and launched on 9 June 1891. *Avoca* was 5,324 tons, 128m (420ft) in length with a beam of 14.7m (48ft). The ship was of steel construction, with four-cylinder, quadruple-expansion engines powering a single screw at 13 knots. There was a single funnel, three masts and accommodation for 400 third-class passengers.

The *Avoca* made its maiden voyage on 25 August 1891, first to Calcutta and onward to Brisbane. From then on the ship went through numerous changes of role, name, owner and operator. First *Avoca* was chartered briefly to Cia Transatlantica in 1895 and renamed *San Fernando* for trooping voyages to Cuba. The ship's name reverted to *Avoca* and during 1899–1900 she made four trooping voyages between India and South Africa for the Boer War, with a fifth as a hospital ship. *Avoca* was sold to East Asiatic Co., Copenhagen, in 1907, renamed *Atlanta* and painted white. During this time the ship was used briefly as the royal yacht for the visit of King Christian of Denmark to Greenland. In 1908 there was a short charter to the New York & Continental Line, when the ship was renamed back to *Avoca*. The ship was sold to the North West Transport Line in 1909 and renamed *Uranium*, and in 1910 the company was taken over by the Uranium Steamship Co. Finally, in 1916, the ship was sold to the Cunard Line, along with the rest of the Uranium fleet and renamed *Feltria*, sailing from Avonmouth to New York.

Prior to the sale to Cunard *Avoca* experienced an incident on 12 January 1913, when she ran aground in thick fog near Halifax while going to the aid of the Allan liner *Carthaginian*, which was on fire. The ship was salvaged, refitted and improved, and later resumed her regular service.

On 5 May 1917 at 7.30 p.m. the *Feltria* was sunk by *UC-48* (Commander Kurt Ramien) 8 miles south-east of Mine Head, Waterford at 51.56N, 07.24W while sailing from New York to Avonmouth with general cargo.

The *Feltria* was sailing in very heavy seas when she was struck by the submarine torpedo and it was not easy launching the lifeboats in such weather. The No.1 lifeboat capsized while being launched and the No.4 lifeboat had been destroyed by the explosion of the torpedo. Fortunately the crew managed to get lifeboats Nos 2, 3, 5 and 6 successfully away from the ship's side. Although most of the crew were in lifeboats No.3 and No.5, the master Captain Walter Price and chief steward were alone in the No.2 lifeboat, which had also been damaged by the force of the explosion. No.6 lifeboat had the chief officer, second officer, purser and three sailors. The submarine surfaced alongside lifeboat No.6 and

Diver Harvey Leonard and Captain Ron Warwick with dinnerware raised from the *Oregon*, in the captain's cabin aboard the *QE2* during an Atlantic crossing. *(Warwick Family Collection)*

questioned the chief officer about what cargo they were carrying. As they were sailing away the submarine picked up one of the engineers from the water and took him to one of the lifeboats.

During the night three members of crew in the No.6 lifeboat died from exposure, and the No.2 lifeboat containing the captain and chief steward was not seen again, but the remaining three crew members in lifeboat No.6 were rescued by SS *Ridley* and landed at Barrow. Out of the crew of sixty-nine there were forty-five lives lost, including the master.

Feltria Wreck

The wreck of the *Feltria* rests 10 miles off the south-east corner of Ireland between Dungarvan and Waterford. There are hundreds of shipwrecks in the area, many of which are also from the First World War and many that have not yet been positively identified. This stretch of the Celtic Sea is notorious for poor underwater visibility and many of the wrecks are in depths of 50m (164ft) or more.

The maximum depth to the seabed around the *Feltria* is 67m (220ft) and it is possible that the wreck may have been visited in the early 1990s by divers pushing the limits on air. These days trimix is a safer gas to breathe on a dive of this depth and a typical bottom time would be thirty minutes, requiring an hour of decompression. The *Feltria* is not a wreck that is visited very often, probably because divers have so many other choices in the area. A popular wreck nearby is the *Manchester Engineer*, also known locally as the 'Glass Wreck' and sometimes confused with the *Feltria*.

The main challenge for divers visiting the *Feltria* is the consistently poor visibility, which is often less than 1m (3ft). This is compounded by the mono-filament fishing line that is snagged on the wreck. Divers have to swim slowly and cautiously, and consequently only small sections of this 128m (420ft) long wreck can be safely explored on each dive. Occasionally visibility can be a bit better, and for divers who are prepared to make the effort the *Feltria* is a very worthwhile and interesting wreck to explore.

The *Feltria* is upright with a list to port and is relatively intact despite the damage caused by the torpedo. The bow is clearly recognisable and the chain lockers can be easily identified. There are numerous mooring bollards on the decks and occasionally guard rails are seen still standing upright and intact. In some places the teak decking is still evident, along with various brass fixtures.

Left, from top

The *Feltria* was previously the *Avoca* and served in the Boer War between 1899 and 1900, including one voyage as a hospital ship. *(Ian Lawler Collection)*

Before being purchased by Cunard *Feltria* operated for the Northwest Transport Line as *Uranium*. *(Ian Lawler Collection)*

Forty-five people lost their lives when *Feltria* was torpedoed by *UC-48* in 1917. *(© Timmy Carey)*

A lamp from the *Feltria*.

The forward mast lies collapsed across the seabed, along with parts of wreckage that have collapsed and slid down the gently sloping decks. Finning across the decks, it is possible to peer down into holes and hatchways looking for interesting features and artefacts from *Feltria*'s varied service history. Divers have reported seeing the remains of fine bathrooms and sinks complete with high-quality brass taps, possibly remnants of *Feltria*'s time as a royal yacht. Surprisingly not much china or cutlery has been found. The hull is lined with portholes that are firmly attached and there is distinctive fantail stern. Other notable features of the wreck are the three large double-ended boilers (technically *Feltria* had six boilers). Large quantities of phosphorous have been seen on the wreck, probably part of the ship's cargo of general government supplies.

Diver Timmy Carey, who has made over ten dives on the wreck, feels that he has only just started to scratch the surface of what the *Feltria* has to offer and that every dive offers something different. This is a sentiment shared by local diver Eoin McGarry, who regards the *Feltria* as one of his favourite wrecks. Eoin recovered an Admiralty anchor from the forward deck, which is on display in the town of Dungarvan.

This Admiralty anchor was raised from the wreck of the *Feltria* and is on display in Dungarvan. (*Eoin McGarry*)

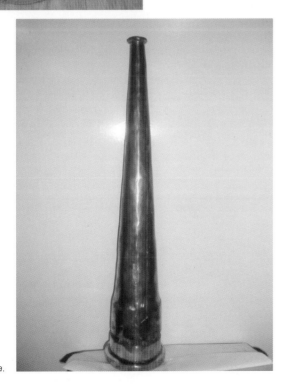

Firehose nozzle from the *Feltria*.

Campania

1893–1918, Scotland

The *Campania* was the fastest passenger liner afloat when she entered service in 1893. Shown here in her home port of Liverpool.

CAMPANIA WAS BUILT for the Cunard Steamship Co. by Fairfield Co. Ltd, Glasgow, and launched on 8 September 1892 by Lady Burns, wife of the chairman of Cunard. The steel ship was 12,950 tons, with a length of 183.2m (601ft) and beam of 19.8m (65ft). There were two funnels and two masts. The *Campania*'s twin screws were powered by a ten-cylinder, triple-expansion engine, giving an impressive service speed of 21 knots. On her trials, *Campania* reached speeds of up to 23.5 knots. The passenger accommodation was for 600 first-class, 400 second-class and 1,000 third-class passengers, with a crew complement of 423.

With the introduction of twin propellers, the *Campania* became the first Cunard Line steamship to relinquish the use of sails. If the engine of a single-propeller vessel broke down, wind power then became the alternate method of propulsion. Dispensing with the sails had the added advantage of allowing the shipbuilders to add more decks and so the image of the modern liner started to take form.

At the time of launch the *Campania* had the largest triple-expansion engines ever fitted to a Cunard ship, and also the largest in the world at the time. However, to protect them from any possible breach in the hull, each of the engines was placed in a separate watertight engine compartment. This would have the advantage, should there be a problem with a breach and one engine room flooded, that the other could keep working and produce enough power to see the ship back to the safety of the nearest port. Other safety measures introduced were watertight compartments to seal off any flooded compartments and keep the ship afloat.

The *Campania* 'in frame'.

Below The *Campania* almost ready for launch on the banks of the Clyde at Glasgow.

Both the *Campania* and her sister ship *Lucania* had the Brown Bros of Edinburgh quadrant-style steering gear, and this became the main steering gear used in ships until well into the twentieth century. All the steering gear was below the waterline. This was a condition laid down by the Admiralty, who also part funded the building of the *Campania* as it was designed to act as an AMC (Armed Merchant Cruiser) in time of war.

The Germans, who were competing with the new designs of ships, were building larger vessels year on year and this led to the four-funnelled liners. However, the *Campania* and her sister ship could be identified from quite a distance by the large size of their two funnels. At the time they went into service not only were they the world's fastest ocean liners, but also the world's largest ships.

The public rooms included a spacious lounge, music room, smoking room and a library. Upon entering service both the *Campania* and her

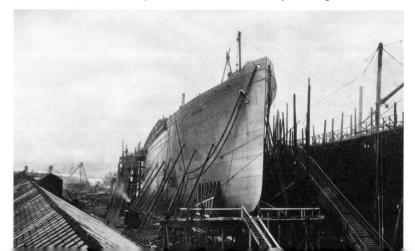

The first-class drawing room on board the *Campania*.

identical sister ship *Lucania* provided the most luxurious first-class passenger accommodation available at the time, including panelled public rooms and staterooms, velvet curtains and thick carpets. Although the main style of design was art nouveau, other styles were seen, including French renaissance. The first-class dining saloon was spectacular with its central part rising three decks to a skylight, and the smoking room included the first ever open fireplace on an ocean liner.

Campania and *Lucania* were the first twin-screw ocean liners and the largest and fastest passenger liners afloat when they entered service in 1893. The *Campania* left Liverpool for her maiden voyage on 22 April 1893 for New York, calling at Queenstown (Cobh) and New York. On her second voyage, 6–11 May 1893, she broke the eastbound record from Sandy Hook to Queenstown, averaging 21.5 knots, taking five days, seventeen hours and twenty-seven minutes. On 18–23 June 1893 she also took the westbound record from Queenstown to Sandy Hook, with a time of five days, fifteen hours and thirty-seven minutes, averaging 21.12 knots and taking the record from the Inman Line's *City of Paris*. The following year *Campania* reduced her time further, with the westbound voyage on 12–17 August 1894 from Queenstown to Sandy Hook taking five days, nine hours, twenty-nine minutes and averaging 21.44 knots.

Both the *Campania* and *Lucania* served as Cunard's primary transatlantic passenger liners for fourteen years, during which time they were superseded in both speed and size by a succession of four-funnelled German liners, starting with the Norddeutscher Lloyd ocean liner *Kaiser Wilhelm der Grosse* in 1897.

In 1901 *Lucania* became the first Cunard liner to be fitted with a Marconi wireless system, shortly after followed by the *Campania*. The use of wireless began to prove its importance when both the *Campania* and *Lucania* exchanged information about ice dangers at sea. Late in 1905 *Campania* became the first liner to have a permanent radio connection to coastal stations on both sides of the Atlantic.

The Cruel Atlantic

The rough seas of the North Atlantic often took their toll on ships, passengers and crew, and unfortunately *Campania* was involved in several incidents that resulted in loss of life.

While returning from New York in July 1900, under the command of Captain Henry Walker, *Campania* ran into thick fog 207 miles west of Queenstown and collided with the barque sailing ship *Embleton*, cutting her in half and causing her to sink immediately. The captain and ten members of the eighteen-man crew were drowned, the remainder being saved in lifeboats. The *Campania* incurred some damage to the bow, mast and rigging, but the captain managed to get the liner safely to Liverpool.

On another crossing in September 1901 the liner was making a typical voyage from Liverpool to New York when an unusually heavy sea broke over the ship's starboard bow. The boatswain's mate George Davis was standing near the chart room when a large wave struck, hurling him against some machinery and killing him instantly. Moments before, the Marconi wireless operator H.M. Downsett had only just avoided a similar fate. The passengers organised a collection and generously raised over £1,000 for Davis' family.

On 14 October 1905 initial reports reached New York by Marconi wireless that a giant wave had swept over the *Campania* in mid-Atlantic and injured twenty-eight steerage passengers. The next day Captain Robert C. Warr sent a further communication with the tragic news that five passengers had been washed overboard to their deaths. Their names were Margaret Cleary, Mary Cosgrove, Neils Ekberg, Elizabeth Grunadotter and John Graham. Many of the injuries were very serious and one young girl's legs were so badly broken that amputation was required by the ship's doctors. At the time the wave struck at least 100 of the 680 steerage passengers were out on deck and although the winds were strong there was no warning of the imminent danger from the freak wave. Only through the swift actions of the officers and crew of the *Campania* was further tragedy averted and their conduct was praised by the passengers.

John Graham was a resident of Milwaukee who was returning home from Europe with his wife Susan on the fateful voyage. She was with him on deck at the time of the accident and suffered injuries to her hip that bothered her for the rest of her life. To make matters worse, Mr Graham had $500 in his pockets which was all the family's fortune and was lost with him. It was common for steerage passengers to keep all their money upon their person and one man who was saved had $20,000 on him. The cabin passengers organised a collection for their fellow passengers in steerage and $1,500 was raised, of which $1,200 was awarded to Mrs Graham, probably on account of her status as an American citizen. This was poor consolation to the Graham family's seven children who had lost their father. One of John Graham's daughters described the event in a local newspaper report:

John Graham, a steerage passenger who was swept overboard by a freak wave in 1905. (Patrick Lynch)

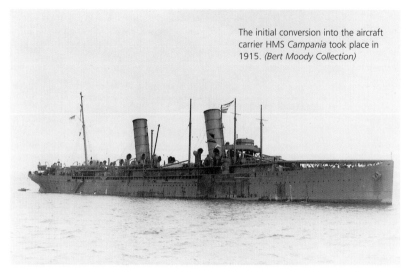

The initial conversion into the aircraft carrier HMS Campania took place in 1915. (Bert Moody Collection)

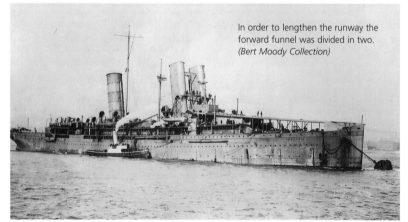

In order to lengthen the runway the forward funnel was divided in two. (Bert Moody Collection)

HMS Campania sank in the Firth of Forth in 1918 after colliding with a Navy vessel.

Mamma was below decks looking out at the storm from the window when papa called to her and said 'Mamma, just come up here and look at these angry waves.' Mamma didn't want to go at first, but she wanted to be with papa, so she put her shawl about her and went to him. They stood there by the gangway, mamma with her arm entwined about the railing, watching the sea, laughing and talking, with no thought of fear, when suddenly there was a great wave swept over them, carrying them both off their feet and causing great confusion, so she could neither see nor hear anything; she felt papa clutch at her shoulder, then he was swept away from her, with the shawl in his fingers. She, too, was carried off her feet and almost into the sea, and would have been gone with father had it not been that in the nick of time a man caught her by the arm and pulled her back.

HMS *Campania*

A list of 1912 New York to Liverpool sailings showed *Campania* had been scheduled for nine crossings, but with reduced numbers of passengers thoughts of her being taken out of service were considered. The *Campania* left on her last voyage from Liverpool to New York in April 1914. *Campania* was then chartered to the Anchor Line for two Glasgow to New York sailings in 1914 and returned to Cunard's Liverpool to New York service, taking over from the *Aquitania* which had been requisitioned for war service. *Aquitania* had only undertaken three voyages before she was taken up for conversion to an AMC. *Campania* was then called to take the place of the *Aquitania*, but unfortunately only managed three voyages before being sold for scrap.

Her final transatlantic voyage started on 26 September 1914, and she arrived back at Liverpool on 15 October 1914. After this voyage she was sold for scrap, but was then resold to the British Admiralty and converted to an aircraft carrier to carry seaplanes. The aim was for floatplanes to be lowered by crane into the water from the ship and also lifted up after landing on the water to be then stowed on board.

The conversion was undertaken by the Cammell Laird shipyard in Birkenhead, and this included gutting the inside to make room for the storage of aircraft. The armaments originally consisted of eight 4.7in guns.

As part of her Admiralty refit, her forward funnel was removed and replaced by two smaller ones. A 48.76m (160ft) wooden flight deck was added at the bow, allowing aircraft to be launched from the deck of the *Campania*, removing the requirement to lower the seaplanes into the sea. However, the length of the flight deck was proven to be too short and further work was undertaken to lengthen the flight deck to 67m (220ft). It was from the *Campania*'s flight deck that the Sopwith Pup biplane fighters took off. At this time the two forward guns were removed and a single 3in gun was added.

Once the conversion was completed at the end of April 1915, HMS *Campania* sailed under the command of Captain Oliver Swan RN to join the Grand Fleet in Scapa Flow. Interestingly, his first officer was Charles H. Lightoller, who had been second officer on the *Titanic* when she sank in April 1912.

Soon after joining the Grand Fleet HMS *Campania* made Royal Navy history, being the first ship to launch aircraft while under way. The importance of being able to launch aircraft while at sea was to have the aircraft flying ahead to scout for the German fleet.

In the early twentieth century tests were undertaken to establish the usefulness of man-carrying balloons for observational purposes, and these were being used in the battlefields of France. It was decided during the conversion also to remove the aft mast from the aft deck to use for observation balloons, and so HMS *Campania* also served as an observation balloon ship.

HMS *Campania* sonar survey from 2008 rendered with WreckSight visualisation software. *(Courtesy of ADUS and Historic Scotland)*

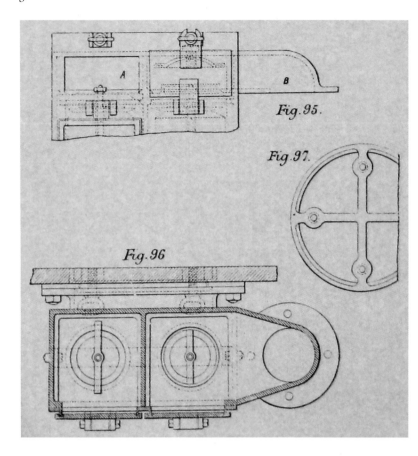

Left The hull of the *Campania* was lined with a series of unique ventilation system intakes.

Above Many of these have become home for crabs and lobsters. *(Video: Sam Warwick)*

HMS *Campania* operated out of Scapa Flow for most of the war, but by October 1918 she was transferred to operating out of Burntisland in the Firth of Forth, and it was there that she met her fate on 5 November 1918 when she was sunk after a collision with a Royal Navy vessel.

On the morning of 5 November HMS *Campania* was anchored off Burntisland, along with a number of other Navy vessels, when a sudden force-10 squall caused her to drag her anchor. *Campania* collided with HMS *Royal Oak*, then HMS *Glorious* and finally her hull was punctured by the forefoot of HMS *Revenge*, causing her engine room to flood, with the loss of all electrical power. *Campania* began to settle by the stern, sinking just a few hours after the collision. All the crew were safely rescued.

A Royal Navy inquiry into the sinking found the watch officer responsible for the accident and recorded his failure to order the dropping of a second anchor when the ship had started to drag her anchor and drift towards the other ships.

It was a sad ending to HMS *Campania*, especially as the sinking occurred just six days before the Armistice was signed on 11 November 1918.

The unfortunate fate of *Campania*'s sister ship *Lucania* came about in 1909, when the ship caught fire and capsized at her pier in Liverpool, subsequently being scrapped.

Campania Wreck

Following her sad demise, *Campania* caused an obstruction in the busy shipping lanes of the Forth. Large parts of the wreck still protruded above the surface and the masts and funnels could clearly be seen. So explosive charges were laid and detonated to disperse the wreck, which was eventually cleared to an acceptable depth by 1921. Further clearance was again carried out in 1947 and the site was then 'swept' to ensure an acceptable level of clearance (12m, or 39ft) for ships navigating the channel. It is understood the wreck was acquired for salvage sometime in the 1960s and that metals of value were removed. One salvage diver working the wreck was reported to have laid a series of lines over the site to aid navigation.

The *Campania* has been known to recreational divers for several decades, but it is not clear when the wreck started to be regularly visited. There are very few reports of any artefacts of any significant value or historic interest being removed from the wreck. The Receiver of Wreck only has one item declared from the *Campania*, which is a porthole. It is unlikely that any ephemera relating back to the Cunard years would have remained on a ship that had been in naval service for several years. In 2001 *Campania* was designated a protected wreck under the Protection of Wrecks Act of 1973 and in 2013 reclassified as a Historic Marine Protected Area. Designation does not prevent public access, but divers must not remove artefacts or interfere with the wreck in any way.

A brief entry for the *Campania* in *Dive Scotland* (1992) concludes: 'One visit is usually one too many, even for the most experienced of divers.' But the current author dived on the wreck several times in 2011 and would happily return for further exploration.

Despite her relatively shallow depth of 30m (98ft), the *Campania* is indeed a challenging wreck to dive. However, for divers with suitable experience it is worth making the effort. First forget all thoughts of finding an intact and recognisable aircraft carrier awaiting you at the bottom of the shot line! There are a number of factors that require careful consideration when planning a dive on the *Campania* and these are mostly due to the wreck's location in the mouth of the Forth. This area is very tidal, with a range of up to 6m (20ft), so strong currents are prevalent on the site. Therefore dives need to be planned for times of the year when tides are low and there is a reasonable slack-water window for diving. The visibility is seldom good on the wreck and divers should expect the worst and hope for the best. The fact that the wreck lies on a flat and muddy seabed makes matters worse and divers need to avoid disturbing the silty sediment. This is one of those dives where sometimes you will literally not even be able to see your own hand in front of your face. To help offset the poor visibility diving in the late spring when the sun is strongest will help provide more ambient light. Ironically, the dive is also a popular night dive with the local divers. This is largely due to the natural luminescence provided by the marine life on the wreck. The tides and low visibility lead into a final important point for consideration, which is the physical structure of the wreck itself. It is very easy to find yourself inadvertently penetrating parts of the wreck. Thermal protection also needs to be considered in these cool Scottish waters. For example, in June the water temperature is typically around 8°C (46°F). Divers also need to be aware that the wreck is located right on the edge of a major shipping lane and extra caution needs to be taken when surfacing. The southern end of the wreck is within metres of the green starboard channel marker buoy.

Some early accounts suggest that the wreck lies in two distinct sections 200m (656ft) apart. However, subsequent side-scan sonar surveys of the wreck prove

Right, from top

Many of the portholes still contain glass, but it is easy to miss them since the wreck is covered in dead man's fingers. *(Catherine de Lara)*

Diver Johno de Lara carefully exploring the dark wreck. *(Catherine de Lara)*

One of the 4.7in guns that was added during *Campania*'s conversion to HMS *Campania*. *(Catherine de Lara)*

this to be incorrect. The wreck is in one complete section approximately 200m (656ft) long by 20m (66ft) wide, lying on the starboard side with the bow to the north. Depth to the seabed is 30m (98ft) and the highest point of the structure stands up to 20m (66ft), occasionally shallower towards the bow. Descending to the wreck, the green ambient light soon fades and darkens, depending on the prevailing conditions on the day. Since the visibility is seldom more than a few metres most divers will concentrate on one area of the wreck around the shot line. This is not the sort of wreck you can realistically attempt to see in one dive. In fact, even divers who visit the wreck regularly are still learning the layout and features.

A typical dive will start amidships. On arrival on the wreck you immediately notice the intense covering of dead man's fingers and plumose anemones. These are so dense that they often hide features and obscure portholes. To the western side of the wreck the hull slopes down steeply, almost vertical in places. Exploring these wide expanses of hull, intact portholes (some with glass) can be seen. A row of ventilation vents the size of dinner plates was observed on one dive by the author. Behind each one a crustacean resident could often be found, typically lobsters and edible crabs. Moving to the eastern side of the wreck the structure is less defined and more broken. Towards the bow at the north divers have reported that the structure is more intact with anchor chains in evidence. Kelp can be found growing on some of the shallower parts of the wreck.

Reminders of *Campania*'s final role as a naval ship and aircraft carrier are often encountered. The ship was armed with seven guns, with two placed on either side at the bow, amidships and stern. The guns are often seen by divers but can be hard to distinguish between sections of mast, which are also in evidence. Remains of the cranes used to recover the Fairey Campania seaplanes launched from the ship can be found towards the forward end of the wreck. There is a very long section of one of the main masts that lies across the wreck, sloping down at a shallow angle, and this can be followed for some distance.

There is little fish life on the wreck, but it is a haven for all manner of other marine life. Lion's mane jellyfish are often present. Seals are often reported by divers, typically appearing playfully around the shot line.

A typical bottom time on the *Campania* is around thirty minutes. Although the relatively shallow depth combined with a nitrox mix would normally allow for a longer dive, the tides and temperature become limiting factors.

In addition to the *Campania* there are many other interesting wrecks and dive sites in the Firth of Forth. Many of these are worth a visit, typically as a second dive after visiting the *Campania*. In keeping with the aircraft theme, a Grumman Avenger plane is intact and upright on a shallow seabed at 14m (46ft). The search and rescue tug HMS *Saucy* is also an excellent dive. The bow is particularly impressive, being upright with both anchors hanging down from the hawse pipes. There is a prominent gun on the bow.

 # *Thracia*

1898–1917, France

THE *THRACIA* WAS originally built as the *Orono* for the Plate Steamship Co. by Sir Raylton Dixon & Co., Middlesbrough, and launched on 30 August 1898. It was a cargo ship with no passenger accommodation. The vital statistics were 2,891 tons, 94.4m (310ft) in length, with a beam of 13.4m (44.1ft). The ship was constructed of steel with one funnel and two masts. A three-cylinder, triple-expansion engine powered a single screw at 10 knots.

The *Orono* was purchased along with her sister ship *Oceano* in 1909 by Cunard to operate on its Mediterranean cargo service routes and renamed *Thracia*. The *Oceano* was renamed *Lycia* (1) and both vessels were sunk by German U-boats in the First World War. The *Lycia* (1) was sunk first on 11 February 1917, and *Thracia* just one month later on 27 March 1917.

The *Thracia* met her fate while sailing at 7 knots in convoy from Bilbao to Glasgow with a cargo of iron ore when she was torpedoed by *UC-69* (Commander Erwin Wassner), a coastal minelayer. The attack occurred at 8 p.m. on 27 March 1917, 12 miles north of Belle Ile, Brittany, at position 47.31N, 03.17W, with the loss of thirty-six crew, including the captain. *UC-69* was a Type UCII coastal minelayer, built by Blohm and Voss, Hamburg, in 1916. *UC-69* was later sunk off Barfleur, Normandy, in December 1917, after being involved in a collision with *U-96*.

The captain of the *Thracia* was a young man called Richard Nicholas, who joined Cunard in 1908. He first served on the *Thracia* as second officer in May 1912 and worked his way up through the ranks on *Ivernia* (1) and *Alaunia* (1). When he joined the *Thracia* on 26 December 1916 it was his very first command.

There were just two survivors from the sinking of the *Thracia*: one was picked up by a French fishing boat and the other by the Norwegian steamer *Nordborg* and landed at Barry, South Wales.

The first survivor was Douglas Valder Duff, who later went on to become a prolific author of maritime fiction, writing over eighty books. He also wrote two autobiographies, *May the Winds Blow* and *Swallow the Anchor*, the former of which dedicates a chapter to the sinking of the *Thracia*. Duff had joined the *Thracia* as a cadet the year before, just a few months short of his fifteenth birthday, having completed his training at HMS *Conway*. He managed to survive the night clinging to the wreckage of an upturned lifeboat and, when he was rescued the following day, he assumed himself to be the sole survivor of the *Thracia*. Just over a year later Duff was again the victim of enemy action when the Cunard ship *Flavia* was torpedoed off the west coast of Ireland.

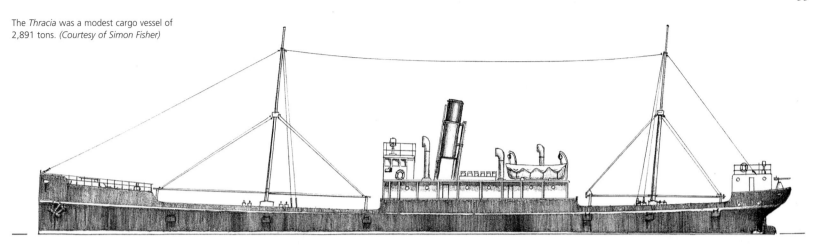

The *Thracia* was a modest cargo vessel of 2,891 tons. *(Courtesy of Simon Fisher)*

There is a full account of the sinking of the *Thracia* in the book *The Merchant Seaman in War* by Leslie Cope Cornford, published in 1918. This book confirms that there was a second survivor who was a Royal Marine gunner:

The events of March 27th, 1917, are, like the night that covered them, darkly clear, with here and there significant and daunting glimpses opening between great spaces of blackness and again obscured. And those glimpses are the reflection of a reflection in the mind's mirror of two men.

One was the gunner of the steamship *Thracia*, a private of the Royal Marines. The time was between eight and nine o'clock at night; the ship was in the Channel, bound to a home port; the gunner was on duty, stationed at his gun on the poop. He heard a sharp detonation, which (he said) sounded like the crack of a pistol fired somewhere forward. A column of water mingled with black smoke shot up forward of the bridge to starboard. Four short blasts sounded on the siren, signifying 'Abandon ship'. The gunner ran forward, mingling with a crowd of hurrying figures in the dark, felt the ship sinking downwards towards the bows beneath his feet as he ran, and understood that she would go down ere the boats could be lowered. He turned and ran back to the gun to fetch his lifebelt, slung it on, climbed on the rail to dive, and before he knew exactly what had happened he found himself in the sea. Events, as they do on these occasions, succeeded one another more swiftly than consciousness could register.

The gunner was drawn deep down in the icy water, came up again, and struck out, shouting for help with all his strength. He swam and shouted during what, with a seaman's particularity, he estimated to be a period of twenty minutes, rising and falling with the lop of sea, fighting for his life, and then there came answering calls, a boat loomed above him, and he was hauled on board. She had been lowered from a neutral steamer, which afterwards landed the sturdy Marine at an English port. He thought at first he was the sole survivor of the *Thracia*.

When the gunner on deck heard a detonation like the report of a pistol, the acting fourth officer, a boy of fifteen, who was just getting into his bunk below, felt a shock as of a small explosion about the main bunker. As he ran up on deck in his shirt, the siren blew the signal 'Abandon ship'. The next thing the boy knew he was being drawn down with the sinking vessel.

Struggling to the surface, he saw a capsized boat, swam to it, and found it was part of the starboard lifeboat, of which the stern had been blown off. The fourth officer climbed in the boat and lashed himself to it. Other men swam to the boat and hung on. The fourth officer counted seven. He made out that two among them were badly hurt. The other men could give them no help, and the two wounded men were washed away and drowned. The rest hung on for a while. Then the black hulk of a steamer loomed about a mile distant, and three of the men resolved to swim to her. They dropped off and started. Five minutes afterwards the steamer vanished. The three men were never seen again.

At this point, the fourth officer, drenched by the sea and stabbed by the sword of the frozen wind, became partially unconscious. When he revived a little the two remaining men of the seven were gone.

What woke the lad to some perception was the sound of a voice, calling in English. He saw a long, dark shape heaving to leeward, and understood that it was a German submarine, and that a German officer was asking him questions.

The German asked what ship he had sunk, whence she came, whither she was bound, and what was her cargo. The fourth officer gave the information. 'Are you an Englishman?' asked the German officer.

The boy replied that he was. 'Then,' said the German, 'I shall shoot you.' 'Shoot away,' said the fourth officer. So disrespectful an answer naturally hurt the sensitive German. 'I shall not waste powder on a pig of an Englishman,' was the German officer's majestic retort.

At this point, the German seems to have permitted a just indignation to overcome his natural delicacy of feeling. 'Drown, you swine, drown!' he shouted, and sheered off.

Douglas Valder Duff was just fifteen years of age when the *Thracia* was torpedoed by *UC-69*. He was one of only two survivors from a crew of thirty-six. *(Courtesy of Elizabeth O'Reilly Family Collection)*

The officer of his Imperial Majesty's Navy in command of the submarine left the child adrift on his bit of wreckage. There the boy drifted, lashed, helpless and to all appearance dead, all that night. The sun rose on that spectacle in the bitter March morning, and still the boy tossed and tumbled in the breaking sea.

There, at half-past ten (the fourth officer of course marks the time, though he was very nearly dead), a fishing boat espied the castaway, bore down and took him on board. He had been more than thirteen hours in the water.

Of thirty-eight persons, these two were saved: the gunner and the acting fourth officer, aged fifteen and a half years.

Although no names were given, the fourth officer was Douglas V. Duff, but the identity of the Royal Marine, who was saved by the *Nordborg*, has not been ascertained.

Thracia Wreck

The wreck of the *Thracia* lies off the French coast in the Bay of Biscay, with the Brittany peninsula of Quiberon to the east and Belle Isle to the south. This is an area rich in shipwrecks, with many resulting from enemy action in the two world wars.

The wreck was located after the war and worked by a salvage company for scrap metal using explosives, destroying much of the superstructure. After that the wreck was forgotten until being rediscovered by French diver Jean-Pierre Cariou, who reported, 'The wreck is now in poor condition under 40 meters (131 feet) of water. The two big boilers and the engine are the highest points.

There is a twelve-pounder gun on the poop. The fore part is completely broken and not in line with the keel.' Some portholes were known to have been recovered at this time.

During the First World War *Thracia* was armed with a Vickers machine gun to defend against attacks by submarines. In 1996 the Société de Recherches en Histoire Maritime (the Maritime History Research Society, aka SORHIMA), led by Gildas Gouarin, was granted a licence to recover the gun. It was fully restored and is now proudly on display in the Musée de Quiberon. Both of the *Thracia*'s 4,700kg (10,340lb) anchors were also raised. One is on display at the local municipal swimming pool in Quiberon; the other was donated to the community of Grand Bornand in Haute-Savoie.

The wreck lies at an angle of 315 degrees, with the bow pointing to the north-west and the maximum depth to the seabed is 36m (118ft). The bow section is badly broken up and is mainly just a confusing tangle of beams and plates. Evidence of the iron ore cargo can be found in what remains of the flattened forward holds. There are various winches, derricks and mooring bollards that would have once been placed along the decks. Moving towards midships, one of the most distinctive features of the wreck is the two large boilers that lie side by side and stand a good 5m (16ft) proud. Immediately aft of the boilers and leaning over to the port side is *Thracia*'s distinctive triple-expansion steam engine. Conger eels can often be found in amongst the connecting rods. Aft of the engine is the propeller shaft and part of the enclosing tunnel still remains. This terminates in a three-bladed propeller, with two of the blades sticking out of the sand at 45 degrees. The third is firmly embedded in the sandy seabed. Just off to the starboard side of the wreck lies the rudder.

The *Thracia* makes a pleasant dive with lots of interesting identifiable features to discover. The visibility is normally good and there is plenty of marine life. The site is quite exposed so calm weather is required as there is no shelter from any swells rolling in off the Atlantic.

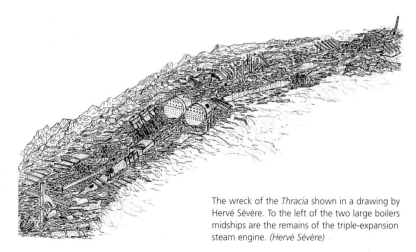

The wreck of the *Thracia* shown in a drawing by Hervé Sévère. To the left of the two large boilers midships are the remains of the triple-expansion steam engine. *(Hervé Sévère)*

Fish life surrounding one of the two large boilers on the wreck of the *Thracia*. (Hervé Sévère)

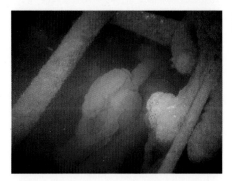

An engine connecting rod. (Hervé Sévère)

Winch gear. (Hervé Sévère)

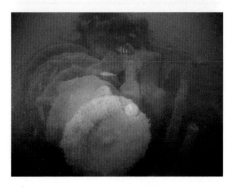

A lone sea urchin clinging to winch gear. (Hervé Sévère)

Flavia

1902–1918, Ireland

FLAVIA WAS 7,347 tons, 143.3m (470ft) in length, with a beam of 17.3m (56.8ft). There was a single funnel, four masts and the vessel was of steel construction. The engines were six-cylinder triple expansion, powering twin screws at 13 knots. The ship was built by Palmer Co. Ltd, Jarrow, and launched on 29 August 1901 as *British Empire* (3) for British Shipowners Co., entering service in 1902. There was passenger accommodation for 125 first-class and 900 third-class passengers. The ship met its end on 24 August 1918 when it was torpedoed off the north-west coast of Ireland.

In 1906 the vessel was sold to Navagazione Generale Italiana, when she was renamed *Campania*, sailing from Genoa to New York and calling at Naples. From 1909 she was chartered to the Northwest Transport Line, sailing the Hamburg to New York route and calling at Rotterdam. In 1910 the company became the Uranium SS Co., and changed the name of the vessel to *Campanello* to avoid confusion with the Cunard *Campania*.

When the First World War started the Hamburg to Rotterdam service ceased and the ship was bought by the Royal Line and started to sail out of Avonmouth. In 1916 she was acquired by Cunard and renamed the *Flavia*, sailing from Avonmouth to Canada. However, her service with Cunard was short because on 24 August 1918, on her voyage from Montréal to Avonmouth, she was sunk by *U-107* (Commander Kurt Siewert) 30 miles NW by W of Tory Island, Ireland.

A young cadet serving on *Flavia* was Douglas Duff, one of only two survivors from the wreck of the *Thracia* the previous year. The young Duff joined the *Flavia* during a refit at Tilbury in 1918 and found the experience of working on a large passenger liner 'the antithesis of *Thracia*'. As *Flavia* was armed with more than one gun, Duff was rated midshipman, Royal Naval Reserve, when the ship set sail for Montréal.

Duff described the final few days leading up to the sinking in his second autobiography, *On Swallowing the Anchor*:

> We loaded ammunition, several hundred horses and mules in Québec as we returned, and some troops, mainly Serbians, enlisted in the American Army, and a few American nurses at Sidney, Cape Breton Island, before we joined a convoy and sailed east for Glasgow. It was a lovely trip, the ships were all big liners or very large cargo ships, and we had an adequate escort, including a battleship. There was none of the amateurism and clumsiness of eighteen months before, when close-formation was new to Merchant Masters. The North Atlantic was almost perfect as it sometimes is in summertime.

The *Flavia* had several different names before being purchased by Cunard in 1916, the last of which was *Campanello*. *(Ian Lawler Collection)*

Duff came on duty at 4 a.m. on 24 August and was manning the gun at the aft of the vessel. Chief Officer Bennerman advised him to keep a special lookout for U-boats as they neared the Western Approaches. It was just before breakfast on a warm sunny day with a calm sea when the U-boat struck:

> With devastating suddenness a column of water, laced with brown smoke, flew into the air as high as our fore-cross-trees and *Flavia* faltered in her stride, shook and began to tremble. A second later, another column flew up, near the first, just forward of the bridge and on the same starboard side. *Flavia* listed sharply, still pushing purposefully through the water at good speed. The four tall masts canted over, lay down to starboard – her bridge and deck beneath my feet all listed. I scarcely heard the thud of the explosions, though I felt their terrific shock run through her hull.

The first officer sent Duff to the bridge to seek instructions from Captain Fear for the aft guns. Duff described the captain as a tall, rather gaunt man and one of the best sailors with whom he had served. Along the way he witnessed scenes of panic amongst some of the men, most notably the soldiers, several of whom had 'apparently gone mad'. Some were even fighting with the seamen who were doing their utmost to lower the lifeboats. Above all the other noise was the squealing of hundreds of distressed horses. On arrival at the bridge the captain gave the order to commence the abandon-ship routine. Duff duly fired four distress rockets to inform the rest of the convoy that they were abandoning ship. Then the captain sent him to his assigned boat station port-side aft to get the boat away.

Upon reaching the lifeboat Duff encountered a khaki-clad Serbian soldier who was completely out of control brandishing a yard-long steel bar. Duff was shocked to see the man taking swings at a nurse who was trying to descend the Jacob's ladder to the boat. She managed to dodge the first blow but when the soldier swung a second time Duff shot him dead. The incident had a calming effect and the lifeboat was loaded with seventy-three people, although it was only certified for forty-six.

With the boat safely away, Duff witnessed the final moments of the *Flavia*:

> Her bows were now submerged, the water above the fore-deck frothing with the air pouring up through ventilators and broken hatchways. It broke in creamy surf against the forward end of her bridge superstructure. The fore-dodgers of the bridge sank to water-level, were buried – the wheelhouse slid beneath the white waves. The foremast-truck was almost gone, the mainmast down to the cross-trees, the single funnel pointing at an angle of forty-five degrees towards the sunken bows, like the cartoon of a great gun. Her stern was rising, the rudder and two propellers already in the air. I could see the far horizon through the gap between her stern-post and the water.

On board the sinking vessel was the sight of a solitary human figure dancing wildly on the top of the radio house on the upper deck. This was one of the crew who had gone mad during the crossing, and been confined in the hospital as a lunatic. He was released when the ship was struck but refused to enter a boat.

> Then, all at once a great jet of soot and black smoke shot from the funnel, whose root was already below the surface. It spewed out for a hundred yards – *Flavia*'s stern rose higher and higher, the grim shapes of the guns on her stern clear-cut against the sky, the lunatic dancing even more frantically on the uptilted after-bulkhead of the radio-shack, the Ensign streaming in the increasing speed of the plunge. For a few moments she looked as though she had stopped; almost as if her bows had touched the sea bottom, which was impossible in those soundings, and then – she was gone!

Having survived the sinking of the ship Duff then described fighting 'one of the most nauseating, dangerous and difficult battles I have ever known' as they tried to fend off the maddened horses and mules that threatened to overturn the crowded boat. This was made that much harder by the presence in the boat of 'panic-stricken landsmen whose greatest fear was the salt water so near to their bodies'.

It had taken twenty-seven minutes to lower the boats and get clear. Despite the danger of stopping a vessel in convoy, HMS *Convolvulus* picked up the survivors and landed them safely in Ardrossan. A few days after landfall Duff was appointed to an even bigger Cunard ship, the 20,000-ton liner *Caronia* (1). Luckily this ship survived the war, eventually being scrapped in 1933.

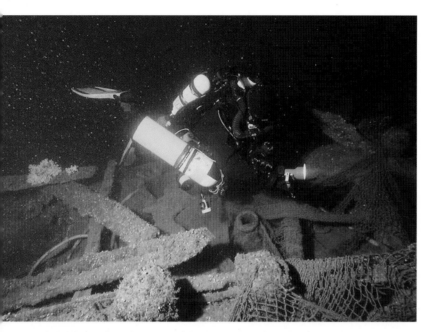

A technical diver explores the remains of the *Flavia*. Damage from the two torpedoes is evident on the wreck. *(Paul Mee)*

Inspecting one of the *Flavia*'s four boilers, at a depth of 105m (344ft). *(Paul Mee)*

It can be established from Duff's account that at least two people lost their lives during the disaster: the lunatic crew member and the murderous soldier. Most official reports state there was only one loss, yet others put the number at a much higher figure. A letter written to one of the crewmen, seaman H.W. Black, two days after the sinking said, 'My word it was a bang wasn't it. I understand there were 126 rescued in the boats, how many would that be missing?'

Since there were known to be 300 Serbian soldiers, 100 cattlemen and a crew of over 100, this puts the total number of souls on board at well over 500, meaning at least 374 lives were unaccounted for and assumed lost. One theory is that the number was deliberately falsified at the time of loss as part of military propaganda.

Flavia Wreck

The remains of the *Flavia* rest in water just over 108m (354ft) deep off the north-west coast of Ireland. The wreck was first found and dived by an Irish technical diving team in June 2008 and as such is one of the most recent Cunard wrecks to be found and dived.

The *Flavia* lies with a list of about 20 degrees to port. Most of the upper decks are completely gone, leaving the boilers and machinery proud and completely exposed. Only a metre or two of the hull can be seen sticking out of the sand on the port side, whereas the starboard hull is 4–5m (13–16ft) high in parts. The bow area is sinking into the sand and is simply a lattice of steelwork with large winches, chain and some unusual 'inverted bell-shaped' features, possibly fairleads, being the only recognisable features. The stern stands higher than the bow and one propeller is visible, with two of the blades sticking out of the sand.

Paul Mee described his first dive on the wreck:

> The dive was amazing, we hit the wreck just in front of the boilers at 105m (344ft) in the dark. I was the only person to go towards them whilst the other members made for midships which was broken up. All the port holes were in a long line as far as the eye could see on the port side and the starboard, with viz around 30m+ (98ft).

Being a newly discovered wreck there is still a lot of brass to see, and several divers have noted the row of at least a dozen intact portholes. One diver also reported being accompanied by a large seal as he scootered the length of the wreck. In common with other offshore wrecks in this area, the visibility is normally excellent.

Some of the items recovered from the wreck include: several portholes, a telegraph, a pistol grip and a 6in gun cartridge. A small J. Roby porthole has also been raised, a distinctive design that were manufactured in Liverpool. The bell has not yet been found.

The stern telegraph recovered from the *Flavia*.

A 6in shell cartridge, probably from the aft gun manned by Douglas Duff.

 # *Carpathia*

1903–1918, North Atlantic

CARPATHIA WAS BUILT by Swan & Hunter, Wallsend-on-Tyne, and launched on 6 August 1902. The vessel was 13,555 tons with a length of 164.6m (540ft) and a beam of 19.7m (64ft), of steel construction, a single funnel and four masts. The engines were eight-cylinder, quadruple expansion, built by Wallsend Slipway Co., and powered twin screws, giving a maximum speed of 16 knots, with a service speed of 14 knots. Passenger accommodation was originally for 204 second-class and 1,500 third-class passengers. In 1905 the passenger accommodation was changed to 100 first-class, 200 second-class and 2,250 third-class passengers, resulting in an increase in tonnage to 13,603 tons.

Carpathia sailed on her maiden voyage from Liverpool to Boston via Queenstown (Cobh) on 5 May 1903. Also in 1903 the Cunard Line was appointed the official agent for Hungarian emigration. This started with the *Aurania* (1) sailing from Fiume, Trieste, Venice and Palermo and on to New York in November 1903. She was then followed by the *Carpathia* after she had completed her summer season from the Liverpool to New York or Boston route. It was for the winter season that she transferred to carrying Hungarian immigrants from Fiume and Trieste to New York.

From 1904 to 1914 *Carpathia* mainly covered the Trieste to New York and Liverpool to New York routes. Summer cruises to Europe were popular with the wealthy Americans and further calls were added to Mediterranean ports such as Gibraltar, Genoa and Naples. *Carpathia* alternated itinerary several times between the New York to Liverpool and New York to Trieste routes, returning annually to Liverpool for a refit.

From 1914 the Mediterranean service was undertaken by the *Ivernia* (1), *Saxonia* (1), *Carpathia*, *Ultonia* and *Pannonia*. However, of these five Cunarders only two, *Pannonia* and *Saxonia* (1), survived the First World War. *Ivernia* (1) became a trooper and was sunk on 1 January 1917 by *UB-47* (Commander Wolfgang Steinbauer) 58 miles south by east off Cape Matapan, Greece, in 1916, with 125 lives lost. *Ultonia* was sunk by *U-53* (Commander Hans Rose) 190 miles south-west of Fastnet on 27 June 1917, with the loss of one life.

On the night of 14/15 April 1912 *Carpathia* was en route from New York to the Mediterranean with 740 passengers, when at 12.25 a.m. the ship's radio officer picked up the *Titanic*'s SOS call. The radio officer took the SOS message to the officers on the bridge, which was located at the forward end of the bridge deck, between mast No.2 and the funnel. The officers then woke the master, Captain Arthur Rostron, in his cabin below, located immediately below the ship's bridge.

It was calculated that the *Carpathia* was 58 miles from the *Titanic* and Captain Rostron ordered full speed towards the reported distress position. In order to provide additional steam for the engines the hot water supply was cut off to the passenger cabins and the *Carpathia* powered across the Atlantic faster then she had ever done before. However, when she arrived at the *Titanic*'s last reported position at 4 a.m. the *Titanic* has nowhere to be seen. Soon the lifeboats were spotted and *Carpathia* took the 705 survivors on board. *Carpathia* then left for New York while the *Californian*, under the command of Captain Stanley Lord, stayed in the area to search for any further survivors.

The modest *Carpathia* entered service in 1903 and achieved eternal fame for rescuing 705 *Titanic* survivors. Shown here berthed in New York.

Above, right Captain Arthur Henry Rostron and his officers with the silver cup presented to them in May 1912 by survivors of the *Titanic* in recognition of their rescue. *(Library of Congress)*

Replica of the *Carpathia* rescue medal. The inscription reads: 'Presented to the Captain, officers & crew of R.M.S. Carpathia in recognition of gallant & heroic services. From the survivors of the S.S. Titanic, April 15th 1912.'

On Thursday 18 April 1912 *Carpathia* arrived back in New York with the *Titanic* survivors. To the surprise of the gathering crowds the ship made straight for the White Star dock, where she unloaded the *Titanic* lifeboats. These were to be the only part of the doomed liner that completed the voyage. The *Carpathia* then moved to her usual dock at Pier 54, where she disembarked her own passengers followed by the *Titanic* survivors. After Captain Rostron had testified at the first day of the United States inquiry, the *Carpathia* left New York to continue her voyage to the Mediterranean. Captain Rostron was to become famous for his actions in the *Titanic* disaster, and was eventually knighted and appointed as commodore of the Cunard fleet.

For the next few years *Carpathia* returned to the Mediterranean service and remained in her commercial service in the First World War, sailing from Piraeus in Greece. The *Carpathia* commenced her last Piraeus–Messina–Palermo–Naples–Genoa–Lisbon–New York voyage on 13 April 1915 and then transferred to the Liverpool to New York service in July 1915. Although the *Carpathia* was never fitted out as a troopship, her design allowed for conversion should it be required.

When travelling in convoy out of Liverpool, bound for Boston on 17 July 1918, the *Carpathia*, while under the command of Captain William Prothero, was struck by two torpedoes fired by *U-55* (Commander Wilhelm Werner) 170 miles west by north of Bishop Rock at 49°41N 10°45W. The torpedoes struck within thirty seconds of each other, the first one on the port side between No.4 hold and the stoke hold, and a second in the engine room, killing three trimmers and two firemen.

Captain Prothero ordered everyone to the lifeboats, but just as the last were safely in the lifeboats a third torpedo struck the ship. The surviving 218 crew and

57 passengers were picked up by HMS *Snowdrop*, which fired several shots at the U-boat that was surfaced and then took the survivors safely back to Liverpool.

A letter was later received from the Admiralty stating that the discipline and organisation on board the *Carpathia* had been of a very high order, and that Captain Prothero was to be publicly commended in the *London Gazette* for recognition of his conduct in the crisis.

Carpathia Wreck

Search and Discovery

The circumstances and details of *Carpathia*'s sad ending were typical of the many thousands of merchant vessels sunk by enemy action in the First Word War. Consequently, stories of more publicised and controversial losses, such as the *Lusitania* in 1915, tended to dominate public attention. However, the significant role that the *Carpathia* played in the *Titanic* disaster would always ensure that this modest Cunard vessel would never be forgotten. The wreck was of obvious interest to salvors and divers, but the remote offshore location and depth meant that no serious attempts were made to locate or dive the wreck for many decades. However, the discovery of the *Titanic* wreck in 1985 and advances in diving equipment created renewed interest in discovering what remained of *Carpathia*.

In 1979 the best-selling American novelist Clive Cussler founded the National Underwater and Marine Agency (NUMA), a non-profit organisation dedicated to discovery and preservation of maritime heritage. The *Carpathia* was a natural target for NUMA and in 1999 a search team was put together in conjunction with a new television series, *The Sea Hunters*. The team included Cussler himself, archaeologist James Delgado and commercial diver Mike Fletcher. In September 1999 NUMA sponsored an initial search for *Carpathia* by the British explorer Graham Jessop. The expedition located a wreck that they thought to be *Carpathia*. However, a subsequent visit to the site utilising underwater cameras established the wreck to be the *Isis* of Hamburg-America Line, which foundered in a storm in 1936.

In May 2000 Mike Fletcher lead the NUMA team out to search for the wreck once more. One of the biggest challenges in locating the wreck was the lack of an accurate starting location. At the time of the sinking a number of different positions were recorded by *Carpathia*'s radio officer, the German submarine *U-55* and HMS *Snowdrop*. A search area had to be defined on a chart covering all possibilities so that a systematic survey could be undertaken using side-scan sonar and a magnetometer. The part of the ocean being searched was a rich hunting ground for U-boats, so the presence of a wreck on the seabed would still require positive identification as that of *Carpathia*. After a month of searching the wreck was located and was conclusively identified by further ROV footage taken in September. On 22 September 2000 NUMA issued a press release stating that the wreck of the *Carpathia* had been found.

The First Dives

The wreck of *Carpathia* was dived for the first time by a team of British technical divers in August 2001. As part of the preparation for such a deep dive, the ten-man team carried out a build-up dive the year before on HMS *Dasher*, a 12,000-ton aircraft carrier in 144m (472ft) in the Firth of Clyde. The trip to the *Carpathia* could only be undertaken with perfect weather, but when the scheduled date approached the conditions were not favourable and the expedition was aborted. A few days later the weather improved and a reduced team set sail for a last-minute attempt at the wreck.

The group travelled the 268 miles from Plymouth aboard the *Loyal Watcher*, skippered by Steve Wright, with all divers taking spells at the helm. When they arrived at the wreck site the conditions were perfect, with just a gentle Atlantic swell. As the divers made their final preparations it was with a degree of apprehension as they did not know what conditions awaited them deep in the ocean and so far from shore. Four divers descended to the wreck: Rich Stevenson, Ric Waring, Zaid Al-obaidi and Bruce Dunton. Fred Buckingham and Dave Whitney took on the important role of safety divers. Ric Waring was the last to enter the water and described his dive:

When I got down to the wreck I was amazed to find myself in ambient light. I hadn't turned my torch on and could see the wreck stretched out around me, two huge telegraph heads lay on top of the wreck, we were right on the bridge! Zaid was nowhere to be seen, Richie was returning back toward the shot line and Bruce had gone off the side of the wreck trying to get down to the sea bed. Two huge ling were patrolling the wreck like guard dogs obviously curious about our arrival. I managed to turn my torch on as Richie gave me a salute as he began his ascent. The wreck was full of very hard shells and coral and crawled with brittle stars. I spotted some plates and found one with the Cunard line's crest.

All divers breathed mixed gas (trimix 6/80) on closed-circuit rebreathers and managed to spend about twenty minutes on the wreck at an average depth of 153m (502ft). Such a deep dive imposed a heavy decompression penalty of five hours in open water. The water temperature on the seabed was 13°C (55°F), warming to 20°C (68°F) for the final decompression stops in the last 10m (33ft). The divers finally broke the surface to a beautiful sunny afternoon and the sight of dolphins playing across the bows of the *Loyal Watcher*.

A china plate with the Cunard crest was recovered, proving conclusively the wreck's identity as *Carpathia*. This dive in itself was a considerable technical achievement and at the leading edge of underwater exploration on scuba. It was also believed to set a record for the deepest ever UK wreck dive at the time.

Ownership

In May 2001 RMS Titanic Inc., a wholly owned subsidiary of Premier Exhibitions Inc., attained acquisition rights to *Carpathia*. RMS Titanic Inc. was granted Salvor-in-Possession rights to the wreck of the *Titanic* in 1994 and has subsequently recovered over 5,000 artefacts from the *Titanic*. In February 2007 Premier Exhibitions sold their interest in *Carpathia* to Seaventures Ltd for $3 million. At the same time Seaventures authorised RMS Titanic Inc. to conduct an expedition to the wreck to recover artefacts for the mutual benefit of both companies.

Joint Expedition 2007

Following the success of the 2001 expedition, plans were put in place to explore and record the wreck in greater detail. Due to bad weather and logistical challenges it was not until September 2007 that divers finally managed to return to the *Carpathia*. This time the team had grown to ten divers, including members from Britain, Italy and Germany, led by Ric Waring. RMS Titanic Inc. were on site with *Janus II* at the same time, conducting their own survey work using ROVs and recovering artefacts for restoration and public display.

The vessel *Ocean Dancer* was chartered as the dive boat and included a decompression chamber on board. This was a vital safety precaution since the wreck site was beyond the 200-mile range of Sea King helicopters, making air evacuation impossible and the nearest point of land was at least a thirty-hour journey by sea.

Six days of diving were completed, with bottom times ranging from twenty to twenty-eight minutes and total in-water times of between four and a half to six hours. Again, all divers used rebreathers, including the Inspiration Classic, Inspiration Vision and Megalodon. One of the highlights of the expedition was the recovery of a double-headed bridge telegraph by Jeff Cornish. Various other smaller items, such as china plates, were also brought up and handed over to RMS Titanic Inc. Divers reported seeing numerous artefacts scattered across the wreck, including loose portholes. The highly prized ship's bells proved

elusive and none were located by the divers or the ROV operators. Some previous ROV footage had suggested a bell was lying in the sand to one side of the wreck, but this turned out to be the base of an oil lamp.

In order to survey as much of the wreck as possible within the restricted bottom times, the divers made use of underwater scooters or diver propulsion vehicles (DPVs). Using a DPV meant that the whole 164m (538ft) long wreck could be circumnavigated on a single dive. Unfortunately the depth took its toll on the underwater cameras, with many imploding beyond 130m (427ft). Some underwater lights also failed, along with a few contents gauges. Fortunately none of the equipment issues compromised diver safety and all dives were completed successfully without incident. In his dive report, Rich Stevenson stated:

Above Divers running through their final rebreather safety checks prior to descent to the deep wreck in 153m (502ft). *(Helmuth Biechl)*

Left Helmuth Biechl explores the wreck of the *Carpathia*, which is seen here covered in brittle stars. *(Ric Waring)*

Clockwise from above

Tim Cashman videoing the wreck and using a diver propulsion vehicle (DPV). In the six years since the wreck was first dived it is already showing signs of further collapse. *(Ric Waring)*

A small hatch cover on the forward port side of the cargo hold. Remains of trawler nets are evident all over the wreck. *(Ric Waring)*

Winch gear. *(Ric Waring)*

The ling fish on the wreck followed the divers 'around the wreck like guard dogs'. (Ric Waring)

The wreck itself is starting to collapse in on itself quite a lot now. On the dive I made in 2001 we never really explored much beyond the bow area but this time I managed to get two scooter laps around the wreck to get a real impression of how she is and at 600' long there is a lot of wreckage to see. At the bow she is very flat now with just the winches standing off the sea bed. As you move aft the midships gets higher and more intact, nearly 10m off the sea bed and the stern is perfectly intact with a list to port but is very obvious and easy to navigate around. The stern is the shallowest part at 143m and the deepest anyone got was 156m so she is still standing high.

Stevenson also reported the temperature on the bottom as being 10°C (50°F), a few degrees colder than the dive in 2001.

RMS Titanic Inc. recovered more than fifty artefacts during the 2007 expedition. These were put on display in 2008 as part of a new travelling international *Titanic* exhibition. Items included: a telegraph, porthole and personal items such as a sterling silver and glass flask.

Clockwise from bottom left

A brass porthole that was raised by Zaid Al-obaidi from his dive in 2001, now in the posession of RMS Titanic Inc., who are the legal owners of the wreck. *(Zaid Al-obaidi)*

The china plate that was found on the wreck during the first expedition in 2001, confirming the identity of the wreck beyond doubt. The text below the Cunard lion reads: 'The Cunard Steamship Company'. *(Carpathia Expedition 2001)*

Examining the telegraph that was recovered by Jeff Cornish during the 2007 expedition. *(Helmuth Biechl)*

Cunard china plates recovered during the 2007 expedition. *(Ric Waring)*

Lusitania

1907–1915, Ireland

HE *LUSITANIA* WAS built by John Brown & Co. Ltd, Glasgow, and when she was launched on 7 June 1906 she became Cunard's largest vessel to date, with a gross tonnage of 31,550 tons. The vessel was 232.3m (762ft) long, with a beam of 26.8m (88ft) and had accommodation for 2,165 passengers – 563 first class, 464 second class and 1,138 third class. Steam turbine engines powered quadruple screws, giving a service speed of 25 knots.

In 1897 the North German Lloyd (NDL) vessel *Kaiser Wilhelm der Grosse* gained the eastbound transatlantic record from Cunard's *Lucania*, followed by the westbound record the following year, with speeds in excess of 22 knots. From then on German ships reigned supreme on the North Atlantic, with further records from Hapag's *Deutschland* and NDL's *Kronprinz Wilhelm*. Cunard's fleet instantly appeared dated and slow by comparison, so the line began negotiations with the government in 1902 for financial support to build two new 'superliners' to challenge the Germans. These new ships were to be the *Lusitania* and the *Mauretania* (1), ships that could reach a speed of 24–25 knots and regain the Blue Riband for Great Britain.

The British design was similar to the German's with regard to the funnels, as the *Lusitania* was also to have four, but evenly spaced and not in two distinct pairs, as was the German style. The government agreed to help, but there were to be conditions. The government would give annual payments to Cunard, but the two ships were expected to be capable of being armed and requisition for war service if needed.

Work began on building the *Lusitania* in June 1904 and the vessel was launched two years later. After trials in the Clyde, *Lusitania* left Liverpool on 7 September 1907 on her maiden voyage to New York, calling at Queenstown. Due to rough seas *Lusitania* did not capture the Blue Riband on her first voyage, but on the second crossing in October she gained the westbound record from the *Deutschland*, with a time of four days, nineteen hours and fifty-two minutes, with an average speed of 23.99 knots. The same month she took the eastbound record from the *Kaiser Wilhelm II* with a time of four days, twenty-two hours and fifty-three minutes, at an average speed of 23.61 knots. In November 1907 the *Lusitania*'s sister ship, *Mauretania*, came into service and the '*Lucy*', as she was affectionately known, only held the eastbound record for a short while due

Right, from top

The 31,550-ton *Lusitania* was only in service for eight years before being torpedoed by *U-20* on 7 May 1915.

The grand dining room on board *Lusitania*. (*Mick Lindsay Collection*)

An artist's impression of the wreck of the *Lusitania*. *(Stuart Williamson)*

to the *Mauretania* taking it in December 1907, in four days, twenty-two hours and thirty-three minutes, at an average speed of 23.69 knots – just ten minutes faster. *Lusitania* held the westbound record until the *Mauretania* took it away two years later, in September 1909, a record that stood another twenty years, until the NDL *Bremen* recaptured the Blue Riband for Germany in July 1929.

During her service *Lusitania* was to become a very popular ship and a transatlantic favourite with her passengers. In November 1908 Captain William Turner was appointed as *Lusitania*'s new master on the recommendation of her first master, Captain James Watt, who was retiring as commodore of the Cunard fleet. Having joined Cunard in 1878, Captain Turner had served on a number of vessels in various positions, including the *Umbria*, *Carpathia* and *Ivernia* (1). Captain Turner was awarded the Liverpool Shipwreck and Humane Society's medal in 1912, while captain of the *Mauretania*, for saving the lives of the crew of the steamer *West Point*, which had caught fire.

With the start of the First World War, the *Lusitania*'s last voyage during peacetime found her arriving at Liverpool on 4 August 1914, the very day that war was declared. Both the *Lusitania* and *Mauretania* were at first requisitioned for war service, but when *Lusitania* arrived back at Liverpool the Admiralty decided that they did not need the ship as an AMC, however they still required

the vessel to remain at Liverpool to be used as and when needed. She was still listed by the Admiralty as an AMC, but continued her transatlantic crossings on a monthly basis between Liverpool and New York, even after the Germans warned that all shipping around the British Isles would be open to attack. The *Mauretania* went on to serve as a hospital ship for the duration of the war.

Due to the high cost of the fuel that was required to run the express-service vessels, the Admiralty made the decision to use smaller liners as AMCs instead and although the *Lusitania* remained on the official Admiralty AMC list she was reclassified as an auxiliary cruiser. There were some worrying incidents during this time as the seas around the British Isles were stalked by German U-boats, but this became more worrying when the German Embassy in New York published warnings that passengers travelling transatlantic did so at their own risk.

The warning stated:

Travellers intending to embark on the Atlantic voyage are reminded that a state of war exists between Germany and her allies and Great Britain and her allies; that the zone of war includes the waters adjacent to the British Isles; that, in accordance with formal notice given by the Imperial German

Government, vessels flying the flag of Great Britain, or any of her allies, are liable to destruction in those waters and that travellers sailing in the war zone on the ships of Great Britain or her allies do so at their own risk.

Imperial German Embassy
Washington, D.C. 22nd April 1915.

This was just before the *Lusitania* was boarding passengers for the homeward voyage to Liverpool. The *Lusitania* left at Pier 54, New York, on 1 May 1915, under the command of her master, Captain William Turner, who had been reappointed as master in April 1915 for the voyage from Liverpool after taking over from Captain Dow who was going on leave. Captain Turner had previously been in command of the *Lusitania* in 1907 before being promoted to the *Mauretania* and *Aquitania*. On board were 1,257 passengers, including 440 women, 129 children, a crew of 702 and general cargo. However, the ship's manifest for the voyage showed that she was also carrying a large consignment of rifle cartridges, including empty shell cases and non-explosive fuses, but Cunard did not classify that as ammunition.

In the meantime, the German navy was concerned about the possible cargo that *Lusitania* was carrying and ordered the commander of *U-20*, Walther Schwieger, to attack and sink her.

By 7 May *Lusitania* entered the Danger Zone, where German submarines were likely to be waiting to attack ships. Captain Turner was concerned about the possibility of U-boats in the area and took all precautions, such as ordering all the lifeboats to be swung out, all bulkhead doors to be closed, doubling the lookouts and ensuring the steam engines were ready to gain full speed in the shortest possible time to get away from any enemy submarines should they be detected.

Captain Turner had in advance calculated exactly where he wanted to be at a particular time and reduced the speed to 18 knots so as to arrive at Liverpool at 4 a.m. the next day. The course was changed during the night, which brought the *Lusitania* closer to the coast, just 15 miles from the Old Head at Kinsale, when the captain was informed that a torpedo had been seen approaching the ship. The torpedo had been fired by *U-20* at 2.10 p.m. and it struck the *Lusitania* on the starboard side just below the bridge.

A second explosion was heard that was initially thought to be a second torpedo, but later, after the *U-20* commander's log had confirmed that they had only fired one torpedo, it was thought to be a boiler exploding. The *Lusitania* immediately started to list to the starboard and sank in just eighteen minutes at position 51.24'N, 08.31'W, with the huge loss of 1,198 lives, including 123 Americans. Although there were enough lifeboats, the listing of the vessel prevented those on one side from being launched.

Within hours of learning of the catastrophe the Admiralty decided to make Captain Turner the scapegoat for the loss of the *Lusitania* as they had sensitive information to conceal. The chair of the Board of Trade inquiry was to be Lord Mersey, who had also presided over the *Titanic* investigation and he promptly received a private letter from the Admiralty stating: 'The

government would consider it politically expedient if the captain of the *Lusitania* were promiscuously blamed for the accident.'

During the inquiry Captain Turner admitted that he had received the Admiralty memos to zigzag, but thought that this instruction need only be followed after a submarine had been sighted. Captain Turner also said that the second explosion may have been internal, but denied that the *Lusitania* was carrying explosives. The captain further stated that his four-point bearings were more accurate than the other bearings. Ultimately the Admiralty's shameful tactics proved ineffective, with Lord Mersey concluding: 'He exercised his judgement for the best. It was the judgement of a skilled and experienced man, and although others might have acted differently and perhaps more successfully he ought not, in my opinion, to be blamed. The whole blame for the cruel destruction of life in this catastrophe must rest solely with those who plotted and with those who committed the crime.'

The United States Government was very angry that American citizens were lost in the disaster and protested that *U-20* had attacked an innocent passenger-carrying ship. The German Government stated the case that the second explosion was caused because the *Lusitania* was carrying munitions, but the British Government denied this. There have been suggestions in the book *Lusitania*, by Colin Simpson (1973), that the *Lusitania* had been taken secretly into dry dock in 1913 to have her No.1 boiler room converted into a magazine, and the same with her mail room, including gun mounts for 6in guns. It is true that the *Lusitania* had been fitted with gun mounts and she was listed as an AMC, but the guns were not thought to have been fitted.

The suggestion that she was carrying high explosives was not proven at the time, but the anger in Britain and America that an unarmed vessel had been attacked and sunk contributed to America's decision to eventually join the Allies in the war.

Later the same year, on 17 November, another vessel with the name *Lusitania* (1,834 tons) was sunk by mines laid by *UC-5* (Commander Herbert Pustkuchen) off the Flanders Flotilla, 1 mile east of Folkestone Gate. She was a cargo ship carrying general cargo from London to Cádiz. Fortunately there were no casualities.

After the loss of the *Lusitania* the commander of *U-20* (Walther Schwieger) became known throughout the world as 'the German submariner who sank the *Lusitania*', but more sinister was the nickname 'The Baby Killer' given to him by the British. He was also recorded as a war criminal on the Admiralty list. Later Walther Schwieger became commander of *U-88* and on 5 September 1917 *U-88* is thought to have been sunk by a mine off the German coast. There were no survivors.

Lusitania's master, Captain William Turner, was later to be the captain of another Cunarder, the *Ivernia* (1) (14,058 tons), when she was torpedoed by *UB-47* (Commander Wolfgang Steinbauer) on 1 January 1917, off Cape Matapan, Greece, with the loss of eighty-five troops and thirty-six crew members.

With the alarming loss of shipping from attacks by U-boats at random, Winston Churchill brought out his secret weapon, the Q-ship. The Q-ship was disguised to look like an ordinary merchant ship, but was secretly manned by a naval crew. Should a U-boat surface to challenge the vessel the naval crew would immediately open fire with the aim of sinking the enemy U-boat with no attempt at rescue, nor did they take any prisoners.

Lusitania Wreck

There was never any doubt that a wreck of a grand ocean liner such as the *Lusitania* would be an obvious target for underwater exploration and salvage. There was also the added mystery of the second explosion and questions over her cargo manifest to be solved. The ship had gone down within sight of land in an area where the depth to the seabed, although nearly 100m (328ft) deep, made the wreck accessible.

Early Diving

The first serious attempt to dive on the wreck of the *Lusitania* was proposed as early as 1931, just sixteen years after her loss. An American submarine inventor named Simon Lake had devised a special steel tube down which divers could descend direct to the seabed. Lake had already used the tube to salvage cargo from wrecks off the coast of Connecticut. Along with Captain H.H. Railey, the Lake–Railey Lusitania Expedition was formed with the objective to recover the purser's safe and other historic artefacts. They also hoped to take photographs and motion-picture footage. Official approval had been granted from various sources but for reasons unknown the expedition never progressed beyond the planning stages.

In the 1930s a Scottish salvage company called Tritonia Corporation was given a contract by the British Government to salvage ships that were sunk in the First World War, which included *Lusitania*. Tritonia commissioned an old lighthouse service boat called *Orphir* and after several months of searching using early depth-sounding equipment the wreck of the *Lusitania* was found at a depth of 95m (312ft). On 26 October 1935 British diver Jim Jarratt became the first person to dive on the *Lusitania*. For his dive Jarratt used the cutting-edge underwater diving technology of the day, which was the Peress dive suit, named after its inventor Joseph Salim Peress. The suit was made of metal that fully enclosed the diver at normal atmospheric pressure and was capable of reaching depths of up to 400m (1,300ft). The diver had to be lowered to the wreck, where he had limited movement using articulated joints in the arms and legs. Steel claws were used instead of hands. The suit also included a telephone communications link between the diver and the surface. Jarratt alighted on the wreck at a depth of 73m (240ft), where he was able to measure the size of the rivets, aiding positive identification of the wreck as the *Lusitania*. Unfortunately the weather soon took a turn for the worse and no further diving operations took place. A memorial service was held on board *Orphir* to commemorate the tragic loss of 1,195 lives twenty years earlier.

Tritonia had plans to visit the wreck again and contracted American salvage diver John D. Craig to take photographs. Craig and his partner Gene Nohl

Right Gregg Bemis, the owner of the wreck, dived the *Lusitania* himself in 2004 at the age of seventy-six and 'gave the old lady a loving kiss'. *(Courtesy of Gregg Bemis)*

Below Boat deck first-class cabin window with its filigreed detail above. *(Leigh Bishop)*

Lusitania's steam whistle now lying off the wreck on the seabed debris field. *(Leigh Bishop)*

had ambitious plans for a new kind of suit and proposed the use of alternate breathing mixtures involving helium. In a contemporary magazine article in 1937 Craig described his strict physical and dietary regime for diving:

> All of us are in the pink of condition. We have trained for months, working off every ounce of fat. Those of us who do the diving, like myself, have given up tobacco, alcohol and mixed foods. That is most important. For weeks we shall have nothing for breakfast but a glass of orange juice and a pound and one-half of honey in the comb which we chew thoroughly, spitting out the wax. The honey provides a carbon background for the oxygen to burn upon and prevents its burning our tissues. When we come up from the seas we are given nothing to eat except a half-tumbler of strained honey, lemon juice and rain water. We carry crocks of rain water in the ship's refrigerators because it is not only pure but contains a high degree of oxygen. When we emerge from the water our body temperatures have fallen from 98 degrees, normal, to 85, although we do not feel cold. The rain-water-honey mixture warms us up, and then, after a massage, we go to bed. After a brief rest we eat, but we must stick to one thing at a meal – proteins or carbohydrates, not both. We immediately feel it if we take the combination and we suffer nausea or weakness. Our physical discipline is most severe.

However, sadly, with the onset of the Second World War, no further dives on the *Lusitania* came to fruition.

The Royal Navy are known to have carried out some operations on the *Lusitania* wreck site during the late 1940s and early 1950s. In keeping with normal military operating practice, details of their activities are not readily known to the general public. It would appear that the wreck was subjected to a

series of depth charges, supposedly for practice and testing. A number of dives to the wreck also took place using a team of hard-hat divers. Surface support was assisted by Teddy Tucker of Bermudan treasure salvage fame, although he did not carry out any dives himself.

First Scuba Dive

The first ever scuba dive on the *Lusitania* was carried out by American John Light on 20 July 1960. Light used the conventional scuba equipment of the day, which consisted of a wet suit, fins, cylinders and a double-hose regulator. He breathed conventional air, which not only has extreme narcotic effects at such depth but is also extremely hypoxic. It is also worth noting that at a minimum depth of 73m (240ft) this was already 18m (60ft) deeper than the standard navy dive tables. It is a dive that would be unthinkable in modern times.

Light started his diving career with the US Navy. He later became a civilian salvage diver and from 1956 an underwater cameraman. Like many before and after him, Light had become gripped by the intrigue surrounding the circumstances of the *Lusitania's* loss that bordered on obsession. He was determined to take photographs and film that would hopefully solve some of the mysteries. Light had no interest in salvage or artefact recovery.

Over the course of three diving seasons Light completed forty-two dives on the wreck. He was also joined by several other divers, including Palmer Williams, who made twenty-five dives. The bottom times were typically limited

A stern docking telegraph of the *Lusitania* now on the seabed. *(Leigh Bishop)*

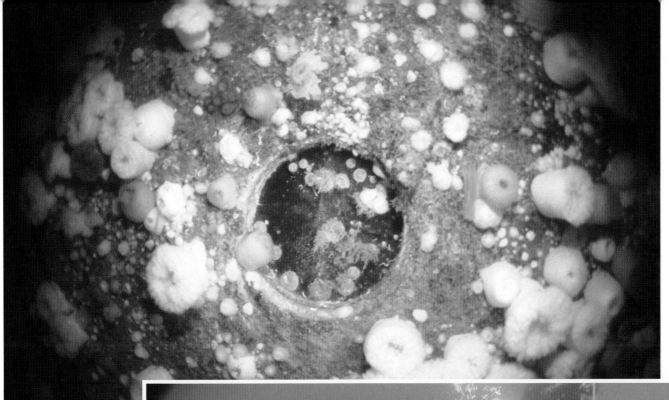

A porthole on the bow of *Lusitania* is now covered in marine life. *(Leigh Bishop)*

Technical rebreather diver Timmy Carey decompressing after a dive to the *Lusitania*. *(© Timmy Carey)*

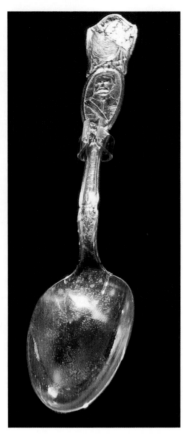

Above, from left

A telegraph recovered from the wreck by Oceaneering in 1982, on display in the company headquarters. *(Andrew Trent)*

Kitchener silver spoon recovered by Oceaneering in 1982. *(Andrew Trent)*

to ten minutes in duration. Nitrogen narcosis was a consistent limiting factor to any meaningful work being achieved at such depth, which is ten times greater than normal atmospheric pressure. Many divers failed to carry out simple tasks such as attaching lines. Some divers simply lost all memory of their dive, a classic symptom of being inflicted with the 'rapture of the deep'.

Sadly, despite all his best endeavours, Light never managed to make the film he so much desired. Ultimately his drive and ambition could not conquer the limitations of the equipment and diving practices of the period. Neither did Light manage to dive the *Lusitania* again, despite having purchased the salvage rights to the wreck from the Liverpool & London War Risks Insurance Association for £1,000.

In later years the question of ownership and salvage rights to the *Lusitania* became hotly contested, resulting in various court cases in America, England

and Ireland. Finally, on 14 May 1996, it was recognised in the Irish courts that Mr F. Gregg Bemis of New Mexico was the legal owner. Bemis had been a former partner of John Light in the late 1960s.

Commercial Salvage

During the months of September and October 1982 the first full-scale commercial salvage operation was conducted on the *Lusitania* by Oceaneering International, who were headquartered in Aberdeen, Scotland. The enterprise was jointly funded by a variety of investors from America and Britain and resulted in the production of a television documentary called *The Lusitania File*.

Prior to the actual dives, Oceaneering conducted two phases of survey work earlier in the year. These consisted primarily of using a remotely operated vehicle (ROV) called *Scorpio* to photograph and video the wreck. During the second phase *Scorpio* recovered the signal bell from the crow's nest.

The divers operated in saturation from the salvage vessel *Archimedes*. This is a standard commercial diving practice and allows divers to remain under pressure for the duration of diving operations and negates the need for lengthy decompression between dives. It also facilitates extended bottom times and divers typically worked the wreck for eight hours at a time. The main objective of the salvage operation was to recover items of value and provide a return on investment for the investors. Oceaneering were indiscriminate in doing whatever was required to find and raise anything of commercial value. Consequently, a lot of explosives and underwater cutting tools were used to open up parts of the wreck, such as the specie room. Some of the larger items raised included two anchors and three of the four bronze propellers weighing in at 16 tons each. Literally thousands of smaller items were raised and included: brass portholes, Cunard china, silver cutlery, glassware, all manner of brass fixtures and fittings, watches, souvenir 'Kitchener' spoons, rare chronometers and the ship's steam whistle. Sadly, a lot of the items were not conserved properly and their condition deteriorated rapidly after being recovered.

Most of the items were auctioned off at Sotheby's but failed to generate the kind of financial returns that were anticipated. One of the propellers was bought by a company who melted it down to create a set of 3,500 unique golf clubs. A lot of the remaining artefacts languished in the gardens of various Oceaneering employees over the years and some items still remain on display in the company's offices to this day.

Ballard Expedition

In 1993 National Geographic commissioned the filming of a television documentary about the *Lusitania*. A key element of this was to be a two-week exploration of the wreck employing the latest film and lighting technology. Unlike previous visits to the wreck, this one did not involve divers as a mini submarine called *Jason* would be used instead. *Jason* was complemented by two unmanned ROVs, *Media* and *Homer*, and all operations took place from the support vessel *Northern Horizon*. The expedition was led by Robert Ballard, famous for his part in the discovery of the wreck of *Titanic*.

There is no doubt that the National Geographic expedition brought back the best underwater images of the wreck seen so far. The wreck was systematically recorded by sonar, photograph and video, and three-dimensional models were made on computers of the wreck's profile on the seabed.

The abundance of lost fishing lines and nets that hung suspended above the wreck was a constant threat to the underwater vehicles. On one dive *Jason's* propeller became totally ensnared, requiring the sub's tail section to be jettisoned in order to return safely to the surface.

A key objective of the dives was to seek an answer to what had caused the second mystery explosion immediately after the fatal torpedo had struck. The final conclusion drawn by the team was that it was due to exploding coal dust, a theory that is contested by some. Further to the documentary Ballard wrote a book with Spencer Dunmore titled *Exploring the Lusitania*, which contains numerous underwater photographs of the wreck and illustrative paintings by renowned marine artist Ken Marschall.

Technical Diving

The 1990s heralded a new age in amateur recreational diving with the increased use of breathing gas mixtures other than regular compressed air for deep diving. The main benefits were reduced nitrogen narcosis at depth and shorter decompression times. Finally a diver had the complete freedom of movement provided by scuba, combined with the clear head required to function safely at depth. This formed the foundation of what is now commonly known as 'technical diving'.

Some of the ammunition that was raised from the *Lusitania* in 2008. (© Timmy Carey)

While Ballard and his crew were exploring the *Lusitania* from the relative comfort of a submarine and ROV monitor screens, a British team of technical divers was already in training for a unique underwater exploration of their own. The group was called Starfish Enterprise, founded by divers Simon and Polly Tapson in 1990. In June 1994 a dive team led by Polly Tapson assembled in Kinsale, Ireland, consisting of eight British divers and four American divers. The American contingent included Gary Gentile, who was already known to Tapson due to the publication of his book, *Ultimate Wreck Diving Guide*, in 1992.

During the course of a two-week period the team completed 120 dives from ten days of diving. The dive boat was *Sundancer II*, skippered by local man Nic Gotto, grandson of famous wreck salvor Risdon Beasley. The divers managed bottom times of between twenty and twenty-eight minutes, and typically spent around ninety minutes decompressing. All used similar equipment, which consisted of back-mounted twin 15-litre (120cu ft) cylinders of trimix, side-slung tanks of nitrox and decompression gas of pure oxygen. Using a trimix blend of 13/52 gave the diver an equivalent narcosis depth of 37m (121ft) at a depth of 90m (295ft). Some also used a fourth gas, argon, for dry-suit inflation, chosen for its insulation properties.

Gentile took a significant amount of high-quality underwater photographs, many of which can be seen in his book *The Lusitania Controversies – Book Two*. One of these was of the bridge telegraph and showed the last acknowledged command to be 'ahead'. Another member of the American dive team, John Chatterton, recorded video of the wreck.

A second, smaller group by the name of Irish Technical Diving (ITD), led by Desmond Quigley, also dived the *Lusitania* later in 1994.

On a second Starfish expedition Polly Tapson saw some long metal tubes on the wreck. This sparked considerable international interest as *Lusitania* was known to be carrying famous works of art owned by Sir Hugh Lane stored in sealed lead tubes. Subsequently, on 25 January 1995, the Irish Government issued an Underwater Heritage Order to protect the *Lusitania* under the National Monuments Act.

Technical divers continued to visit the wreck throughout the 1990s and into the new millennium. The equipment used continued to evolve with the introduction of rebreathers and it is now rare for divers to dive to such depths on open-circuit scuba. Not only do rebreathers considerably reduce the amount of gas a diver has to carry, it alleviates some of the logistical challenges of having to fill so many cylinders and mix gas at the end of each day's diving.

More recently controls over diving the wreck have become more rigorous. Any diving requires permission from the appropriate authorities and must be carried out with the sanction of the wreck's owner, Gregg Bemis.

Having owned the wreck for thirty-five years and being an active participant in the numerous technical diving expeditions, Bemis decided it was time to see the wreck for himself. Considering he was aged seventy-six at the time, this was an impressive accomplishment. Bemis commenced a comprehensive training

This first-class cabin window was recovered by Stewart Andrews during the August 2011 expedition to the wreck. The bottom time of forty-nine minutes at 90m (295ft) required a decompression of four hours. *(Courtesy of Petr Stach and Creative Differences)*

always publicly known to be carrying 4,200 cases of rifle ammunition. However, reports from the divers did seem to suggest that the large quantity and variety of ordnance on the wreck was more than they expected.

In 2009 the Discovery Channel sponsored an expedition to the wreck with Odyssey Marine International, which resulted in the production of the documentary *Lusitania Revealed*. No manned submersibles or divers were used and ROVs were employed exclusively. A detailed systematic survey of the entire wreck site was carried out using the latest in hi-tech imaging equipment and the amount of fishing net draped over the wreck proved that fishermen were ignoring the wreck's heritage status. One interesting discovery was a number of long cylinders that were thought to be the tubes seen in 1994 by Polly Tapson. It was established that they were not the containers for the lost paintings. Graphic footage showing the degradation of the wreck also helped present the case to Dúchas, the Irish Heritage service, that time was running out to preserve artefacts and solve the mystery of the second explosion.

One of the most recent and extensive expeditions to the wreck took place in August 2011 and featured technical divers, commercial divers using Nuytco atmosphere suits, manned submersibles and ROVs. The project was sponsored by National Geographic and resulted in the documentary *Dark Secrets of the Lusitania* (2012). The team were licensed to perform penetration dives into

programme with technical diving instructor Hal Watts in Florida, where he made dives to 73m (240ft). In addition to learning the physical and theoretical rigours of deep mixed-gas diving, Bemis also had to familiarise himself with a dry suit in preparation for his descent into the cold Irish waters. When the day finally came to make the dive to the *Lusitania* the weather was perfect and Bemis entered the water with Watts and photographer Dan Burton. Bemis carried out his dive using open-circuit scuba and described his experience for *Dive New Zealand* magazine:

> Hal and I proceeded to the bottom making a gas switch from our Nitrox 37 to our Trimix 13/55 as we passed through the 80–100 foot (24–30m) level. We spotted the flashing strobe light secured to the shot line in plenty of time to slow down for a soft landing on one of the several large ventilators scattered about the wreck. After giving the old lady a loving kiss (its been 35 years) we explored the immediate vicinity including a massive skylight with varied portholes, the glass windows of which are long gone. All the wreck is covered with a scattering of sea growth and with a delicate layer of silt or dead plankton, or whatever. When stirred up it takes a few minutes to disperse but does not significantly interfere with visibility except very locally.

Dive expeditions in 2006 and 2008 identified an abundance of .303 rifle ammunition scattered on the wreck. Although this caused a stir in the press it was not considered a major development by historians since *Lusitania* was

The crew of the August 2011 *Lusitania* expedition, which included commercial and technical recreational divers. Towards the left at the rear is a bright yellow Nuytco atmosphere suit. Front left is a Nuytco two-man submersible. Second from the left in the front row, kneeling is Gregg Bemis, owner of the *Lusitania* wreck. *(Photograph courtesy of Petr Stach and Creative Differences)*

the wreck and recover artefacts. The plans included cutting a hole into the side of the vessel to get access to the forward holds. As usual the weather and tides played a part, but early reports indicated that the expedition had been a success. Some of the items raised included the bronze telemotor, telegraph and one of the ornate first-class cabin windows. The recoveries were made by an Irish technical dive team lead by Eoin McGarry and overseen by an archaeologist and preservation specialist.

Wreck Today

The final resting place of the *Lusitania* is in the Celtic Sea 12 miles from the Old Head of Kinsale off the southern coast of Ireland. This part of the ocean is tidal so the wreck can only be dived during periods of slack water. The wreck lies with the bow pointing to the north-east and stern to south-west, resting on the starboard side at angle of roughly 30 degrees. The wreck has already collapsed further since John Light's pioneering dives of the 1960s. At the time he reported a minimum depth of 73m (240ft), whereas the highest point is now at 82m (270ft). Depth to the seabed is 93m (305ft).

The visibility can be up to 10m (33ft), but 3m (10ft) is much more typical. It is always dark. The best times of year are often accompanied by a plankton bloom, which further restricts the amount of ambient light reaching the wreck. The remains of snagged fishing nets, trawler tackle and mono filament lines remain a constant threat to exploring divers. Divers need to look upwards as well as down to avoid the consequences of swimming in under a net.

The most intact and recognisable area is the bow, where the outline of the name *LUSITANIA* is still visible on the port side. The starboard anchor is still firmly in place. The foredeck capstans and mooring bollards are clearly recognisable, some still wrapped with neatly coiled ropes. One of the huge anchor chains runs across the deck and descends down into a hawser pipe.

Most of the bridge structure has slid down the starboard side of the wreck into the debris field scattered on the seabed. One of the ship's telegraphs remained here for many years, along with one of the whistles. Oceaneering removed at least one telegraph and the other whistle during their time on the wreck in the 1980s. Aft of the bridge area are *Lusitania's* distinctive ventilation outlets, which resemble oversized dustbins.

Portholes and windows of all shapes and sizes line the length of the wreck, many of which still contain their glass. There are numerous holes and openings along the starboard side of the hull, some original, others due to salvage work. A few of the ship's railings still stand proud. Occasionally tiled areas are exposed, including the mosaic tiling in areas once well trodden by the first-class passengers. One of the first-class baths, complete with an unusual shower cage, lies scattered amongst other debris.

Parts of the engine room are exposed and remains of collapsed catwalks are in evidence. The curved tops of the huge boilers can also be observed. Nothing remains of the four enormous funnels. Aft of the first funnel opening are three fresh-water tanks complete with valves.

The modest marker for the mass *Lusitania* grave in Cobh graveyard. (© *Timmy Carey*)

Little remains of the stern docking bridge, but the telemotor and telegraphs have been seen amongst the tangled debris towards the aft end of the wreck. At the stern, part of the rudder is still in place but a section has broken off and lies on the seabed below. The prop shafts terminate in featureless stubs since three of the four powerful propellers have been removed by salvors. Two blades from the remaining propeller are visible poking out from underneath the wreck.

Scattered all over the wreck are numerous small artefacts, such as light fittings, Cunard china and the occasional personal effect.

Care should be taken of unexploded hedgehog mines found scattered on the seabed amongst the debris field. These provide evidence of the depth charging that took place in the 1950s.

Marine life is plentiful with an abundance of pollack swimming in and out of the wreckage. Conger eels are frequently seen hiding in recesses. Small red starfish and delicate sea urchins seem out of place on such a deep, dark wreck. In fact, the marine life is so prolific that it can actually be a hindrance to divers surveying the wreck.

Most divers fortunate enough to have visited the wreck of the *Lusitania* rate it as one of the highlights of their diving experience, and affectionately refer to her as the '*Lucy*'.

Folia

1907–1917, Ireland

As the Canadian Northern's *Principello*. The ship was sold to Cunard in 1917 and renamed *Folia*. *(Ian Lawler Collection)*

THE *FOLIA* WAS originally named *Principe di Piemonte* when she was built for the Lloyd Sabaudo Line of Italy in 1907. The vessel was 6,365 tons, 131m (430ft) in length and had a beam of 16.4m (53ft). There were two funnels, two masts, and a six-cylinder, triple-expansion engine powering twin screws for a service speed of 14 knots. The ship was built by Sir James Laing & Sons, Sunderland, and launched on 28 February 1907. The accommodation was for 120 first-class, 50 second-class and 1,500 third-class passengers. The maiden voyage left Genoa on 19 June 1907 bound for New York, calling at Naples, Palermo and Gibraltar.

In 1913 the ship was sold to Canadian Northern Railways, renamed *Principello* and chartered to Uranium Steamship Co. for their Rotterdam to New York service, replacing the *Volturno*, which had been lost at sea. *Volturno* was an ocean liner that was also under charter from the Canadian Northern to the Uranium Line when she caught fire and sank in the North Atlantic on October 1913. The *Volturno* radio officer had sent out SOS signals that were picked up by eleven ships that arrived and rescued 520 passengers and crew. Sadly 130 passengers, mainly women and children, were lost due to problems launching the lifeboats.

From 1914 passenger services commenced operating from Bristol to Montréal, calling at Québec. Then in 1916 the *Principello* was acquired by Cunard to help replace the many vessels they had already lost in the war. Cunard renamed the ship *Folia* and it was used on the transatlantic route sailing from Bristol to New York. Cunard also bought two other Uranium Line vessels: *Uranium* (5,254 tons), which was renamed *Feltria*, and *Campania* (9,285 tons), which was renamed *Flavia*.

The *Folia*, commanded by Captain F. Inch, left New York for her return voyage to Bristol carrying 4,400 tons of general cargo. It was on Sunday, 11 March 1917 when she was sailing 4 miles ESE of Ram Head near to Youghal Island, Ireland, that she was torpedoed at position 51.51'N, 07.41'W without warning by *U-53* (Commander Hans Rose).

An eyewitness account was given of the attack in Sir Edgar T. Britten's *A Million Ocean Miles* (1936):

> It was 7.15 a.m. that the Third Officer observed the periscope of a submarine some 500 feet from the ship and nearly abeam. Immediately afterwards he saw the feathery wake of a torpedo approaching, and a second later the *Folia* was hit amidships, the explosion smashing two of her lifeboats. Seven of the crew, including the Second Engineer, were also killed by the explosion, and

the *Folia* herself began rapidly to settle. Four boats were at once lowered, and the rest of the officers and crew were safely embarked. While the lifeboats were still in the neighbourhood the submarine came to the surface, motored rapidly round the ship and fired four shots into her. She next backed away and fired a second torpedo into the sinking vessel. The U-boat then cleared off, but Captain Inch got his boats together and instructed the officers in charge to steer on a Nor'west compass bearing. Three of them made fast by painters so as not to get adrift from each other, and in this manner the frail boats stood on their course. About 11 a.m. the Captain, under the fog that had crept up, sighted breakers ahead. Creeping along the line of breakers they at last sighted smooth water at the base of towering cliffs. Pulling for these they saw the outline of a house high above, with people standing in front of it. Shouting in unison the crew succeeded in attracting attention and learned that the place was Ardmore, Youghal, Co. Cork, and from there they proceeded to Dungarvan, where they arrived in time to hear the church bells that evening.

Although armed with a 12in stern gun, the *Folia* was no match for the submarine when it surfaced and sank the ship by gunfire, with a loss of seven crew and sixty-eight survivors.

U-53 was built in Germaniawerft, Kiel, launched on 1 February 1916 and commissioned on 22 April 1916. The first commander was Hans Rose from 22 April 1916, and he was commanding *U-53* when she sank *Folia* in March 1917. On 1 December 1918 *U-53* surrendered and was eventually broken up at Swansea in 1922. It is thought that Hans Rose was a decent submarine commander who would wait and see that all the lifeboats of a ship he had torpedoed had got away safely, and was known to throw a tow line to keep all the survivors' boats safely

A diver illuminates the wreck with a powerful torch. *(David Riordan)*

Divers decompressing on the shot line at the end of a dive on the *Folia*. *(© Timmy Carey)*

Evidence of the *Folia*'s cargo, which included cast-iron shell casings. *(David Riordan)*

Above The gun was unveiled in Ardmore in March 2017 to commemorate the *Folia* centenary. *(Alan Peacock)*

Left In July 2014 a team of divers led by Eoin McGarry raised the 12lb anti-aircraft stern gun from the *Folia*. *(Eoin McGarry)*

together until a rescue ship, often a destroyer, arrived in the distance. He would then let go the ropes and submerge to leave before the U-boat was attacked.

Both the other two ex-Uranium vessels, *Feltria* and *Flavia*, were also sunk by submarines during the First World War.

Folia Wreck

The wreck of the *Folia* lies 4 miles off the coast of southern Ireland, to the east of Cork. The nearest point of land is Ram Head and dive boats often depart from the fishing village of Ardmore in County Waterford.

The maximum depth to the seabed is 40m (131ft) and the visibility has been reported to be as good as 20m (65ft), although this is rare. The area is tidal so diving needs to take place during slack water. The exposed location also requires good weather conditions.

The *Folia* was known to be carrying a large quantity of brass bars, which were heavily salvaged by Risdon Beasley in 1977. The salvage was carried out using a grab, which resulted in a lot of damage to the wreck. Much of the brass that remained was removed and sold commercially by local divers in the 1980s. The brass bars are in two main sizes; the large ones are 183cm (72in) long, 5cm (2in) in diameter and weigh 33kg (72lb), while the smaller bars are 155cm (61in) long, just over half the diameter of the large bars, and weigh 18kg (26lb). Occasionally they can still be found hidden amongst the wreckage scattered

around the stern. The other main cargo carried by the *Folia* was trench-digging machinery, the remains of which can be seen on the wreck, although it is hard to distinguish individual parts.

With a length of 131m (430ft), the *Folia* is one of the largest wrecks in the area within sport-diving depths and takes several dives to appreciate fully. In some places the wreck stands up to 5m (16ft) proud of the rocky seabed. The bow is one of the most intact parts of the wreck and easily recognisable. There are lots of scattered steel plates, but the boilers are prominent in the middle of the wreck. The salvage efforts are most evident aft of the boilers, where most of the superstructure has been destroyed. Shell casings are still found in this area. The rudder can still be at the stern but the 12lb anti-aircraft gun was recovered in 2014.

Plenty of porcelain has been found on the wreck over the years, although what remains today is mostly just broken shards. Interestingly, all the china that has been recovered bears the inscription of 'Canadian Northern', which was the name of the company that owned the *Folia* before the ship was purchased by Cunard in 1916. Since Cunard acquired the *Folia* in the middle of the war they would have seen little value in replacing all the dinnerware at that time. Brass fittings have also been observed stamped with the vessel's first name, *Principe di Piemonte*.

There is plenty of marine life on the wreck and like so many shipwrecks in this part of the world the *Folia* is a popular habitat for conger eels. The abundant shoals of fish make the wreck popular with local anglers. Thus, divers need to be careful of becoming entangled in lost fishing line and tackle.

Ascania

1911–1918, Canada

Pieces of broken porcelain still lie scattered on the wreck of the *Folia*. (© *Timmy Carey*)

The crockery still bears the mark of Canadian Northern, the *Folia's* previous owner.

CUNARD LINE'S FIRST *Ascania* was 9,111 tons and originally laid down as *Gerona* for the Thomson Line, prior to being taken over for completion by Cunard as *Ascania*. This ship was 142m (466ft) in length with a beam of 17m (56ft) and possessed two funnels and two masts. *Ascania* was built of steel, had twin-screw propellers, powered by two triple-expansion steam engines, providing a service speed between 12 and 13 knots. She was built by Swan Hunter & Wigham Richardson, Newcastle, and launched on 4 March 1911. The passenger capacity was for 200 second-class passengers and 1,500 third-class passengers. There was provision for 2,080 tons of cargo. The second-class cabins and public rooms were amidships and the cabins were fitted with electric radiators. The smoking room was fitted with rectangular windows, with furniture and panelling in oak. The expansive promenade deck featured a veranda café.

In the original inward and outward ledgers at Southampton Docks for 1911 it was recorded that the *Ascania* had arrived from Newcastle under the command of her first master, Captain W.R.D. Irvine, on 22 May 1911 at 7.15 a.m., carrying a cargo of ballast. The passengers embarked at Southampton and the ledgers record that the *Ascania* left Southampton Docks at 3.25 p.m. on 23 May for her maiden voyage to Québec and Montréal. From then on Cunard provided a fortnightly service to Québec and Montréal.

During the First World War, the *Ascania* was used as an AMC sailing across the North Atlantic, but on the eastbound voyages all the third class was occupied by Canadian troops on their way to the battlefront in France. In May 1918 the *Ascania* also carried a detachment of the US 119th Infantry from Hoboken, New Jersey, first to Halifax, Nova Scotia, and then made up a transatlantic convoy to their destination at the port of Liverpool. They were attacked by submarines on the night of 26 May, but arrived safely at Liverpool on 27 May 1918.

The *Ascania* was wrecked during the night of 13–14 June 1918 in the Breton Strait, 20 miles east of Cape Ray, Newfoundland. The keel of the vessel was broken so she could not be refloated and was declared a total loss. All hands were saved.

First and Last Voyage on the *Ascania*

Hugh Williams Humphreys (1901–93) was a young seaman on his first voyage to sea on board the *Ascania* at the age of seventeen, when he had the unfortunate experience of being shipwrecked in 1918. However, this did not deter him

Ascania pictured sailing westbound off Rose Blanche lighthouse near her final resting place at Gull Island, Petites. The Robert G. Lloyd painting was commissioned to celebrate the September 2006 diving expedition to the wreck. *(Author's collection, courtesy of Robert Lloyd)*

because he returned to sea in September that year. He went on to serve a further fifteen years until he was forced to leave after suffering a serious accident on board the RMS *Montrose*.

His son, John Humphreys, talks about his father:

My father went to sea without the permission of his parents, although his mother tried to stop him, but the ship had already sailed. His first voyage was on the Cunard liner *Ascania*, during which she was wrecked off the south coast of Newfoundland on the 14 June 1918. After his experience on the *Ascania* he went back to sea in September 1918 on the SS *Quilpue* of the Pacific Steam and Navigation Co., and for the next fifteen years had a career at sea. He was seriously injured when serving on the Canadian Pacific Line RMS *Montrose*

Ascania shown here on a postcard sent from a voyage to Canada in 1911. The sender writes: 'going now up the river St Lawrence, very foggy'.

in 1933 when an accident occurred while carrying out a lifeboat drill in dock in Liverpool. On my father's retirement, he wrote a book about his time at sea, in Welsh, his native language. It was titled 'My First Voyage and Others' and contains a graphic account of the grounding of the *Ascania*.

Extracts from John Humphreys' translation of his father's account are reproduced below.

Hugh Williams Humphreys:

When I was a young boy, if anybody asked me what I wanted to do when I grew up I would always reply, 'Go to sea'. After all my Grandfather Captain Hugh Williams was the Captain of the '*Polly Preston*' a famous Nefyn and Porthdinllaen sailing vessel. My Father was also a sailor, and when they came home, the conversations were all about the sea and sailing ships. However, I faced an insurmountable obstacle in the form of my mother, who was adamant that I would never go to sea. Her objection was based on the tragedy of losing her younger brother Hugh David Williams who was drowned when his sailing ship the *Edward Seymour* was lost off the Island of Anticosti in the Gulf of St Lawrence in October of 1902. This objection was the only source of disagreement that ever came between us.

When Hugh Humphreys was seventeen he had been attending the Pwllheli Grammar School and the First World War had been going for four years. He was offered work as a cashier with a famous Welsh company, Morris & Jones, at their head office in Liverpool: 'I leapt at the chance that this would give me to leave home and go to Liverpool, with the attendant opportunity of going to sea.'

With his wages at only 10 shillings, he was able to gradually save up enough to buy the contents of a reasonable sloop chest in his preparation for going to sea. However, he had an opportunity to achieve his ambition of a mariner's life when visiting Pier Head at Liverpool one Saturday. Hugh Humphreys:

I was down on the Pier Head at Liverpool when the White Star liner *Canada* docked, her captain was my uncle, so on Sunday I went to his home in Seaforth to see him. Much to my own surprise I told him a white lie, I said to him that my mother had told me to ask him if he could help me to get a berth. He told me to be down at the Shipping Office on the following Monday. He met me at the Shipping Office and introduced me to a friend of his, Captain Mathias a shipping agent, who turned out to be the brother of the local butcher in Pwllheli whom I knew very well.

Captain Mathias very quickly obtained me a berth on the H.M.S *Ascania*, which was lying in the Huskinson Dock. The *Ascania* was a Cunard liner, which had been requisitioned as an armed merchant cruiser. I wrote home and told my Mother what I had done, and then on the following Friday I joined the ship just before she moved from the dock out into the River Mersey.

The smoking room on *Ascania* featured oak panelling.

On boarding the ship Hugh Humphreys was shown his quarters in the forecastle, where he met five other boys who had arrived before him. These boys were all from the correctional ship *Cleo*, anchored in the Menai Straits:

Boys were sent to the *Cleo* by the courts because of truancy and bad behaviour. The bosun called us out on deck where we were 'inspected' by the Staff Captain and the Second Officer, who divided us into Port and Starboard watches. The Staff Captain who knew both my Uncle and Capt Mathias was looking out for me, he told me to report to the 'Yeoman of the Signals' on the bridge.

One of the reasons Hugh Humphreys was chosen to become a runner from the radio shack to the bridge was because he had a good education and could read and write:

The yeoman was a very helpful and pleasant person; he helped me to obtain my uniform and showed me around the bridge and the radio cabin. The Second Officer who was also Welsh, and went to the same Church as me in Liverpool, came and had a long conversation with me, during which he warned me about my fellow cabin mates from the *Cleo*.

When the *Ascania* was converted to an AMC, the third-class smoking room was adapted to take the supports for the gun mounting, but also acted as the mess hall. At dinnertime Hugh Humphreys went down to the mess hall:

The dinner was very good indeed, far better than what I expected, with plenty to eat with no rations. In the mess store there were two identical wooden

Left When Hugh Humphreys joined the *Ascania* at age seventeen it was his first trip to sea. *(John Humphreys)*

Below Ascania tie pin worn and owned by Hugh Humphreys when he was shipwrecked. *(John Humphreys)*

At about this time we were also issued with life jackets, and given instructions that we were to wear them all the time we were at sea. I was allocated as a crew member on lifeboat No 3. One of my duties was to make sure that the automatic plug was working correctly, every day! We also had numerous boat and fire drills.

The Ascania *sets sail*

Hugh Humphreys:

We set sail early on Sunday morning and were the lead ship of the convoy carrying the convoy commodore; consequently I was kept very busy taking messages to the radio room, and helping the yeoman with the signal flags. While crossing Liverpool Bay the convoy was escorted by eight American lease lend destroyers, which were called 'Wills Woodbine' ships, presumably because of their long low profile.

We turned west past the Fastnet Rock and the convoy was given orders to disperse with every ship taking its own course. Apparently, the range of the U-Boats was very limited, and the threat did not justify a convoy after sailing through home waters.

One evening, at about six o'clock, just after finishing their evening meal the bell sounded for 'Action Stations' and almost immediately the gun above the mess hall was fired:

The noise was deafening, the place shook, and the mess hall filled with cordite smoke. We all ran to our action stations; mine was on the bridge alongside the Yeoman. When I arrived there, he pointed out to me a submarine lying low and grey in the twilight. It fired three shots at us in quick succession, one was short and the others went over us, meanwhile the *Ascania* had turned broadside on to the U-Boat and every gun on that side began to fire. When the spray from the shells had died down there was no U-Boat to be seen, the opinion was that it had crash-dived. There followed a lively debate on the bridge as to why the U-Boat had not tried to fire torpedoes at us, it was concluded that either we had probably surprised it, both with our presence and our reaction, or probably it had already used up its torpedoes.

It was on 13 June 1918, after crossing the North Atlantic, that the *Ascania* ran aground in fog near Rose Blanche, off the south-west coast of Newfoundland. Hugh Humphreys:

As we were approaching Newfoundland in the dark, I was sent up to the crow's nest to the forecastle lookout man, with instructions to tell them that they were to keep a sharp lookout for a certain lighthouse whose name I now forget. On returning as I climbed up the ladder to the bridge the ship gave an enormous shudder and bucked up, there was a roaring tearing, grinding noise.

buckets one containing 28lbs of strawberry jam and the other marmalade. There was also a 7lb block of butter and several containers of pickles and a plentiful supply of bread, so whatever happened to us we were going to be well fed.

After having his lunch he returned to the bridge where he found a number of officials. Hugh Humphreys:

There was the Convoy Commander, a Pilot and the Captain, and the place was a hive of activity. The ship was moved out of the Dock and taken to the middle of the Mersey where she was anchored just off the Landing Stage. In the meantime, the Yeoman showed me how the signal flags were folded and kept, and how to use the message pads between the bridge and the radio room. I was also taken down to the first class saloon where there was a big chart of the North Atlantic from which I was to obtain the ships position at mid-day every day, and at any other time if required by the Yeoman.

While the *Ascania* was anchored off Pier Head fourteen Canadian nurses and several army officers who were returning to Canada after service in France embarked, confirming to Hugh Humphreys that the likely destination was to be Canada:

I was thrown down onto the deck. When I picked myself up there was steam everywhere and the ship was in darkness. I made my way to the bridge, and was immediately ordered to go with the yeoman to the lower wheelhouse to get the distress rockets, set them up, and fire them. The ship had clearly gone aground.

The ship had been plunged into darkness and remained so until a dynamo on the boat deck was brought into action. Hugh Humphreys:

It was apparent that the stokers from the engine room had broken the lashings that secured one of the lifeboats and had attempted to launch one. In the process, several stokers had been injured by being crushed between the boat and the ship.

Although the sea appeared to be quite rough there was no motion to the ship and for the time being everyone on board appeared to be reasonably safe. Hugh Humphreys:

There was considerable confusion on the bridge. It was clear that nobody knew where we were, there were no lighthouses visible and there did not appear to be any reaction to our distress rockets. The carpenter reported to the bridge saying that there was water in all the bottom tanks, and that the ship was holed along its length. The second officer and the quartermaster also came onto the bridge and said that we were hard aground fore and aft but she was clear of the seabed amidships.

The *Ascania* fired maroons and after fifteen minutes they received a radio message telling them where they were. The message confirmed that they were aground to the east of Port Aux Basque and told them a steamer would arrive within the hour. Hugh Humphreys:

The tide was going out and there was considerable concern about the position of the ship. Although the ship was stationary with very little movement, she was groaning and making terrible grinding noises. About three o'clock in the morning the amidships section of the ship settled down ominously to such an extent that the two funnels were now touching, it was feared by the captain that her back was broken. At about this time the steamer arrived and anchored astern of us and told us to stay where we were until daylight.

Why did Ascania run aground?

This was the question that the captain and his officers discussed during the night while waiting for the daylight and arrangements to transfer passengers to the steamer waiting alongside. Hugh Humphreys:

During the last few days before our grounding, the carpenter had been repairing and putting up new shelves on the bridge. He had been keeping a

large canvas bag of tools in a cupboard alongside the compass binnacle and it was being alleged that this bag had caused a big compass error. To my knowledge, it was never resolved as to why the ship was so far off course as to run aground where she did.

The following day the steamer SS *Kyle* was moored quite close to the stern of the *Ascania* with a hawser rigged between her stem and the steamer. Hugh Humphreys:

On to this hawser the steamer ran her dory, which was then pulled backwards and forward between the two ships. Throughout most of the day most of the passengers and crew were taken off in this manner.

It was not until the evening of the second day that Hugh Humphreys was told that he was to disembark:

I took as much clothes and belongings as I could carry and went down the Jacob's ladder and into the dory. As I left the ship she was a sorry sight, she was visibly sagging in the middle and had settled deep in the water. Both her propellers were visible, although I had only been on her a few days I was close to tears. Boarding the steamer was dangerous as there was quite a swell running. We were hoisted via a harness up from the dory onto her deck. When my turn came, I was hoisted into the air, but I was thrown violently against the steamer and when I came on board I was almost unconscious. The Doctor diagnosed two broken ribs and several strained ribs, and gave me a morphine injection and I was placed in a bunk. I never said goodbye to the *Ascania*!

Sam Warwick points out the location on Gull Rock where *Ascania* grounded and where the wreck lies today. The abandoned coastal community of Petites is to the left. *(Catherine de Lara)*

Rick Stanley and Sam Warwick prepare to 'splash in' on the wreck of the *Ascania*.

Right, from top

Spare propeller blade. *(Catherine de Lara)*

The giant steering quadrant stands up on its side and is a very distinctive feature of the wreck. *(Catherine de Lara)*

One of the *Ascania's* large boilers. *(Catherine de Lara)*

The steamer took the passengers and crew to North Sydney, Nova Scotia, where they received an enormous welcome, both as shipwrecked survivors and because their passengers were the first Canadians to return from the war in France. However, Hugh Humphreys was sent to hospital, where he spent a few days recovering.

Hugh Humphreys was given $5 expenses by Cunard and informed that his wages ceased when the ship ran aground: 'I wrote home to tell them what had happened and that I was safe, but the letter did not arrive until after I got home.' Leaving for home was undertaken with swift precision and gave Hugh Humphreys and the surviving crew little time to prepare:

> One night without warning, we were given a few minutes to pack and then we were bussed down to the docks and on board a ship. It was quite a while before we realised that we were onboard the Cunard liner *Mauretania* which was jammed with American troops on the way to France. We had an uneventful crossing of the Atlantic berthing back in Liverpool.

After returning safely to Great Britain, Humphreys had no further involvement in the *Ascania* story:

> I was never interviewed about my time on the *Ascania*, as far as I know, no inquiry was ever held into her loss. I never found out why she was so far off course that night.

Captain Horace Mills Benison

The master of the *Ascania* (1) when she was wrecked in the Breton Strait was Captain Horace Mills Benison. Benison was born in 1857 and commenced his career with Cunard as fourth officer on the *Etruria*. In 1892 he joined the RNR (Royal Navy Reserve), serving as lieutenant on HMS *Curlew* for twelve months, and a further four months at Portsmouth, finally returning to Cunard on 26 June 1893. After serving as second officer on *Campania* he re-joined the *Etruria* as first officer on 15 January 1895. Between 4 and 18 January 1900 he resigned to take a command, returning to Cunard again as chief officer on the *Carpathia* on 14 April 1903.

Benison's first Cunard command was the *Veria* on 28 July 1905. He then went on to command *Pannonia*, *Carpathia*, *Ivernia* (1), *Pavia* and *Saxonia*. Captain Benison was in command of the *Alaunia* (2) when the vessel was mined in the English Channel on 19 October 1916 with a loss of two crew members. He first took command of *Ascania* (1) on 23 June 1917 before serving as master on *Mauretania* (1), then *Aurania* (2), before returning to the *Ascania* (1) one last time. Captain Benison retired on superannuation in May 1920.

Early Salvage Attempts

It has been stated that after the *Ascania* ran aground all the crew and passengers had been rescued and the ship could not be refloated, and was therefore declared a total loss. However, in his book, *The Coast of Newfoundland: The Southwest Corner*, Clarence Vautier has written about what happened after the *Ascania* was wrecked off Cape Ray in June 1918.

It appears that at first the *Ascania* had suffered little serious structural damage, but the middle section of the keel was balancing on a ledge. However, as the *Ascania* was not taking on water Captain Benison did not need to give the order to 'abandon ship' and the passengers remained on board until the next morning, when they were able to board the SS *Kyle*.

The grounding was reported to Lloyd's the next day and after an inspection was carried out it was decided to refloat the *Ascania*. The salvage contract was awarded to the Reid Co., which operated around the Great Lakes.

Although the contract was worth $1 million there were conditions this would only be paid for a successful salvage operation. This was going to be a risky operation because of the stormy weather conditions to which the area was often subjected.

Right, from top

Wolf fish are a common sight among the rocks around the wreck. *(Catherine de Lara)*

Section of the hull towards the shallower forward part of the wreck. *(Catherine de Lara)*

There is a lot of ordnance scattered among the wreckage. *(Catherine de Lara)*

The aim was to seal all the cargo holds and pump compressed air into the vessel to raise her from the ledge. However, on 26 June the open area where the *Ascania* had run aground was struck by gale-force winds and all inspection work was halted.

The divers eventually returned to continue their examination of the *Ascania*, but found that the storm had caused further damage to the ship. This included a broken rudder and stern frame, but more seriously, where the keel was resting on the ledge the engine room floor had buckled upwards, and areas of the cargo holds were split open.

The seriousness of the damage required additional salvage equipment to be brought in for the operation. The Reid Co. were able to acquire a 100ft coaster, the *Mary Battle*, from a shipyard in Montréal. However, this was to take precious time in loading the vessel with the equipment needed for the operation. It was at least three months before the *Mary Battle* was ready to sail with Thomas Reid, his partner in the company, Louis Meyer, and a crew of forty-six. They eventually arrived at North Sydney on 5 September, but were delayed there for a further four days due to high winds. The *Mary Battle* and crew finally arrived at Petites on 10 September 1918.

Once they had arrived and disembarked, the job of the crew was to set up their accommodation tents for the time they were to spend on the project. However, they were still open to the elements when the wind blew all the tents down the next night. The crew then had to look for alternative accommodation and finally rented houses in the nearby Harbour le Cou.

The supplies were transferred from the *Mary Battle* to the *Ascania* on 13 September, but again the weather deteriorated and high seas forced the crew to leave the vessel. It was a further ten days before they could return to unloading the equipment.

Continuous bad weather caused further delays to the salvage operation, and all the time the costs were increasing; it was almost the middle of October before all the equipment was finally aboard the *Ascania*. Some work was carried out and divers continued their underwater inspections. By the beginning of November they were ready to refloat the vessel on the next spring tide, but the local Petites residents warned that a severe storm was approaching that would stay around for some days. This was confirmed on 14 November when the whole area was hit by south-easterly winds, causing serious damage to the *Ascania*'s hull. Furthermore, high westerly winds followed the first storm, causing further damage.

When the crew were able to return to the ship they found that the *Ascania*'s stern had settled 7ft deeper and other equipment the salvage workers had set up had been destroyed. It had become clear that the salvage operation was in serious trouble, but on 28 November this was confirmed when a fire broke in one of the holds and spread throughout the vessel with all wood on board burned away and further damage to the salvage equipment.

It was a great disappointment to the salvage company, who had lost the battle – and the million dollars! The *Mary Battle* left Petites on 1 December for Port aux Basques and then on to North Sydney.

Diver Johno de Lara is holding a bottle of champagne found on the wreck by Catherine de Lara. It is still intact and complete with cork, despite nearly a century underwater. *(Catherine de Lara)*

As for the wreck of the *Ascania*, further damage from the storms caused the vessel to slip off the ledge and into deeper water. However, for the local residents they were able to collect smaller items from the wreck and some lifeboats that were intact were sold to the locals. Clarence Vautier:

One of the lifeboats was sold to my great-grandfather William Vautier, who at the time had just given up going to sea to work on the Anglo-Newfoundland Telegraph Line as a repairman. The boat was named the *Johnny Walker* and was used to travel along the bays until 1946, when it was dismantled.

Ascania Wreck

Following the original salvage at the time of loss, the *Ascania* was largely forgotten until the 1960s. This time she was again the target of commercial salvors, whose main interest was removing all remaining metal of value, namely brass and copper. Due to its remote location in a sparsely populated area of south-west Newfoundland, the *Ascania* is seldom visited by recreational divers. However, it is known that small groups of divers have been visiting the wreck occasionally since the 1980s.

The remains of the *Ascania* lie in shallow water surrounding Gull Island, where the ship originally ran aground. Gull Island is a small rocky outcrop a few kilometres from the coastal community of Petites, which is only accessible

by boat. At its peak Petites had a population of over 200 people, but was depopulated by the Canadian Government in the early 2000s, along with many other similar fishing villages. The closest places on land accessible by road are Harbour Le Cou and Rose Blanche, 50km east of Port Aux Basques.

The wreck lies with the bow section in shallow water of 3m (10ft) to the north-west and the stern deeper as 15m (49ft) to the south-east on a rocky seabed. Due to the shallow depth and exposure to strong Atlantic swells the wreck has become very broken up and scattered. Both propeller shafts remain complete and in place, running parallel across the top of the wreck. At the stern the propellers have been removed but the steering quadrant and part of the rudder remain. The steering quadrant is an impressive feature of the wreck, standing vertically proud and over 2m (6ft) tall. Two spare propeller blades can be found lying on the seabed amongst the wreckage. There is a lot of live ordnance scattered around this area of the wreck. At the side of the wreck parts of the masts can be found and a section of the crow's nest. Forward of the shafts are two boilers, one of which is standing on end. Beyond the boilers the wreck starts to get a lot shallower and specific features become harder to identify. One anchor remains on the seabed, along with some chain at about 3m (10ft). The other anchor was removed at the time of salvage and remained in Petites for many years.

In 1983 divers found five full bottles of wine and intact crockery showing the Cunard crest. Occasionally artefacts can still be found trapped within sections of the ship's hull. An expedition in 2006 found a champagne bottle complete with cork, along with many shards of Cunard china. A brass porthole was also located.

Apart from the logistics of getting to the dive site, the main challenge to diving the *Ascania* is the weather conditions. Even on calm days the onshore swells can be significant, making diving challenging, particularly on the shallow parts of the wreck, forward of the boilers. If the conditions are favourable then the dive can be safely made by all levels of diver. Navigation on the wreck is relatively easy as the twin-propeller shafts provide a good point of reference for a full circumnavigation of the wreck. There are no opportunities to penetrate any parts of the wreck. Divers should be aware of munitions. Visibility is generally in excess of 5m (16ft) and sea temperatures during summer months are typically around 12°C (54°F). The majority of the seabed is solid rock with some gravel patches and in many places the wreckage is fused into the rock. Fish life is quite sparse, with little to be seen apart from the occasional wolf eel and flatty. Urchins, barnacles and starfish can be found clinging to the wreck.

Andania

1913–1918, Northern Ireland

ANDANIA (1) WAS made of steel by Scott's Shipbuilding & Engineering Co. Ltd, Greenock, and launched on 22 March 1913. This ship was 13,405 tons, 158.6m (520ft) in length, with a beam of 19.5m (64ft). There were two funnels and two masts and the engines were eight quadruple-expansion powering twin screws at 16 knots. In total there was accommodation for 2,060 passengers, which included 520 first-class and 1,540 third-class passengers. There was a change in the third-class accommodation from the earlier Cunard ship designs, where previously the third class was in dormitories, with the introduction of four- and six-berth cabins.

Cunard had inaugurated the Canadian service in 1911, but decided to order their own purpose-built ships for the Canadian service. Three vessels, the *Andania* (1), *Alaunia* (1) and *Aurania* (2), were ordered and all were almost identical in construction. *Andania* and *Alaunia* were ordered from Scott's Shipbuilding & Engineering Co. Ltd early in 1912, but the *Aurania* was built a few years later by Swan, Hunter & Wigham Richardson, Wallsend-on-Tyne.

When *Andania* was launched in March 1913 she was the first of the three ships to be completed. She left Liverpool on her maiden voyage on 14 July 1913 bound for Montréal, calling at Southampton and Québec, with representatives of the Canadian Government on board. Plans for the *Andania* to sail from London required the approach channels to the Thames to be dredged in advance of the *Andania* sailing through them. From August 1913 she commenced her first London to Montréal service, calling at Southampton and Québec, and in January 1914 London to Boston, but soon reverted to the original London to Montréal route.

In August 1914 *Andania* was requisitioned as a troopship and used to carry Canadian troops on the transatlantic route to the battlefields in France. A further task for the *Andania* was to act as an accommodation ship for the German POWs in 1915, but this was only for a short time as she was needed to carry the Royal Inniskilling Fusiliers and the Royal Dublin Fusiliers to Cape Helles for the Sulva landings in the Gallipoli campaign. The next year she was back to transporting Canadian troops, but later in 1916 and into 1917 she was used on the transatlantic passenger service from Liverpool to New York.

It was on 26 January 1918 that her fateful journey began, when she left Liverpool for New York. However, the route she had to travel was around the coast of Northern Ireland, where the German submarines would be waiting to attack and sink shipping. *Andania* was carrying general cargo, 40 passengers and up to 200 crew. On 27 January the *Andania* was hit by a torpedo fired by *U-46* (Commander Leo Hillebrand), 2 miles north-north-east of Rathlin Island, North Channel, at position 55°20'N, 06°12'W. Almost immediately the ship began to list to starboard and started sinking. Seven lives were lost.

On 29 January 1918 the *New York Times'* headline read: 'ANDANIA GOES TO THE BOTTOM', and reported the sinking of the vessel, including eyewitness accounts of the torpedo attack.

The *Andania* of 1913 was sister ship to the *Alaunia*.

Andania was struck by a torpedo and sank in deep water off Rathlin Island in 1918. Seven lives were lost.

06°26'W, proving that the U-boat menace was very serious off that part of the coast of Ireland.

U-46 was built at Kaiserliche Werft, Danzig, and was launched on 18 May 1915. Oberleutnant zur See Leo Hillebrand was appointed commander from her commission on 17 December 1915 until 6 December 1916, when Alfred Saalwächter assumed command from 7 December to 15 January 1917. Leo Hillebrand resumed command of *U-46* on 16 January 1918 until 11 November 1918. It was just ten days after he took over command for the second time that the *Andania* was sunk by *U-46*. In total, *U-46* undertook eleven patrols, sank fifty-two ships and damaged one ship, until she surrendered to Japan in November 1918.

The First World War claimed many of Cunard's ships and all three of the purpose-built ships for the Canadian service were sunk. *Alaunia* was the first in October 1916 when she struck a mine and in February 1918 *Aurania* (2) was sunk by a torpedo from *UB-67*.

Andania Wreck

A hydrographic survey by HMS *Bulldog* in 1984 identified a large wreck close to the reported location of *Andania*. The side-scan sonar images showed wreckage that was 155m (509ft) long and 16m (52ft) wide, consistent with a vessel the size of *Andania*. In 1987 local Rathlin Island diver Tommy Cecil confirmed the location of the wreck with sonar, but it wasn't dived until a decade later. Cecil gained international acclaim in 1987 for rescuing Richard Branson and Per Lindstrand when the Virgin Atlantic balloon ditched into the sea off the north coast of Rathlin Island.

The wreck of the *Andania* lies in water 112m (367ft) deep, halfway between Rathlin Island off the north coast of Northern Ireland and Mull of Kintyre on the west coast of Scotland, in the middle of a busy shipping lane. The position in the Western Approaches to the British Isles is subject to extremely strong tidal flows. Thus diving is limited to times of the year when tides are at the weakest and slack water on the ebbing tide is essential. Normally when the slack-water period on a wreck ends, the tide starts to pick up speed gradually, but on the *Andania* it can be very sudden, like 'being hit by a wall of water'. The dive is made even more challenging by being in an area of very poor underwater visibility, with just 1–2m (3–6ft) being typical. As such, the handful of technical divers that have dived the *Andania* consider it to be the toughest wreck dive in the British Isles. For most divers one dive is enough and very few feel the desire to make a return visit.

The *Andania* was first dived by Norman Woods and Oliver McIlroy one evening in September 1997. Diving took place from a Rigid Inflatable Boat (RIB) and Tommy Cecil provided additional boat cover from a second RIB. After completing a bottom time of fifteen minutes the divers faced a lengthy drift decompression, which carried them 6.5 miles. This was made even more challenging since by then night had fallen. The visibility on the wreck was described as 'black'.

It was at breakfast time that the passengers were informed that there would be a boat drill at 10 a.m. However, it was when many of the passengers were making their way to their lifeboat stations that the torpedo struck the ship. Dr J. A. Harker of the American branch of the Ministry of Munitions was one of those on the way to his boat station:

> The vessel immediately took a list to starboard and I proceeded to boat 6, which was the first to get away, with fifteen passengers. We rowed an hour and a half and managed to rescue several persons who were struggling in the water before we were taken aboard a patrol vessel, which took us to an Antrim coast town, where we arrived at 5 o'clock Sunday afternoon.

The *New York Times* on 14 February 1918 reported that 107 survivors of the U-boat attack were landed safely. Some passengers were in the lifeboats for four hours before being picked up by a patrol boat, which then took them to Larne, near Belfast. It was while the passengers were on board the rescue ship that an SOS was picked up from the Anchor Line vessel *Tuscania*. *Tuscania* was torpedoed later the same year by *UB-77* (Captain Wilhelm Meyer) on 5 February 1918, 7 miles north from the Rathlin Island at 55°37'N,

The *Andania* rests on a muddy seabed and lies across the tide in an approximately east–west direction. The wreck stands 13m (43ft) proud, making the shallowest point just under 100m (328ft). It is upright with a slight list to starboard and the bow is badly damaged, probably as a result of the torpedo that sank the vessel. A lot of the superstructure has gone and has most probably been swept over the sides of the wreck. No significant artefact recoveries have been made and the wreck seems surprisingly barren. With the constant threat of the changing tide many divers elect to stay within a close distance to the shot line.

Andania is one of many wrecks in the North Channel and Western Approaches that is visited by a group of British technical divers called Dark Star, led by diver Mark Dixon. In August 2011 Dark Star became the first group to dive the *Empress of Britain*, a 42,348-ton Canadian Pacific liner in a depth of 161m (528ft).

A diver descends down the shot line to the *Andania* into the pitch black darkness below. *(Video: Tim Cashman)*

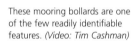

These mooring bollards are one of the few readily identifiable features. *(Video: Tim Cashman)*

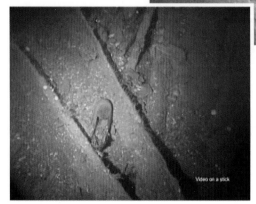

A lone shoe amongst the *Andania* wreckage. *(Video: Tim Cashman)*

Alaunia

1913–1916, England

THE *ALAUNIA* (1) was the second of the three 'A'-class ships to be built by Scott's Shipbuilding & Engineering Co. Ltd, Greenock, and was launched on 9 June 1913. The ship's vital statistics were 13,405 tons, 158.6m (520ft) long and with a beam of 19.5m (64ft). *Alaunia* was very similar in appearance to *Andania* (1) and had two funnels and two masts. Quadruple-expansion engines powered twin screws, giving a service speed of 15 knots. There was accommodation for 500 second-class and 1,500 third-class passengers.

There had been for some years on the older transatlantic steamers a tendency to dispense with the first class and instead have a combined first and second class, which was described as the 'second class'. It was when the *Andania* and *Alaunia* were launched that Cunard announced that 'Cabin Class fares would be charged' for their best accommodation, but these adverts were very quickly changed to 'One Class cabin (second cabin)', possibly due to pressure from passenger groups.

On 27 November 1913 the *Alaunia* made her maiden voyage from Liverpool to Boston, calling at Queenstown and then across the North Atlantic to Portland, Maine.

In August 1914 the *Alaunia* was requisitioned as a troopship and fitted with a 4.7in gun on her stern to help protect the vessel from attacks by German submarines.

Alaunia was at first used to carry Canadian troops to take part in the fighting in France, but by the summer of 1915 she was involved in the Gallipoli campaign, carrying troops for the landings. At the time *Alaunia* was under the command of Captain Arthur Rostron, who had been master of the *Carpathia* in the rescue of *Titanic* passengers. Later the same year it carried troops to Bombay, India. In 1916 *Alaunia* returned to the North Atlantic route carrying troops from Canada and America to the war in Europe. However, *Alaunia* also continued carrying civilian passengers, mail and freight from the USA and Canada to Europe, and it was during one of these voyages that the vessel was sunk.

The final voyage of the *Alaunia* commenced from London to New York, leaving on 19 September 1916. When the *Alaunia* left New York in October 1916 for her return voyage to London she had 180 passengers, 166 crew members and was carrying 8,000 tons of general cargo.

The *Alaunia* safely crossed the North Atlantic and docked at Falmouth on 17 October, where the mail was discharged for conveyance by train to London and other parts of the country. Most of the passengers also left the ship to continue their journey by train to London, which was a much faster way of arriving than staying with the ship for the final leg of the journey to the docks in London.

The ship's master, Captain Horace Mills Benison, was confident that if he kept the *Alaunia* powering at its top speed of 15 knots throughout the voyage he would outrun any German submarine. That had been his practice, which was successful in the ship safely docking at Falmouth from its transatlantic voyage.

However, it was not a submarine that was to sink the vessel, but a mine, and therefore speed turned out not to be the top priority. Maybe a more cautious speed may have given the officers on the bridge time to assess any potential dangers, especially as it was known that the Germans had been laying mines in the English Channel.

The *Alaunia* left Falmouth on 18 October and proceeded up the English Channel at full speed. In the early hours of the morning the captain and first officer were on the bridge and sailing close to Beachy Head when they saw the *Royal Sovereign* light vessel. As the ship came closer to the lightship, the captain was unaware that he was heading directly towards a line of German mines that had been laid and positioned close to the surface. It was 4.30 a.m. when the vessel passed over the mines and at least one exploded under the keel of the *Alaunia*. Captain Benison's first thought was that the ship had been torpedoed and this would have surprised him as he had maintained top speed to avoid such an occurrence.

Immediately Captain Benison sounded the general alarm, which the passengers and crew knew was a signal to make for their allotted boat stations. Still thinking that they had been torpedoed, he instructed the radio operator to send an SOS stating that they had been attacked and torpedoed south of the *Royal Sovereign* light vessel. The SOS alerted the Eastbourne and Newhaven lifeboats, which were immediately launched.

By then the captain had been informed by the chief engineer that the engine room was flooded and this alerted him to order the crew that it was time to get the lifeboats launched and abandon ship.

No sooner was the order to 'abandon ship' given than the first patrol boat of the Dover Patrol arrived at 5 a.m. and also started to take off the few passengers that had remained on board and the crew. The captain ordered that the anchors to be lowered to hold the ship in position, but by this time the *Alaunia* was sinking by the stern.

The SOS had also brought five Royal Navy destroyers to the scene, but due to the need to transfer the few passengers and crew from the *Alaunia* to the rescue boats, one of the lifeboats was already being lowered from the ship when it tipped up and all the occupants fell into the sea. All the occupants were rescued except a steward and trimmer, who were never seen again. These were the only two casualties that resulted from the loss of the *Alaunia*.

On 21 October 1916 the *New York Times* reported the information they had received from the Cunard Line's agents that the *Alaunia* had been sunk and that all passengers had been landed at Falmouth, but two members of the crew had been lost. They were second steward Frederick Morris and coal trimmer White.

The 13,405-ton *Alaunia*, shown here in Royal Albert Dock, was built in 1913 and struck a mine three years later.

Above The launch of the *Alaunia* on the Clyde in 1913.

The *Alaunia*'s expansive promenade deck.

Silver plate dish recovered from inside the wreck of the *Alaunia* in the 1980s. The hallmark dates to 1913, the year the ship entered service.

After the remaining fourteen passengers and crew were rescued they were taken to Dover, but Captain Benison remained behind after boarding the Dover Patrol boat to witness the final moments of the *Alaunia*.

The *Alaunia* was still on the surface, although settling by the stern with a slight list. Another patrol boat arrived in the early hours of the morning. Its commander considered that it would be possible to tow the *Alaunia* to beach her, but commented that he could not understand why the order had been given to abandon ship earlier as she was still on the surface, although with some settling at the stern. Captain Benison was upset by his remarks, but expressed his concern that he considered it too dangerous to try to tow the vessel. However, the patrol boat commander was adamant and ordered a party of sailors to board the *Alaunia* to prepare for the tugs that would tow her in and beach her.

With attempts to raise the anchors proving difficult and the list of the ship increasing, Captain Benison protested that it was much too dangerous to continue as the ship was likely to capsize and sink at any moment. This did not deter the patrol boat commander, who still did not believe it was as risky as the captain had said, but added that had the effort been initiated a few hours earlier he was certain she could have been successfully towed and beached. By this time the boarding party had discovered the gaping hole in the hull and the water pouring in, and they realised that the *Alaunia* could not be towed. They were taken off by the Eastbourne lifeboat. It was at approximately 9 a.m. that tugs arrived to undertake the towing operation to beach the ship, but it was all too late as the *Alaunia* rolled over and sank by the stern at 9.30 a.m.

It was unclear at the time whether or not the ship had been torpedoed. However, crew members on watch had not observed any periscope on the surface of the water near the ship at the time, and experience of torpedo attacks from submarines was such that it was known that the wake of the torpedo was often visible as it approached a ship, but none of these clues had been observed. Furthermore, U-boat commanders were known to be proud of their successes and would be sure to claim the ship as their prize, but this did not occur either.

It was possible that the ship could have hit an underwater obstruction, but the massive explosion that ripped open the hull, flooding the engine room, pointed to some form of attack. Thus by then attention had turned to the possibility that it could have been an explosion from a mine when the ship passed over a minefield. It transpired that *Alaunia* had hit a mine that had been laid by *UC-16* of the Flanders Submarine Flotilla. It was in 1915 that the German Navy recognised the importance of minelaying and the Flanders Submarine Flotilla was formed, operating out of Zeebrugge. *UC-16* was launched on 1 February 1916 and commissioned on 18 June 1916 and its first commander was Captain Egon von Werner.

The UC boats were designed mainly for minelaying, but were also armed with torpedoes. They carried eighteen VC200 mines in vertical racks in the bows of the submarine. In addition its armaments included an 8.8mm deck gun. Most of their minelaying was done at night and for speed they would keep on the surface at 11 knots, but if danger was detected or submarine

It appeared that Frederick Morris was well known in New York when the *New York Times* report stated:

Frederick Morris had been coming to this port for many years on the *Carmania*, *Lusitania*, *Aquitania*, and *Laconia* before he went to the *Alaunia*. The steward had a Belgian sheepdog as a pet on the ship. It was given to him by the crew of the *Queen Elizabeth*. The dog was called Hoodoo Nelly because she had been on five warships that were sunk before she went to the *Queen Elizabeth*. Morris was about 43 years old, and had a wife and family in London. He was well liked by passengers who sailed on the Cunard line and esteemed by shipmates.

It is worth noting from the report above that the 'Queen Elizabeth' referenced was HMS *Queen Elizabeth* and not to be confused with Cunard Line's own *Queen Elizabeth*, which was not built until after the war. HMS *Queen Elizabeth* was named in honour of Queen Elizabeth I and was one of the dreadnought battleships, launched on 16 October 1913 and entered service in January 1913. She was to serve in both world wars and was eventually scrapped in 1948.

nets seen they would submerge, where they could maintain 6.5 knots. Mines were laid regularly down the east coast and into the English Channel. In total *UC-16* had sunk forty-three ships, with the *Alaunia* being the largest passenger ship claimed by the mines she laid. The end came for *UC-16* when she was believed to have been sunk by mines off Zeebrugge in October 1917 with the loss of all her crew.

It was not an easy time for Captain Benison after the *Alaunia* was sunk because the questions asked by the Admiralty regarding his conduct and decision making were not very positive for him. The Admiralty had paid particular attention to and appeared to believe the Dover Patrol ship commander's version that the *Alaunia* could have been saved if the decision to tow and beach her had been given earlier. They set up a full inquiry into the loss of the *Alaunia*, but this was not to take place because all the eyewitnesses had been posted to other war duties and it was not possible to trace them all.

On 9 November the *New York Times* published an interview with Captain Benison the day after he arrived in the port in command of the Cunard liner *Saxonia*:

Captain H. M. Benison, who commanded the Cunarder *Alaunia* when she was sunk by a mine in the English Channel on October 19, arrived here yesterday in charge of the *Saxonia*, bringing the first details of the disaster to this port.

He said the *Alaunia* was about 2 miles south of the Royal Sovereign Lightship, near Beachy Head, about 4.30 in the morning when the mine struck her aft and exploded with terrific force. Capt Benison said it was a German mine which had been laid by a submarine over night, right in the track of ships bound up Channel. He saw a minesweeper explode one three hours after the ship had been struck.

'I ordered the 12 boats to be lowered,' Capt Benison continued, 'and had the crew get into them, because it is difficult to know just how long a ship will be afloat after she is struck. The fifth engineer was in the tunnel at the time. He saw the tail shaft go up with the stern into the air and he came on deck in quick order. In 20 minutes a patrol boat was alongside, and half an hour later we were surrounded by destroyers. When ninety of the crew of 180 on the *Alaunia* had got away in the boats a patrol boat came alongside and took the remainder on board. The steamship kept afloat until 9.30 in the morning and I would have had her towed into shallow water if the tugs had arrived in time. When they eventually came out from Newhaven the decks of the *Alaunia* were awash, and, with the heavy cargo in the bottom of the hold, there was no chance to save her.

Fred Morris the second steward and White the coal passer, were killed through falling overboard while getting into the boats and striking their heads against the side of the ship. The two stewardesses were in the water over half an hour, and had nothing but their night dresses. One of them had left the Cunard service and was living in New York. She was making the round

voyage on the *Alaunia* as a holiday by permission of Captain D. J. Roberts the Marine Superintendent, to see her relatives in London. Mrs Scott, one of the stewardesses is on board the *Saxonia*.

Alaunia Wreck

The *Alaunia* is probably the best diveable Cunard Line wreck in inshore UK waters and has been a popular destination for divers for many years. She is ranked number twenty-two in Kendall McDonald's top 100 UK wrecks and featured among Rod Macdonald's ten entries in 'Dive England's Greatest Wrecks'. The wreck is visited regularly by dive clubs and the many charter dive boats that operate in the area. Like most wrecks on the south coast of England, the *Alaunia* has been stripped of most removable non-ferrous material, but there is still a lot to enjoy, including the abundant marine life.

The wreck of the *Alaunia* lies on her portside at an angle of 45 degrees on a sand and shingle seabed. The maximum depth is typically around 36m (118ft), with the highest point of the wreck standing a good 10m (33ft) proud. *Alaunia* lies roughly east–west, with the bow to the east and within sight of the *Royal Sovereign* light tower. *Alaunia* is the biggest wreck off the Sussex coast and most dive boats depart from Eastbourne. Commercial salvors have taken full advantage of the easy access to the wreck. Both the propellers have been removed and explosives have been used to remove cargo and other valuable materials.

Any visit to the *Alaunia* is always exciting and full of anticipation of what will be revealed upon descending to this big old wreck. The most intact part of the wreck is the bow, which lies on its port side with the starboard anchor looped

One of the rectangular brass bridge windows recovered from the wreck. *(Sussex Shipwrecks)*

over and hanging vertically from one of the hawse pipes. The forecastle area in the bow can be easily and safely penetrated. A large foredeck derrick angles up sharply through the green-tinged waters. Moving aft from the bow, two further anchors can be found lying amongst the wreckage. Many sources report that part of the wheelhouse lies on the seabed to the port side of the wreck. This may have been the case once but little evidence remains of anything distinguishable now. Maybe the removal of the large distinctive rectangular portholes aided the collapse. Despite its popularity with tool-bearing divers, a few stubborn portholes still remain in various parts of the wreck, some of which still contain glass. There are also many sections of flat hull plates with empty holes where portholes have long since been removed or fallen down into inaccessible parts of wreckage.

The tops of the large boilers can be clearly seen protruding in big arches from the top of the wreck. One boiler has broken free and rolled over on its side. A lifeboat davit still reaches out to the surface arching high above the wreck. There are numerous mooring bollards and lots of winch gear. Towards the stern a propeller shaft can be seen, leading towards what remains of the steering gear and a large steering quadrant.

Line, ropes and tangled fishing tackle are a constant threat and require the diver to take special care when moving around the wreck, particularly in low visibility. The *Alaunia* attracts a considerable amount of fish, making the wreck a popular destination for fishing trips. The fish life includes wrasse and shoals of pouting and bib. Diver Jerry Gull caught a large turbot on the wreck that was 'big enough to feed 8 people'. It is not uncommon for both fishing and dive charters to be present on the wreck at the same time. Other marine life includes lobsters, which can sometimes be seen confidentially prowling amongst the confusing mass of wreckage. Conger eels are also seen lurking in holes and crevices. Bright white dead man's fingers brighten up the otherwise dull metal plates.

The *Alaunia* is big and definitely requires at least several dives to get a feel for the whole wreck. It is easy to spend a whole dive on just one section, such as the intact and picturesque bow. The wreck is within sport-diving range but demands respect from the visiting diver. Visibility can often be 5m (16ft) or more in the summer months but it can also be less than 1m (3ft), making the dive much more challenging. There is a deep dark scour in the sand at the bottom of the wreck near the stern on the starboard side, where the depth can reach nearly 40m (131ft). The high-water slack often yields the best visibility. Using a nitrox mix will mean bottom times in excess of half an hour can comfortably be made without the need for decompression.

Opposite, clockwise from top left

The bow and foredeck of the *Alaunia*. (Catherine de Lara)

One of the *Alaunia*'s boilers. (Catherine de Lara)

Forward winch gear on the bow, which is lying on its port side. (Catherine de Lara)

The massive starboard anchor hangs down from the bow. (Catherine de Lara)

The steering quadrant at the aft end of the wreck. (Catherine de Lara)

A lobster confidently foraging on the wreck. (Catherine de Lara)

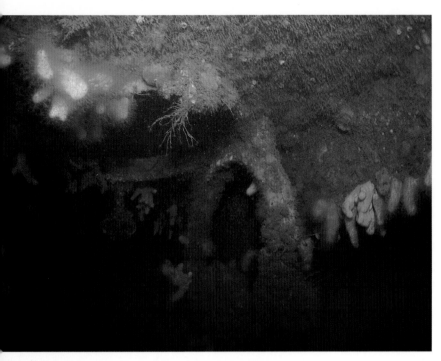

Contrasting conditions and visibility on the *Alaunia*. (Catherine de Lara)

The same porthole on another dive a few years later. (Catherine de Lara)

Aurania

1917–1918, Scotland

THE *AURANIA* (2) was the third of three purpose-built ships ordered by Cunard in December 1913, but due to commencement of the First World War the build was delayed and she was not completed until 1916. The *Aurania* was 13,936 tons and built of steel by Swan, Hunter & Wigham Richardson, Wallsend-on-Tyne. The ship was 158.6m (520ft) long with a beam of 19.5m (64ft) and had two funnels and two masts. Twin-screw propellers were powered by steam turbines with single-reduction engines, giving a service speed of 15 knots. When *Aurania* was launched on 16 July 1916 the accommodation was similar to the other two vessels. However, during the final stages of fitting out the *Aurania* was hired to the government for use as a troopship. The *Aurania* made her maiden voyage from the Tyne to New York on 28 March 1917 in ballast without passengers.

Although the *Aurania* was built as an ocean liner, then fitted out as a troopship, she was still equipped in readiness for passenger service. Below deck, behind an engraved plate marked 'Silver Room', was a securely locked room where all the Cunard Line crested silverware was stored. This included all the silver plate, such as the cutlery and serving dishes, as required for passengers to experience the luxury of ocean liner travel in the early twentieth century.

On each transatlantic voyage from the USA *Aurania* carried 2,000 American 'doughboys' to the battlefields of France. The American 'doughboy' was an informal term used in the First World War for members of the American Expeditionary Force (AEF). The *Aurania* made seven transatlantic crossings before being torpedoed and sunk in February 1918.

In early 1918 the German military commanders had planned for a spring offensive against the Allies. However, they were concerned about the number of American troops that were being transported to the battlefields in France. With America having entered the war in 1917, the number of Allied troops on the battlefront was increasing and there was great concern by the German High Command that their spring offensive would not succeed unless the ships carrying the troops could be sunk before they arrived in Europe. The plan was to use the German U-boats to seek out, attack and destroy the troopships, but this was not an easy task because of the minefields that had been laid in the English Channel, leaving only one safe route to the North Atlantic. That is, until the Northern Barrage had been laid and they then had to find a way of negotiating these minefields.

The *Aurania* left Liverpool on 3 February 1918 en route for New York, unescorted and in ballast. Her course took her around the coast of Northern Ireland, where, on 4 February, about 15 miles north-west of Inistrahull, off the

The *Aurania* (2) was taken up for war service upon completion in 1916, so never sailed in Cunard livery. *(Rich Turnwald Collection)*

coast of Donegal, she was struck by a torpedo from *UB-67* (Commander Gerard Schulz) on her port side. The torpedo hit the engine room area, killing eight firemen in the explosion.

The vessel was left without power and went aground. A line was taken aboard and *Aurania* was refloated, but the trawler that attempted to tow the ship was beaten by a force-9 gale and it was an impossible task. When the tugs arrived they attempted to tow her, but the towline parted and she was driven on the rocks at Caliach Point on the Isle of Mull, by which time everyone had safely left the ship. The gales were very severe and the *Aurania* was broken to pieces, and declared a total loss.

By the time America received the news from Cunard Line officials that the *Aurania* had been torpedoed she had already gone aground. On 8 February 1918 the *New York Times* published a report with the headline 'Aurania torpedoed, but remains afloat':

> The Cunard liner *Aurania*, 13,400 tons, was torpedoed by a German submarine within the last forty-eight hours while bound for the United States, Cunard line officials announced yesterday.
>
> Although badly damaged the ship was not sunk, and is believed to be making her way back to port with the assistance of Government vessels. The ship carried little cargo.
>
> There were thirteen or fourteen passengers aboard the vessel when she was struck.

UB-67 was launched on 16 June 1917, commissioned on the 23 August 1917 and took part in three patrols. The first patrol was with V Flotilla based at Kiel, under the command of Albrecht von Dewitz from 23 August 1917 to 30 November 1917. *UB-67* then became a training unit under the command of Gerhard Shulz from 1 December 1917 to 20 October 1918, and then returned to being in a combat unit under the command of Hellmuth von Doemming from 21 October 1918 to 11 November 1918. On 24 November 1918 *UB-67* surrendered and was eventually broken up at Swansea in 1922.

During her operational service, *UB-67* sank just two ships, the largest being the *Aurania*. The other vessel was HMS *Ascot* (810 tons), a purpose-built paddle minesweeper, built in 1916 by Ailsa Shipbuilding Co. Ltd, Troon. HMS *Ascot*

was torpedoed and sunk off Farne Islands on 10 November 1918 with a loss of fifty-one lives and was the last warship to be sunk in the First World War. The sinking of the *Aurania* took place just before work started on the Northern Barrage, instigated by the US Navy to make it more difficult for the U-boats getting into the North Atlantic to attack transatlantic shipping.

The North Sea Mine Barrage – Northern Barrage

By the time the Americans joined the war in April 1917 they were concerned about the serious loss of transatlantic shipping, and that prompted them to suggest creating a minefield stretching across the North Sea from Scotland to Norway. The aim was to prevent the U-boats from leaving their bases and using the North Sea route to the North Atlantic to wreak havoc on the transatlantic convoys, including the ships carrying American troops to the French battlefields.

The English Channel already had minefields laid to restrict the U-boats from sailing through the Channel to the North Atlantic, and this forced U-boats to use the unprotected North Sea route into the North Atlantic.

The Northern Barrage was essentially one of the largest American naval operations of the First World War. At first the British were not keen on the idea, for reasons of possible restrictions on the movement of the Grand Fleet, but did eventually agree to lay two of the three areas of what was to be a giant minefield stretching from the Orkneys to Norway. Area B was the British responsibility and was in the far west, consisting of 50 miles of deep minefields, started in March 1918. The aim was to have surface patrol vessels that would force the U-boats to submerge towards the mines. Area C was

This sketch was submitted in an August 1918 report to Cunard, assessing the condition of the wreck. The report concluded that there was little hope of saving the ship.

Sharp edges on the rusted wreck can be hazardous to an unwary diver. Occasionally Cunard artefacts can be found by rummaging in the shifting sands amongst the wreckage. *(Ian Derrick)*

The *Aurania* has a colourful coating of dead man's fingers. *(Ian Derrick)*

Although very broken up, the *Aurania* is still a very scenic wreck and attracts plenty of marine life. *(Ian Derrick)*

also a British responsibility and that was to lay mines that were in deep and shallow water near to the Norwegian coast.

The American responsibility was the 130 miles of the middle section of shallow mines. The American minelayers also supported the British with their minelayers in their areas. The whole operation was under the protection of American Battleship Division 9.

American Battleship Division 9 was a group of four, later increasing to five, dreadnought battleships of the United States Navy Atlantic Fleet, and was the American Navy's contribution to the British Grand Fleet during the First World War.

This extended minefield became known as the North Sea Mine Barrage, or Northern Barrage, a large minefield whose aim was to close the North Sea passage to German U-boats. However, it appeared that the Northern Barrage had limited success, with just a few U-boats sunk.

Aurania Wreck

At the end of the First World War the *Aurania* was salvaged extensively by James Gush of Greenock. The wreck then lay largely forgotten at the base of Caliach Point for over half a century before attracting the attention of local salvage divers in the late 1960s. In 1969 the wreck was purchased by Richard Greeves of Aros in Mull and for many years the site was worked for salvage. Recreational divers first started to visit the wreck in the 1970s and it soon became a popular destination for members of the Northampton branch of the British Sub-Aqua Club (BSAC). This was prompted by the discovery of silver cutlery on the wreck in June 1980. The club then initiated a search for the rest of the silver stored in the Cunard silver room described earlier. This involved the excavation of a large hole in the seabed in the general area where the cutlery had been located. This became known as the 'Silver Pit' and it yielded a vast amount of silver plate from the Victorian and Edwardian eras. Items included: tea and coffee pots, jugs, serving platters, toast racks, tea strainers and more cutlery. Some of this was put on show at Northampton BSAC's stand at a London dive show in the 1990s. Much of the collection can still be seen today at the Charlestown Shipwreck Centre in Cornwall.

Inventory of the recoveries from the *Aurania* that were declared to the Receiver of Wreck:

DROIT	DESCRIPTION
A/0401	1 x brass oiler
A/2721	2 x table spoons, 2 x fish forks, 1 x table fork, 1 x fish knife, 1 x serving dish metal small, 1 x side plate metal, 3 x beer bottles, 1 x mineral water bottle
A/2849	1 x porthole
A/1169	1 x hinge, 1 x pipe valve, 1 x spoon, 1 x lamp bracket, 1 x banister bracket
A/0925	1 x brass grill
A/1686	1 x bit plate
A/3109	3 x bottles
A/3122	9 x bits broken pottery, 1 x bit of bottle
A/3277	1 x lid, 1 x light, 2 x portholes, 5 x forks, 5 x spoons
A/1079	1 x brass handrail
A/2570	1 x T joint, 1 x porthole screw
A/1729	3 x serving dishes & lids, 1 x serving dish, ornate, no lid, 1 x toast rack, 2 x milk jugs, 1 x condiment set & holder, 6 x forks, 6 x spoons, 6 x knives
A/3205	1 x brass steam valve, 1 x brass porthole opening light
A/0950	1 x flange, 1 x bottle, 1 x brass item
A/2490	4 x coins, 1 x dish, 1 x plate, 1 x toilet bowl, 6 x bottles, 4 x jars, 1 x prop shaft, 1 x porthole
A/3510	1 x bottle, 1 x brass nut

A diver swims past the massive boilers, the most distinctive feature of the wreck. *(Tom Forwood)*

Close-up of one of the boilers which are covered in dead man's fingers. *(Ian Derrick)*

A silver toast rack recovered from the wreck. *(Eric Sauder)*

Close-up showing the embossed Cunard Line emblem. *(Eric Sauder)*

DROIT	DESCRIPTION
A/3679	1 x door catch, 1 x lamp frame, 1 x post, 1 x thing, 1 x coat hook
A/1391	1 x porthole dog
A/2445	65 x pieces ship's silver (1st & 2nd class), 2 x portholes, 1 x telegraph
A/4425	2 x silver serving dishes, 10 x cutlery, 1 x pair nutcrackers, 1 x sauceboat, 1 x jug, 1 x concretion, 1 x pot, 1 x bottle
A/3058	2 x spoons, 1 x knife, 1 x bottle, 1 x brass valve, 1 x 'A' valve
A/4199	1 x porthole, 1 x cog, 1 x hatch cover
264/01	1 x half a china plate with the 'Cunard Steamship Company' logo
A/4462	1 x bottle champagne & contents, various tableware & cutlery, 1 x concretion, 1 x prop shaft bearing, 1 x part pipe, 1 x porthole, 1 x bearing ring, 1 x nutcrackers, 1 x pottery sherd
133/10	1 x Brass pipe fitting ring/valve seal (?), 54.5mm external diameter, 7mm external height, 43.5mm internal diameter, 3.5mm internal thickness with internal bevelled edge, slight chamfer to one external edge

---

Aurania silver recovered from the 'silver pit' on display at the London Dive Show.

Our combined memory is that it is a smashed up flat pack in a very exposed location off Mull. Shallow-ish covered in weed and kelp, I think the highlight was some broken blue and white crockery and a Spanish Dancer. The boilers are meant to be quite big, but I can't remember them. Gordon thinks he saw one, but can't remember it being very exciting.

A 'Spanish Dancer' is a species of nudibranch, a large colourful sea slug that would not normally be associated with temperate waters of the British Isles. However, the west coast of Scotland is exposed to the warm waters from the Gulf Stream, which encourages a greater diversity of marine life.

The author dived the wreck twice in 1996 and it is the experience on these dives and finding Cunard china that provided the original inspiration for this book, thus demonstrating that one person's broken crockery is another man's treasure. The author is also ashamed to say that in his failed quest to remove a porthole and find more Cunard china he compromised safe diving practices and surfaced with just 10 bar of air remaining (50 bar, or 25 per cent, is the recommended minimum).

Like many wrecks close to shore, the depths on the *Aurania* are relatively shallow and range from 15–20m (49–66ft). The wreck is 100m (328ft) from the steep vertical cliffs of Caliach Point on the north-western tip of Mull. The proximity to cliffs, combined with exposure to strong winds and tides from the west can cause dangerous swells and backwash if the weather conditions are not right. Consequently, the ability to dive on this site is very much at the mercy of the elements.

The wreck itself lies north-west and parallel to the cliffs with the bow to the north. Divers in the 1980s reported that the bow was largely intact and standing 7m (23ft) proud, but contemporary reports indicate that this has subsequently collapsed. The main body of wreck that is distinguishable is around the middle section, where two enormous boilers form an imposing presence standing 7m (23ft) above the seabed. It is also around this area of the wreck that the silver was located and the occasional item can still be found to this day. The majority of the remaining wreckage is spread out over a wide, flat area devoid of many distinguishing features. There are some large winches, quite a few mooring bollards and a lot of flat steel plates. The wreck definitely requires more than one dive to see all that it has to offer.

As with most wrecks and dive sites off the west coast of Scotland, marine life is abundant and octopuses have even been seen on the wreck. The fire tubes in the boilers make a good home for numerous species of small fish and the wreck has a liberal covering of dead man's fingers. Visibility is also good in this area and often in excess of 5m (16ft), with up to 10m (33ft) being common.

The *Aurania* seems to be a wreck that divers either love or hate. Divers Gordon and Moira Simpson recalled:

Recent finds from a dive in August 2011 show that the 'silver pit' still has a few remaining items. Parts of the Cunard Line crest are on the shards of blue and white china. *(Dr Geoff Vernon)*

Lancastria

1922–1940, France

The *Lancastria* was launched in 1920 and requisitioned as a troop transport in 1940. The ship was bombed by German aircraft and over 3,000 lives were lost. *(Bert Moody Collection)*

THE *LANCASTRIA* was built by William Beardmore & Co. Ltd, formerly Robert Napier & Sons, and launched on 31 May 1920 as *Tyrrhenia*. The ship was 16,243 tons, 166.6m (553ft) long and had a beam of 21.3m (70ft). There was a single funnel and two masts. Steam turbines powered twin screws at a service speed of 15 knots. The passenger capacity was for 280 first class, 364 second class, and 1,200 third class.

The *Tyrrhenia*'s maiden voyage commenced on 13 June 1922 from Glasgow to Montréal, calling at Québec, with her subsequent voyages leaving from Liverpool. From 1923 her voyages were from Hamburg–Southampton–Québec–Montréal. Many people found difficulty in pronouncing *Tyrrhenia* and she gained the nickname of 'Soup Tureen'. In 1924 she was given a refit and renamed *Lancastria*. The refit included a change in passenger accommodation to cabin and third class, with 580 cabin-class and 1,000 third-class passengers. Her first voyage left Liverpool on 24 March 1924 for New York, calling at Queenstown. From 1926 to 1932 *Lancastria* sailed from London–Le Havre–Southampton–New York and then became a cruising liner.

The evacuation of the British Expeditionary Force (BEF) from the Dunkirk beaches was very successful and this was what Prime Minister Winston Churchill told the British people. However, he was not entirely truthful because even two weeks after the rescue of troops from the Dunkirk beaches many thousands of British troops and even civilians were still in France, and in danger of being captured. Over a period of two weeks the troops, including RAF ground crew, Royal Marines and some Royal Navy sailors, had travelled for days and suffered lack of rest and food before they arrived at St Nazaire at the mouth of the Loire. Here they hoped that a similar rescue to that of Dunkirk may be possible.

When the troops arrived at St Nazaire many boarded the Cunard liner *Lancastria*, only to be attacked by German Stuka dive bombers flying over the Loire Estuary on 17 June 1940. After the bomber attack, *Lancastria* sank in twenty minutes, and it has been estimated that at least 5,000 troops, including civilians, were on board and more than half lost their lives, some because they couldn't swim.

Coming so soon after the Dunkirk evacuation, Churchill was reluctant to tell the British public of the *Lancastria* disaster because he believed that if they were faced with the news of the sinking it would cause further damage to the country's morale, especially with a threatened invasion of Great Britain by the Germans. The prime minister placed a ban on publication, which he later forgot to lift. However, the story was to surface in a New York newspaper, which alerted the British press and they then took up the story.

There is a memorial to the disaster and an annual commemoration service held in St Nazaire that some of the remaining survivors and their relatives attend. Up until recently the only memorial in the UK to the worst British wartime maritime disaster was the Merchant Navy Memorial at Tower Hill, which contains the names of the crew of the *Lancastria*. On 1 October 2011 a new memorial was unveiled on the site where the ship was built on the Clyde. Each year on 17 June a flotilla of boats goes out to the site of the wreck, which is marked by a buoy, and at the same time as the attack on the *Lancastria* in June 1940 a commemoration service is held.

Captain Rudolf Sharp was master of the *Lancastria* when German bombers sank her. Coming from a maritime family living in the Shetlands, both his grandfather and uncle had served with the Cunard Line, and so he was drawn to a maritime career. He was distinctive by his stature, being stoutly built, 5ft 11in tall, but looked older than his age.

Captain Sharp's merchant navy service included time on the *Mauretania* (1), *Olympic*, *Franconia* (2) and *Queen Mary*. He took command of the Cunard liner *Lancastria* in March 1940 and after returning from a cruise in the Bahamas the *Lancastria* was requisitioned as a troopship and sent to New York to be refitted. On return to England the *Lancastria* was employed to transport troops to Norway, but this was not a successful venture and not long after landing the men she was sent back to pick them up and return them.

Captain Sharp's chief officer was Harry Grattidge, who was later to become Sir Harry Grattidge, captain of the *Queen Elizabeth* and commodore of the Cunard fleet. Captain Grattidge gave his own account of joining the *Lancastria* and what happened at the time of her sinking in his autobiography, *Captain of the Queens* (1956). Grattidge joined the *Lancastria* at the time of the evacuation of Norway. He explained that it just seemed like a matter of a few weeks after landing the Canadian troops that they received the order to evacuate them. Captain Grattidge:

There was something like twenty liners converted into troopships manoeuvring in the cold waters of Namsos; the destroyers did the tough job of running into the mainland and bringing off the soldiers and we on the troopships carried them back – Poles, Canadians, Frenchmen, British troops of the Green Howard Regiment, many nationalities but all of them dirty and depressed, most of them without rifles. It was a relief when the whole sad campaign had ended and the *Lancastria* went into Liverpool for overhauling and dry-docking.

Although the *Lancastria* was berthed in Liverpool for a refit, Captain Sharp was instructed to prepare to leave that evening. Chief Officer Grattidge remembers the date was 14 June 1940 when he had already given leave to as many of the crew as possible. However, he had met the Cunard's marine superintendent in the Cunard offices, who told him of the urgency to recall the crew as they were required for a special mission, and that they would be sailing at midnight. Grattidge went back to the ship and ordered the chief engineer to get up steam. Telegrams were sent to the crew and all but three crewmen managed to get back to the ship before she left Liverpool for Plymouth. She arrived there on the Saturday and they anchored in Plymouth, along with the *Franconia*, which had also sailed at the same time.

Lancastria was ordered to sail that night at approximately 11 p.m., first for Brest, but when they arrived the area was clouded over with smoke from burning oil tanks. A German aircraft flew over and dropped a bomb that effectively put the *Franconia* out of action, and she had to return to Liverpool, arriving in poor condition, but the *Lancastria* made for St Nazaire, anchoring 5 miles from shore.

Captain Sharp had been ordered by Admiralty representatives to take on as many passengers as possible, which was in effect against international maritime law, but they began taking on board troops from the BEF that were being ferried out to the ship by destroyers and smaller vessels, and by midday the decks were packed with troops. A first check by Chief Officer Grattidge of numbers revealed that there were already 5,000 on board, 2,000 over the vessel's normal capacity. As well as the troops, civilians with children began to arrive. German aircraft could already be seen in the sky and then the attacks began on the ships in the Loire Estuary.

Harry Harding

Harry Harding had just turned twenty and was one of the survivors of the *Lancastria* disaster. He talks about his memory of what was Britain's worst wartime maritime disaster:

Although I had previously specialised in all aspects of ammunition examination and storage, I had joined the army in a spirit of enthusiasm, patriotism and every other 'ism' at the time of the Munich crises in September 1938.

A week after the declaration of war, the 10th September 1939, I embarked in Southampton for Cherbourg and after a sort of going from 'here to there' like the proverbial headless chicken we found ourselves in Nantes with our office and storage facilities in the Salle des Fetes. I was in what was then the Royal Army Ordnance Corps (RAOC) now the Logistics Corps. Nantes was Mechanical Transport Sub Depot. There we stayed until the 'phoney war' took on an entirely different dimension, until on the morning of the 16th June 1940 when we were told we were pulling out. It was all very organized, but of course, leaving all our stores behind.

We arrived in St. Nazaire, staying the night near to the dockside. During the night, the oil installation tanks were bombed. On the morning of the 17th June 1940, and quite early we were fortunately taken out to the *Lancastria* and I boarded, along with many others at about 9 am. Being among the first to arrive we were handed a Board of Trade lifejacket. By modern day standards lifejackets were then somewhat primitive, consisting of four cork squares front and back joined together by something like Hessian. Primitive it may have been, but it most certainly helped in my survival. The Cunarder was a cruise liner with a passenger complement of something like 3,000, so they soon ran out of lifejackets. We had breakfast, which I believe was actually served, and later, lunch/dinner.

It was a very hot day and I remember hearing over the tannoy that the canteen would be selling bottles of Bass [beer]. I joined the long queue snaking up and down the gangways and saw those at the head of the queue bringing back these small bottles and thought to myself: God is it worth it,

Harry Harding, one of the *Lancastria* survivors. *(Derek and Adrian Harding)*

The final moments of *Lancastria*. *(Lancastria Association of Scotland)*

suffering here in the heat. I think I'll go up on deck. And that is a decision I have never regretted all my life.

I was on the open 'B' deck and witnessed it all. I saw these two, slowly rotating propellers and saw three bombs descend and said to myself: 'Christ almighty. We are being bombed.'

I could see they were going to strike the ship somewhere, and I buried my head in my lifejacket. There was debris all over the place. And, despite the explosions, everything seemed to be very quiet. I still have the watch I was wearing, and it still shows the time I decided to jump overboard, 4.05pm.

In the portholes I could see bodies wedged, dead or alive I don't know, and behind the bodies, hands, whether pushing the bodies out or pulling them out of the way to make escape possible! Behind that, the flames and I said to myself: 'If there is a hell, it is there.'

Whatever our circumstances we all had one thing in mind: 'Get me out of here, survival' and I clambered over the rail (or did I vault?) and jumped into the waters below. All that I remember was that the water was quite warm, but I felt quite cold when I was rescued. While in the water I saw the *Lancastria* upturned, and there must have been thousands clinging to it in the last minutes of their lives. I also remember, as far away as I was, there were thousands of voices singing, 'Roll out the Barrel' and 'There'll always be an England'. For years afterwards I could not stand the sounds of those songs.

I was rescued by a little French fishing vessel and returned to St. Nazaire after being in the water for about 1½ hours where I had been swimming around and grabbing hold of 'this and that' to keep my head above water.

After being picked up and getting myself 'sorted out' I helped in pulling on board other survivors (or bodies) that happened to be nearby with long handled boathooks. We were taken back to St. Nazaire, boarded the *Ulster Prince* and set sail for the UK in the early hours of the 18 June, the very day when the French capitulated and finally docked in Falmouth in the late afternoon. I remember thinking at the time there was an awful lot of life waiting for me out there. I had just turned 20.

This certainly came true as Harry Harding reached the age of ninety on 21 September 2010.

Captain Sharp and Chief Officer Grattidge were on the bridge when the German aircraft started their assault. At first the aircraft were unsuccessful with their attacks on the *Oronsay*, which survived, but the deadly attack on the *Lancastria* came at approximately 3.45 p.m. Damage to the *Lancastria* after the four bombs had hit was extremely serious as some of the troops were already in the ship's holds. The engine room was put out of action and the order was given to abandon ship. Already the ship was listing to the port side. Many people were lined up on deck thinking that they would have to swim for it, but the German aircraft continued to fly over, machine-gunning those on deck, and at that point many started to dive into the sea.

Grattidge was in the water for some considerable time, but eventually was rescued with others by a rowing boat and taken to a tug that transported them to the *Oronsay*, where the first officer reported to Captain Nicholls, her master, on the serious nature of the injuries to the casualties. After giving his report he returned with the tug to one of the small destroyers, which continued for the rest of that day bringing casualties to the *Oronsay*. Miraculously, many of the casualties, despite their serious burns, survived. *Oronsay* sailed for Plymouth at approximately 8 p.m. and arrived late on the Tuesday night. Harry Grattidge was very pleased to meet up with the chief engineer in Plymouth, having thought he had been lost, and then travelled by train to London where a few days later he met Captain Sharp, who had also survived the sinking to prepare a report of the loss. Captain Sharp recorded 'Latitude 47.09. Longitude 2.20' and asked: 'What time did you enter the water?' The first officer replied: 'Eight minutes past four, I know that. The water stopped my watch.'

Sadly Captain Sharp died two years later when in command of the Cunarder *Laconia* (2) (19,860 tons). In a career with Cunard that spanned almost thirty years, Sharp had been an officer on many famous Atlantic liners, including the *Campania*, *Lusitania*, *Mauretania* (1), *Olympic* and the *Queen Mary*. Captain Sharp had never had any accident with the vessels he commanded, but after the *Lancastria* and the *Laconia* (2), it was all too much for him and he could not face the future after the second disaster at sea. Once he had seen everyone into the boats he then locked himself in his cabin and was not found before she sank.

Harry Harding concluded in 2011:

The tragedy has never officially been recognised by Westminster but not so in Holyrood in Edinburgh where the Scottish Parliament, with the approval of HM, struck a survivors' medal, which I received at the hands of their First Minister, Alex Salmond two years ago.

My story was recorded for the BBC. I say my story, but those who survived seem each to have a different story, all more or less true. It was all dependent upon one's circumstances and location at the time of the attack.

I don't think that I can add to what has already been written and broadcast by survivors and witnesses to what was at that time described by the Prime Minister, Mr. Winston Churchill, as being the greatest maritime disaster ever (at least 4,000 perished).

Harry Harding sadly passed away on 21 June 2011 while this book was being written.

Lancastria Wreck

The sinking of the *Lancastria* resulted in the loss of over 4,000 people, the greatest loss of life at sea in a single maritime incident during the Second World War. Understandably, the subject of diving on the wreck is a sensitive one, especially to families who lost loved ones in the tragedy. However, the wreck itself did not have any legal protection until as recently as 2006, when the French authorities declared a 200m (656ft) exclusion zone around it. As of 2011, the *Lancastria* has still not been designated as an official war grave by the British under the Protection of Military Remains Act, despite ongoing campaigns to do so. This is because the Ministry of Defence does not have any jurisdiction over the French territorial waters in which the *Lancastria* lies.

The exact location of the wreck of the *Lancastria* is 9½ miles south-west of St Nazaire. Coincidentally, St Nazaire is where the Cunard liner *Queen Mary 2* was built between 2002 and 2003. When *QM2* was conducting her sea trials off the French coast the officers on the bridge clearly observed the position of the *Lancastria* on their electronic navigation charts. The wreck site is marked permanently with a bright red buoy bearing the name 'LANCASTRIA' in white letters.

The wreck lies on the port side in water of a depth of 26m (85ft) and rises to 12m (39ft) below the surface. It is in an area that is subject to strong tides and currents.

The quotations below have been translated from the experiences of a French ex-navy diver who dived the *Lancastria* several times in the early 1970s. His first dive was made at the request of a local fisherman who had ensnared his fishing tackle on the wreck.

The wreckage could be seen from the bow to the stern, no penetrations were made as an exploration of this kind is too dangerous without special equipment, given the dilapidated state of the hull. The visibility never

The bell, bearing the *Lancastria's* previous name of *Tyrrhenia*, was returned anonymously with a note. *(Mark Hirst)*

exceeded 4 to 5 metres with a lot of suspended particles. At that time, with calm water at the surface, a rainbow was visible indicating that the drops of oil still went up the hull. The diver commented that the highest point of the wreck was the bridge and that the hull appeared twisted towards the bow. The anchor chains were noted running down into the hawser pipes. He also reported seeing many rows of portholes and large windows lining the hull.

Describing the marine life, the diver went on to say:

This ship is an ideal place for all kinds of fish and shellfish. During the various dives I saw the huge congers, who were not impressed by our presence, many binders, bars, sea bream and swarms of pouting. A large-sized lobster was in the entrance of a well chained to the bow.

Unsurprisingly the diver also observed a lot of fishing line on the wreck.

The ship's bell turned up in unusual circumstances during a Lancastria Association pilgrimage to France in 2005. Two members of the trip were in a military graveyard near St Nazaire making preparations for a wreath-laying ceremony when they saw a man running away from the main gates. He had left behind a heavily encrusted ship's bell bearing the name *Tyrrhenia*, the original name of the *Lancastria*. Sticking out of the top of the bell was a short note in French, that translated to: 'More than 30 years illegal, since I took the bell from the *Lancastria* beneath the sea. The original named the *Tyrrhenia*. I wish to remain anonymous.' Allegedly the man had kept the bell in his possession for thirty years.

Upon returning to England, the Lancastria Association intended to have the bell put on permanent display in Katharine Cree church, London, where the annual June memorial service is held. However, they were soon contacted by the Receiver of Wreck and there was some concern over what would happen to the bell since technically it was still the property of Cunard Line. Fortunately Cunard did not lay any claim to it and it now remains in the church.

Members of the various *Lancastria* associations continue to make regular pilgrimages to the wreck on the anniversary of the vessel's sinking, when they lay wreaths of red poppies in the sea.

The permanent marker buoy over the *Lancastria* wreck site. *(Mark Hirst)*

 # *Carinthia*

1925–1940, Ireland

WHEN SHE WAS laid down as yard build number 586, Cunard had originally planned for the ship to be named *Servia*, but when launched on 24 February 1925 the name was changed to *Carinthia* (2). The vessel was built by Vickers Ltd, Barrow-in-Furness, and was 20,277 tons with a length of 183m (600ft) and beam of 22.4m (74ft). The ship was made of steel and had a single funnel and two masts. Steam turbine engines powered twin screws at 16 knots. *Carinthia* had passenger accommodation for 240 first-class, 460 second-class and 950 third-class passengers, complemented by a crew of 450. When she was launched the *Carinthia* was the largest of the five intermediate liners to be built after the First World War.

First-class accommodation was luxurious and included a smoking room, lounge and restaurant all decorated to represent various themes. The accommodation for third-class passengers was much improved and more comfortable than previously seen, and included smoking room, library and a shop, which was quite an innovation at the time. There were also good facilities for sports, including a swimming pool, gymnasium, tennis courts, and shower and bath facilities, including masseur and massage treatments.

The maiden voyage of the *Carinthia* left Liverpool for New York on 22 August 1925. The *Carinthia* had been being built specifically for cruising in the winter season, sailing from New York. The service included a world cruise in 1926–27 and the occasional cruise from Southampton to the Norwegian fjords.

An interesting story was recounted to members of the entertainment staff on the *Queen Victoria* in 2009, when Mr and Mrs McAllister shared photographs and mementos of Mr McAllister's parents.

Mr McAllister's father, Hugh, was born in 1900 and, like many young people in the First World War, ran away to sea to serve his country, but when his true age was found out he was quickly sent home. Hugh McAllister's determination to go to sea paid off when he applied to Cunard to be a radio officer in 1920. As with many other young mariners, he had no experience or training before going on board and he soon learned 'on the job'.

This was the same year as Hilda James, a member of the British relay team, won the silver medal at the 1920 Olympics. Hilda had been a member of the Garston swimming club and her success in the Olympics was recognised by the Cunard swimming club, which was based in the basement of Liverpool's Adelphi Hotel. Although still an amateur, she was invited to become a life member and became a figurehead of the Cunard swimming club.

Hilda James, her coach and his wife were given free passage on the *Berengaria* to undertake a swimming tour of the USA in 1922. It was while on board the

The *Carinthia* made several world cruises. In 1939 she was hired by the Admiralty for service as an armed merchant cruiser.

This was in recognition of Hugh McAllister being the first radio officer to maintain contact with base from all positions while on the world cruise.

Alterations were made to the passenger accommodation in 1931, changing from first class, second class and third class to cabin class, tourist class and third class.

In 1934 the *Carinthia* transferred to the London–Le Havre–Southampton–New York route, and from 1935 to 1939 she transferred to the Liverpool to New York service, combining that with cruising.

The day war was declared in 1939 *Carinthia* had left New York for Liverpool, but on her arrival she was requisitioned by the Admiralty, fitted out as an AMC and renamed HMS *Carinthia*. After her conversion to an AMC she joined the Northern Patrol from January 1940. She was later to take part in convoy work and it was while on convoy that she met her fate.

Berengaria that Hilda first met and danced with the ship's radio officer, Hugh McAllister. After that they communicated regularly by letter while Hilda went on to become a world record holder, holding ten world records.

Hilda James was very keen to be part of the British Olympic team for the 1924 Olympics in Paris, but the British Olympic Association refused to pay for her mother to accompany her as her chaperon, despite being twenty years of age. Hilda was bitterly disappointed, but not having the opportunity to be a member of the 1924 British Olympics team prompted her to decide to join Cunard on a permanent basis. This came about after she was an invited guest aboard the new *Franconia* for an Irish Sea shakedown cruise prior to the vessel's entry into service in 1923. Cunard had been trying very hard to persuade Hilda to join the company as a celebrity crew member, and finally offered her the world cruise on the new cruise liner *Carinthia* in 1925. Hilda did not tell her parents until the night before the *Carinthia* sailed out of Liverpool.

When the *Carinthia* sailed on her 1926–27 world cruise Hugh McAllister and Hilda James, who had been writing to each other since 1922, became engaged and later married in 1930. It was Hilda James' decision when she became engaged to return to England as it was not the right thing for a wife of a merchant seaman to be on the same ship as her husband.

When he was radio officer on the 1926–27 world cruise, Hugh McAllister was presented with an engraved gold pen which is one of Mr and Mrs McAllister's treasured mementos. It carries the inscription:

W.H. McAllister S.S.Carinthia. Commemorating consistent direct radio communication with New York during world cruise 1926–27. R.C.A.

Hilda James, an Olympic swimmer, married *Carinthia* radio officer Hugh McAllister. *(Courtesy of Ian McAllister, Hilda James Archive)*

The bow of the *Carinthia*, 117m (384ft) down. The bright glow coming from within the forecastle is from a diver's torch. *(Barry McGill)*

HMS *Carinthia*, under the command of Captain Barrett RN, was sailing in convoy from Gibraltar to England when, at 1.13 p.m. on 6 June 1940, she was hit by a torpedo fired by *U-46* (Commander Englebert Endrass) west of Galway. Despite the gunners on board firing at the submarine, after further unsuccessful attempts by *U-46* to sink the ship the U-boat left the area because the ship was burning and settling by the stern and sinking. The crew began to abandon ship, but she did not sink straight away and was taken in tow by one of the four Royal Navy ships dispatched to assist her. It was the next day that she sank approximately 30 miles off Bloody Foreland with the loss of four lives.

Carinthia Wreck

The wreck of the *Carinthia* is one of the most recent Cunard shipwrecks to be discovered and dived. The reason for this is primarily due to its remote location off the north-west coast of Ireland in depths in excess of 100m (328ft). The Outer Approaches to the North Channel were a rich hunting ground for enemy U-boats in both world wars and the seabed is densely populated with wrecks of lost Allied tonnage. With advances in technical diving many of the deeper wrecks are now being dived for the first time. Not far from the *Carinthia* is the wreck of the Canadian Pacific liner *Empress of Britain*, which lies in even deeper water of 160m (525ft).

The *Carinthia* is believed to have first been dived in 2007 by a group of Irish technical divers using the dive charter boat *Rosguill*, skippered by Michael McVeigh and based out of Downings, County Donegal. The wreck was positively identified by the recovery of the ship's bell. The voyage out past Bloody Foreland to the wreck requires travelling a distance of over 50 miles, so the weather has to be monitored carefully. Once on site over the wreck land is no longer visible.

Technical diver and instructor Barry McGill described his dive on the wreck in August 2008:

Descending the shotline through the slightly murkier surface waters, we broke through the thermocline at 48m (157ft) to see the massive intact wreck. This incredible sight was amplified in the 50m-plus (164ft) visibility, with natural light penetrating from the surface to the wreck, which lay in 117m (384ft). The *Carinthia* is collapsing to starboard, with the decks mostly level. Touching down after a long descent on the port side of the ship and seeing the massive hull stretching out in both directions with its countless rows of portholes was extraordinary.

I moved along the port gunwale rail towards the bow. The seabed along the starboard gunwale rail was littered with items from the great ship. I could see the bridge telegraphs and compass housing spread across the seabed. The bow lies on its starboard side, revealing the massive port anchor securely in place. The bow section was the highlight of the dive, because it offered a real appreciation of the huge size of this magnificent ship. But my bottom time was running out, and I had to drag myself back towards the shotline. On the way, the forward mast appeared, sprawled over the seabed and mostly intact.

Fantastic reports kept coming back from divers astonished by the landscape of the wreck. Artefacts litter the decks and the seabed on the starboard side, including brass telephones and ship's logs. Memories of this great dive will stay with everyone for years to come.

Diver Stewart Andrews described the aft end of the wreck:

Most of the mid-ships upper decks are gone leaving a clean 'deck' area across the ship, at and aft of what was the bridge area. Further aft as the ship lowers to the stern area a huge dark void can be seen, when facing forward, as a 'window' inside the hull – even the strongest diver's torch can not make out any decks inside this void, so most of them must have collapsed internally – an eerie uninviting darkness in 114 metres (374ft) of sea water. The port side of her stern stands up well, to about 8 or 9 metres (26 to 30ft) whereas the starboard side is level with the seabed.

One distinctive feature of the wreck is the forward mast in front of the bridge, which sticks out horizontally above the seabed on the starboard side. One of the ship's bells was seen here, hanging in silhouette in its original position above the crow's nest. Patches of grey paint have been observed on some parts of the hull, surprising for a wreck that has been under the sea for over seventy years.

Several excellent recoveries have been made, including the *Carinthia*'s helm and two bells. One diver even managed to find and raise a bell, telegraph and compass all on the same dive!

Left, from top

A telegraph, compass and bell, all recovered in the same dive. *(Michael McVeigh, skipper, Rosguill)*

The fully restored mast bell from the *Carinthia*.

Caronia

1949–1974, Guam

THE *CARONIA* (2) was built by John Brown & Co. Ltd, Glasgow, in 1947. The ship was 34,183 tons, 206.8m (678ft) in length and had a beam of 27.9m (91ft). There was a single large funnel and a prominent mast behind the bridge. *Caronia* had steam turbine engines that powered twin screws at a service speed of 22 knots. There was passenger accommodation for 581 first class and 351 cabin class.

Caronia was launched on 30 October 1947 by HRH Princess Elizabeth on her last public engagement before her marriage to Prince Philip. Following her launch and naming ceremony, *Caronia* spent just over a year being fitted out in a dry dock in Liverpool, but then undertook her trials on the Clyde. The *Caronia* was one of the largest ships built after the Second World War and was significant by her livery, her yacht-like proportions, so distinctive for her role in cruising, and of course her huge funnel, which was later to be a problem in an accident she had in Japan. On 4 January 1949 *Caronia* made her maiden voyage under the command of Captain Donald Sorrell from Southampton to New York, calling at Cherbourg.

After her maiden voyage *Caronia* began her cruises, first to the Caribbean then being extended to longer voyages until she started her world cruises. As the *Caronia* was specifically built for cruising, with her stunning art deco interiors and high crew-to-passenger ratio she became very popular, especially with the wealthy Americans for her 'all first-class' world cruises, which were the ultimate in luxury, especially being the first Cunarder to have private bathroom facilities in all passenger cabins. Apart from her nickname 'Green Goddess' she also acquired further nicknames, including 'the millionaire's yacht', which for the crew was quite noticeable and interesting. *Caronia* was also referred to with fondness by passengers as their 'large private yacht'. This could be borne out by the comments of one American passenger, who told a member of the crew that she went on the world cruise every year, had the same cabin and never left the ship for the whole of the cruise. It was her own 'floating hotel'.

The American millionaires were a different story. One of the stewards told ship's carpenter Gus Shanahan that each year they would have the same group of American millionaires who would start the world tour, but after a month they would get fed up with each other's company and would leave the *Caronia* and fly back to the States.

By cruising from America *Caronia* was also a great dollar earner, both for the company and especially because she brought in the much-needed currency for Britain's economy. In 1951 *Caronia* made her first world cruise,

starting in New York on 6 January and terminating in Southampton on 19 April. She also undertook a European cruise from New York in the summer of 1951. While undergoing her annual overhaul at Liverpool in December 1952 she suffered a fire on board, but this was not serious and was easily dealt with. Of the long line of over twenty masters, each would take the *Caronia* on a world cruise before handing over to the next master. However, Captain 'Bil' Warwick was the only master ever to do two consecutive world cruises and would refer to the *Caronia* as 'My Yacht'.

The cruise schedules were much the same year on year, starting in January when she undertook a three-month cruise, which was often the world cruise, and from May she would then sail to the Mediterranean and Black Sea. Following on in June there would be a six-week Scandinavian cruise around the Norwegian fjords, the Baltic and the northern capitals, culminating at Southampton. After further Mediterranean cruises from New York, *Caronia* would return to Southampton in December for her annual overhaul, before starting a similar itinerary again in January.

Caronia was the first of the Cunard fleet to have a swimming pool on deck, which fitted in well with the cruising season in the tropical heat. Despite the fact that Cunard had her built for cruising, they still intended to use her on the North Atlantic transatlantic service for the summer, which was far busier with more passengers on board. The transatlantic passengers benefited greatly from the luxurious interior of the *Caronia* because when on a transatlantic crossing, despite the fact that it was a two-class sailing, every cabin in both classes had the same full facilities. Following on from the summer schedule *Caronia* then entered her cruising service, when she visited the West Indies and South America. It was in June 1953 that *Caronia* was used to bring American passengers over for the queen's coronation.

In 1956 *Caronia* had air conditioning fitted and cruises after this went from New York to Cape Town, South Africa, on to Japan and then crossed the Pacific Ocean back to America. Quite apart from the wealthy passengers travelling the world, crew members had a wonderful opportunity to see the world without having to pay for it.

Barbara Pedan had joined Cunard as an assistant lady purser in 1953 to work on the *Queen Mary*, but later gained cruising experience on the *Britannic*, which along with sister *Georgic* were the only vessels of the original White Star fleet left working as part of the Cunard fleet that joined Cunard-White Star in 1934. They were still allowed to fly the White Star colours.

Barbara Pedan talks about her experience on one of the world cruises, and as she recalls, the 1958 world cruise was a memorable one:

> The *Britannic* cruises were only a curtain-raiser for when I joined the *Caronia* for the 1958 cruise. *Caronia* was a beautiful ship painted a pale green, sometimes known as the 'Green Goddess'. She had her regular following of very wealthy Americans who sailed in her every year. *Caronia* did one World Cruise a year lasting from January to July.

Passengers were nearly all American with a sprinkling of South Americans. We sailed from New York visiting various places en route to South America. Rio is a wonderful place and one of the most impressive towns to approach from the sea. I had the added thrill of being on the Bridge as we went in. Before each port a local pilot joins the ship to guide it in. It appeared that the Rio pilot did not speak any English, only Portuguese, so the Captain thought it would be a good idea if I went on the Bridge in order to help out if there were any difficulties. He knew I spoke Spanish and was under the impression that Portuguese was more or less the same which, in fact, it is not at all. Fortunately, there were no difficulties and I enjoyed the most wonderful view of the city and the statue of Christ on Corcovada or the Sugar Loaf Mountain.

From Rio we went into the South Atlantic crossing to South Africa, calling at Tristan da Cunha where the islanders came out in their long boats and were treated to a slap up meal. From Tristan da Cunha we went on to Cape Town and had a week there. We went to the Cape of Good Hope and to some of the wonderful beaches. The sea is icy cold but the sun very hot. From Cape Town we sailed on to Durban, and there we hired a car and went to visit a

game reserve for a couple of days. We saw the rare white hippopotami and lots of other interesting animals.

From there we went on to the Island of Zanzibar. I shall always remember the smell of spices such as Cloves and Cinnamon miles before you actually came into port. From Zanzibar we went across to Ceylon, now Sri Lanka. We just had time there to visit Kandy and see the Temple of the Tooth where one of Buddha's teeth is enshrined. The drive there was fascinating with jungle on both sides and lots of elephants working logs. From Ceylon on to Bombay, now Mumbai, and we visited Poona which used to be the H.Q. of the British army but which is now completely Indian.

From India we went on to Singapore, then the Island of Bali, my favourite place. It was then a completely unspoiled tropical island, lush vegetation, beautiful temples, rivers where the very beautiful women were doing their washing, fantastic white beaches bordered by palms. From Bali it was on to Hong Kong, then Manila in the Philippines. Then on to Japan, which everyone looked forward to as one of the highlights of the cruise. We first called at Nagasaki in the South Island. The last port of call in Japan was

Yokohama, from where we were able to visit Tokyo. This is a big modern city, big department stores which were most interesting.

On 14 April 1958 *Caronia* was leaving Yokohama when she collided with one of the lighthouses just as they were leaving the port. Barbara Pedan remembers this incident well:

> We left Japan with the bands playing and started to prepare for the next port but we were still within sight of land when there was a big crash and we had hit one of the small lighthouses which were on the outer edges of the harbour.

Gordon Brown was also a crew member on board and was off duty at the time:

> I was in my bunk on my afternoon break when there was an almighty crack! There were high winds and the ship had six tugs to escort her to the breakwater, but the Japanese pilot had released some of the tugs just after they had left the quayside. At that time the *Caronia* had one of the largest funnels which would almost act as a large sail if hit by a gust of wind. Another crew member was at the bow of the *Caronia* and saw a large American tank landing craft sailing towards the harbour entrance from the sea to the US Naval Base on the port side of the ship. The landing craft kept on the same course, heading towards the *Caronia*. The Officers on the bridge would have had to reduce power if another vessel was entering the harbour entrance and with a combination of the strong wind, reduction in power and too few tugs to pull her back the *Caronia* swung round to the starboard and into the breakwater, damaging the bows of the ship.
>
> We had a great gash in the ship and had to steam back again to Yokohama. There was no ship yard really big enough to take the *Caronia* except the Yokosuka dockyard, a US Navy base, who agreed to allow the ship to be repaired in their dry dock. The *Caronia*'s crew were not allowed to go through the naval base because of security.

Barbara Pedan had mixed feelings about the time in the US base, with passengers' complaints, but then there were some American destroyers in and they were invited on board:

> The trouble was that there were 300 passengers on board and as the hotels were all very full they couldn't be accommodated ashore. So the passengers had to stay on the ship while the repairs were carried out.
>
> All the services stop when the ship is in dry dock so things weren't too easy and the complaining passengers, of whom you always get a few, were in their element with complaints at every turn.
>
> It was nearly three weeks before the repairs were finished so I feel I know Japan better than some of the other countries. Of course, we were pretty busy during the time in dry dock as there were so many arrangements to be made,

The *Caribia* (ex-*Caronia*) being pounded by the waves in the entrance to Apra Harbor.

cables to be sent and passengers to be pacified. But we had some time off every day and time in the evenings. The U.S. Navy had a couple of battleships in and they entertained us very well and we were asked out several times to Japanese homes, which was very interesting. From Japan we went on to Honolulu in mid Pacific. Then it was on to San Francisco on the west coast of America, through the Panama Canal and back to New York.

> In New York we unloaded our American passengers, took another lot on and set off for a Mediterranean Cruise lasting six weeks, back to New York and finally to Southampton in late June. It was a wonderful experience to look back on. If you like travel it is indeed a wonderful opportunity to see the world.

In 1959 the *Caronia* cruised to the Black Sea, calling at Yalta for the first time, and Jim Taylor was a crew member on that occasion:

> Of all the ships I had been on I truly fell in love with the *Caronia*. She was built like a yacht and had that lovely raked bow, like some of the sailing yachts today. I spent two years on there, thoroughly enjoyed it and made lots and lots of friends on board.

Jim Taylor's first voyage was from New York on 3 October 1959 for the *Caronia*'s autumn Mediterranean cruise, which extended into the Black Sea. This was the first time the ports of Odessa and Yalta were opened to cruise ships since the outbreak of the Cold War. Jim Taylor remembers this very well:

The *Caronia* was the first ship to cruise in the Black Sea after the Russians had opened up the ports of Odessa and Yalta. We were approaching the Port of Odessa when there was this turbulence of the sea alongside the ship, and an enormous Russian submarine surfaced alongside of us. About 50 uniformed and smartly dressed crew lined up on the deck of the submarine to welcome us.

It was about this time that the shipping company's transatlantic voyages were having a bleak time, with more and more of the potential passengers changing to jet aircraft in which they could reach America in five hours rather than five days. Similarly, cruise passengers were beginning to prefer flying to a holiday destination, which gave them more time on holiday than if they had to sail there.

This decline in the transatlantic and cruising market caused Cunard to take the *Caronia*, *Carinthia* (3) and *Sylvania* (2) out of service in 1968, with the *Caronia*'s last voyage leaving Southampton on 17 November 1967 under the command of Captain John Treasure Jones. Once she had returned to Southampton *Caronia* was laid up for some time until she was bought by a Yugoslavian group, who had planned to use the vessel as a floating hotel in Dubrovnik.

However, for some reason this did not happen and she was resold to Star Shipping, a Panamanian company, in May 1968 and renamed as *Columbia*. She then sailed to Piraeus in July 1968 to be overhauled and refitted, where she was again renamed, this time as *Caribia*. The intention was for the *Caribia* to return to cruising and she eventually left New York after a number of delays on her first Caribbean cruise on 11 February 1969.

It was not an easy time because there were complaints from many of the passengers due to poor conditions on board. The ship struggled on and departed for a second cruise on 28 February 1969. However, the problems increased, with one crew member being killed when there was a serious engine room explosion while sailing off Martinique, culminating in a loss of power and leaving the ship drifting. Having made temporary repairs, the cruise was cancelled and the passengers flown home. The *Caribia* had to be towed back to New York to face an uncertain future.

Although the ship was bought again, the funds could not be raised to refit her and she remained idle in New York for a further five years, until she was sold for scrap in 1974. The *Caribia* left New York under tow of the ocean-going tug *Hamburg*, under the master Captain Dieter Spannhake, in April 1974 for Kaohsiung, Taiwan. Further problems arose, including the vessel taking on a list near Honolulu, but after repairs she continued on her journey.

On 12 August 1974, when 3 miles off the coast of Guam, *Hamburg* was caught up in tropical storm Mary. While battling strong winds and heavy seas the tug experienced serious engine problems and the captain decided to seek refuge in Apra Harbor to make repairs. But the *Hamburg* no longer had the power to control her tow and was at risk of running aground. With his own vessel in danger, Captain Spannhake made the difficult decision to cut the *Caribia* loose. This resulted in the *Caribia* grounding on the tip of Glass Breakwater at

9.15 a.m. The three crewmen still on board were rescued by helicopter from the water just before the vessel went aground. The next day the *Caribia*'s stern slid off the breakwater into the deep water of the harbour channel.

Caribia (ex-*Caronia*) Wreck

Early Visits by Sport Divers
Imagine waking up to find the wreck of a large ocean liner in the middle of your local harbour. Then add to that the crystal-clear, 30m (98ft) Pacific visibility and sea temperatures of 30°C (86°F). It is also worth noting that at

Above Ron Strong exploring and photographing the wreck in 1974. *(Dianne Strong)*

Left Dianne Strong visiting her favourite part of the wreck. *(Ron Strong)*

218m (715ft) long *Caribia* was even bigger than the *Andrea Doria*, at the time considered by many to be the Everest of wreck diving. Even in their wildest dreams most divers could never conjure up such a great diving opportunity. Thus within days of *Caribia*'s sinking the wreck became a magnet to the many local sport divers on Guam. Salvage buoys placed on the wreck acted as beacons to excited divers arriving by boat or swimming out from the nearby Glass Breakwater.

The *Caribia* started to break up immediately upon sinking. The whole structure could be heard creaking and groaning as the vessel was ravaged by winds and tides. One of the first casualties was the wheelhouse, which was completely ripped off and settled on the bottom away from the rest of the wreck. Eventually the main body of the wreck settled on the port side. The large open promenade windows enticed visiting divers down inside her once glamorous interiors to reminders of past glories. Prior to being sold, *Caribia* had been systematically stripped of most fixtures and fittings of any commercial value. Certainly there was no china or silverware to be found on this wreck. Popular souvenirs amongst divers were the numerous brass plaques that marked doorways and signage around the ship. These bore inscriptions such as 'OFFICERS', 'ENTRANCE' and 'DECK PANTRY'.

In addition to recovering artefacts from the wreck, divers could explore and marvel at the sad remains of this once great ocean-going ship. A popular area to visit was the stern, where the letters 'CARIBIA' and 'PANAMA' were embossed, providing a great photo opportunity. The wreck also rapidly became a haven for fish and other marine life.

Despite its ease of access and newness, the *Caribia* was by no means an easy dive. Divers hungry for souvenirs and portholes were easily distracted and a number of accidents occurred. Within three months five divers had been seriously injured and one even suffered a broken back. The main problem was that such a large structure in a narrow channel of water was subject to strong tidal surges, particularly the shallower parts of the wreck. Other hazards included loose material, such as cables, wires, insulation, piping and swinging doors and hatches. There were also stories of divers really pushing the limits of time and air supply in order to get at portholes from deep inside the wreck. All thoughts of maintaining a safe 25 per cent air reserve were clouded by the quest for more brass. Divers were warned by the authorities to stay away from the wreck but the words fell on deaf ears and a diving ban was never actively enforced.

Sport diving was still relatively new in the early 1970s. Even more in its infancy was the skill and equipment required to undertake underwater photography. However, two of Guam's most active and experienced divers, Ron and Dianne Strong, dived the wreck many times and took many stunning and unique underwater images. Not only do these pictures give an amazing record of the wreck, they also illustrate how diving equipment has evolved over the last three decades. Dianne described the first *Caribia* dive she made with Ron on 22 August 1974:

Various pieces of wreckage can still be found in the entrance to Apra Harbor. *(Sam Warwick)*

Opposite, from top

Hard-hat divers prepare for the work of cutting up the wreck. *(Yasuma Ogawa Collection)*

One of the salvage divers cutting into the hull, which was raised in sections. *(Yasuma Ogawa Collection)*

The salvage of one of *Caribia*'s twin propellers. *(Yasuma Ogawa Collection)*

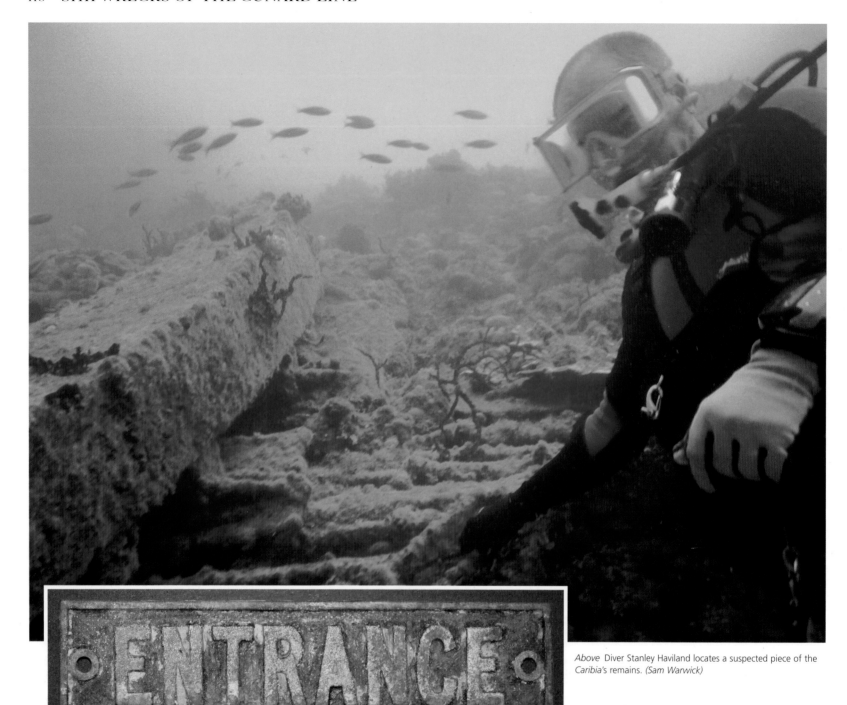

Above Diver Stanley Haviland locates a suspected piece of the *Caribia*'s remains. *(Sam Warwick)*

Left One of the brass doorway signs that were collected as souvenirs by divers in 1974.

As scuba instructors, we were eager to be the first civilian divers to explore this virgin wreck. With underwater cameras in hand, Ron and I submerged carefully, alert for any sea surge being so close to the breakwater. Guam's tropical sun already cast light on the ship's pristine white hull.

As she lay helplessly on her port side, the *Caribia*'s promenade deck windows greeted us, enticing us to enter. Her teak-covered promenade decks looked as if they had just been swabbed. Lifeboat rubble resembled whipped cream as it lifelessly rested in wreckage near her Lido deck in the stern. The ceramic tiles of the swimming pool gleamed. No lifeguard was on duty, but the pool was full of water!

Dianne and Ron's underwater photographs appeared on the front page of Guam's newspaper, the *Pacific Daily News*, the next day.

Sport divers were also involved in shooting 16mm movie footage for a documentary about the impending salvage operation.

Once the commercial salvage agreement was finalised, the honeymoon period was over and the wreck was out of bounds forever to sport divers. However, those who dived the wreck during those brief few months had a unique experience to treasure forever.

Salvage

It was essential for the wreck to be removed as soon as possible since it was causing a major obstruction right in the middle of the entrance to Guam's only deepwater harbour. It was of particular concern to the US Navy since Guam is the site of a large US naval base, which in the 1970s stationed submarines bearing Polaris missiles. Since the *Caribia*'s owners would not take responsibility, this task fell to the United States Army Corps of Engineers (USACE).

During an initial survey dive in November 1974, US Army divers discovered that the wreck of the *Caribia* lay right next to a wreck of a naval landing craft (LSU) that contained 50 tons of live ordnance. This was eventually removed by the navy's Explosive Ordnance Demolition Team and in itself was a massive undertaking. A total of 952 dives were made with 388 hours spent underwater. The wreck site was finally given the all clear in April 1975, but there was always the continued concern that more ammunition may be lying underneath the wreck. The *Caribia* was also seeping oil, so this had to be dealt with using oil booms, skimmers and absorbent pads.

Since the USACE did not have the resources to complete such a large salvage job on its own, the job was put out to tender and eventually granted to the Nippon Salvage Co. of Tokyo. The contract was worth $6.6 million and work commenced on 23 June 1975. The plan was to cut up the 34,000-ton wreck in situ and raise it in 400-ton sections.

The cutting work was performed by divers using both hard-hat dress and standard scuba equipment. Torches and dynamite were used to cut through the steel hull and interiors. Once each section was detached it was raised from the seabed using a huge floating crane. Each section was then taken across Apra Harbor to a dedicated cutting dock to be broken down further. Unsurprisingly, more live ordnance was found as sections were removed. From then on dynamite was used as the sole means of cutting up the ship.

Bad weather often hampered progress and at least 180 days were lost due to storms. One of the biggest delays was caused by super typhoon Pamela in May 1976, with the sinking of several salvage barges causing the loss of most of Nippon's equipment.

The punishing salvage schedule combined with the effort of working at depths of up to 45m (150ft) took its toll on the divers and initially the safety record was poor. At least 195 separate cases of decompression sickness ('the bends') were reported, with sixteen being recorded in one month alone. Nippon addressed this issue by revising the divers' decompression schedules and dive profiles. Safety improved dramatically and there were no fatalities or permanent disabilities.

The salvage operation was officially completed on 30 June 1977, and final records showed that 13,743 dives were carried out over the two-year period.

The Caribia *Today*

Today hardly anything remains of this 34,000-ton ship. The salvage team is to be applauded for its great achievement in removing the wreck, but little of interest was left for visiting divers. Consequently, the wreck is now just a footnote in local dive guides and the area is seldom dived. However, for those hungry to find any final evidence of Cunard's Green Goddess it is still worth a dive.

Divers visiting the site in the 1980s reported finding large flat steel plates, some still containing portholes. It was a good location to visit after typhoons, when the seabed might shift, exposing new pieces of wreckage. Debris was reported to be seen as shallow as 3m (10ft) on the inside point of the breakwater and continuing down into the middle of the harbour to a maximum depth of 50m (164ft).

The author dived the site in April 2011. Commencing the dive just off the inside of the breakwater in about 10m (33ft), small pieces of debris were seen scattered on the seabed. The water was a comfortable 28°C (82°F) and visibility in excess of 20m (66ft). Descending deeper down the sloping ledge into the harbour, bigger pieces of wreckage started to appear at 20m (66ft). It was hard to identify what each item was and which part of a ship it came from. Big rivets could clearly be identified in some pieces of metal plating so there is no doubt that some of the large pieces of metal are from the final remains of *Caribia*. Continuing to a depth of 30m (98ft), further pieces of old metal continued to be found. Unfortunately, with just a single cylinder and the planned dive time nearly up, it was not possible to explore deeper to the bottom of the slope. Maybe future dives will reveal some final surprises.

Note: divers should be aware that unexploded Second World War ordnance is still present in the waters of Apra Harbor!

4

～ OTHER LOSSES ～

～ *Abyssinia* ～

Abyssinia: 1870, 3,253 tons, length 110.9m (364ft), beam 12.8m (42ft), iron hull, steam engine, speed 13 knots. Built by J. & G. Thomson, Glasgow, and launched 3 March 1870, with her maiden voyage in May 1870. Accommodation for 200 first class, 1,050 steerage.

Abyssinia was the fourth of a new fleet of five liners that were built for the weekly Atlantic mail service. Along with her sister ship *Algeria* they became the first to carry steerage passengers. The ship originally served on the Liverpool to New York route, calling at Queenstown. The *Abyssinia* was sold to the Guion Line in 1880.

In December 1891 *Abyssinia* left New York for her transatlantic crossing carrying fifty-seven passengers, eighty-eight crew and a cargo of cotton. In the early hours of 18 December a fire broke out that could not be brought under control. Fortunately the Norddeutscher Lloyd (NDL) liner *Spree* saw the smoke

The sad demise of *Queen Elizabeth*, which caught fire and capsized in Hong Kong Harbour, during conversion to a floating university in 1971. (*John A. Hudson*)

from the *Abyssinia* and saved all passengers and crew, so although the ship sank there was no loss of life.

The Board of Trade Wreck Report for *Abyssinia* in March 1892 concluded 'that the fire had started from a naked light used by one of the trimmers in the compartment where the coal was stowed, in close proximity to the cotton'. Cotton, being a very flammable material, would easily catch fire and spread very quickly. It was not an ideal cargo to be carried at the same time as passengers.

The report gave the position in the North Atlantic as just 47° N, 44° W. With such a vague position and remote location it is unlikely the wreck will ever be found.

～ *Albania* (2) ～

Albania (2): 1920, 12,768 tons, length 159.4m (523.1ft), beam 19.5m (64.0ft), steel hull, powered by two sets of geared steam turbines, speed 13 knots. Ordered by the Cunard Line in 1916, but due to the First World War building was suspended and did not recommence until 1919. Built by Scotts Shipbuilding and Engineering, Greenock, and launched on 17 April 1920, and registered at Liverpool by the Cunard Line on 21 December 1920. Originally designed as a cargo-passenger ship with accommodation for 470 cabin class.

The *Albania* left Liverpool for New York on her maiden voyage on 19 January 1921 and remained on that route until 1922, when the ship was transferred to the Canadian service. Neither route proved viable for the dual-purpose vessel and in 1925 the *Albania* was laid up. The ship was eventually purchased by Navigazione Liberia Triestina S.A., Trieste, Italy, in March 1930 and renamed *California*. For the next four years the vessel operated on the Italy to west coast USA service before being laid up once more in 1934 at Genoa. Between March and October 1935 *California* served as a 'patient transport vessel' carrying wounded and sick troops during the Italian invasion of Ethiopia. In 1937 the Italian Government reorganised their shipping companies and Navigazione Liberia Triestina was dissolved, resulting in the transfer of *California* to Lloyd Triestino.

The *Abyssinia* was built for Cunard Line in 1870 and sold to the Guion Line a decade later. In 1891 the ship caught fire and sank in the Atlantic with no loss of life.

Following Italy's entry into the Second World War the *California* was requisitioned by the Royal Italian Navy and converted into a 770-bed hospital ship in June 1940. The ship was repainted according to the established Geneva Convention for hospital ships with white hull, green band and large red crosses. In July the *California* sailed on the first of several return voyages from Naples to Libya but had a narrow escape in September when the ship was damaged by shrapnel during a British air strike at Benghazi.

On the night of 10 August 1941 the *California* was lying at anchor in the shelter of Syracuse Harbour, Sicily, when the ship came under attack by Fairey Swordfish torpedo aircraft from the 830 Naval Air Squadron of the British Fleet Air Arm. The *California* was struck by an aerial torpedo and sank soon afterwards, the stern coming to rest on a shallow seabed in 10m (33ft) with the upper decks remaining above water. There was one casualty among the crew.

Salvage operations commenced soon after the loss but a serious fire, followed by a heavy storm resulted in the complete sinking of the *California* in October.

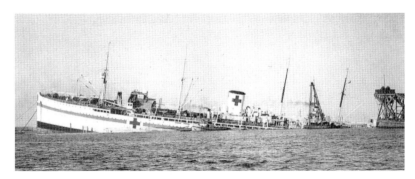

Salvage operations on the Italian hospital ship *California* (ex-*Albania* (2)) commenced soon after the vessel was sunk by British aircraft in August 1941.

Fortunately much of the furniture and medical equipment had been saved and was put to use in the hospital ship *Città di Trapani*. The remainder of the wreck was recovered and salvaged in the post-war period.

During the Second World War the *California* had carried out a total of thirty-two missions, transporting around 24,000 sick and wounded soldiers. Three months after the sinking three airmen from 830 Squadron were captured in Sicily after ditching their plane in bad weather. When questioned why they had attacked a clearly recognisable hospital ship they claimed that the air crews had been provided with an edited identification photo from which the red crosses had been removed!

⌦ *Alpha* ⌫

Alpha: 1863, 653 tons, length 65.8m (216ft), beam 8.41m (27ft), one funnel, two masts, iron construction, two-cylinder oscillating direct-drive engines powering a single screw. Built by Barclay Curle & Co., Glasgow, for Cunard, and registered under the name of William Cunard, the younger of Samuel Cunard's two sons. The *Alpha* was launched in 1863 with accommodation for 25 first-class and 150 third-class passengers, sailing the Halifax–New York–Bermuda service.

In 1888 the *Alpha* was sold to Pickford & Black and operated by the Halifax & West India Steamship Co. for a monthly service from Halifax–Bermuda–Turks Islands.

In 1897 James D. Warren, a marine insurance agent, purchased the *Alpha* for carrying passengers and supplies to the Klondike goldfields. However, when the Klondike gold-rush trade began to diminish Warren sold the *Alpha* in 1899 to Samuel Barber of Vancouver Island, who then used the vessel for trading locally. The *Alpha* was wrecked on Yellow Rock, off the east coast of Vancouver Island, during a gale on 15 December 1900 while carrying a cargo of 700 tons of salted salmon, lumber and coal. There was a loss of nine lives, including the owner and his brother, Captain Yorke, three engineers, a purser and a stowaway.

⌦ *Andania* (2) ⌫

Andania (2): 1922, 13,950 tons, length 158.6m (520ft), beam 19.9m (65ft), one funnel, two masts, steel construction, builders Hawthorn, Leslie & Co. Ltd, Hebburn-on-Tyne. The engines were double reduction steam turbines, powering twin screws at a service speed of 16 knots. Launched on 1 November 1921. Passenger accommodation was provided for 500 cabin-class and 1,200 third-class passengers.

Andania mainly sailed on the London to Montréal route, but sometimes only as far as Halifax. From 1925–26 *Andania* also picked up European passengers and cargo from Hamburg and then sailed to Southampton and on to New York. From 1927 onwards the *Andania* route commenced from Liverpool to Montréal, calling at Glasgow, Belfast and Québec. The 1930s Depression made problems for the Canadian transatlantic trade, causing *Andania* to be laid up for two years.

CUNARD LINE   R.M.S. "ANDANIA"   GROSS TONNAGE 14,000

Andania (2) was sunk by a torpedo in 1940, fortunately with no loss of life.

When the *Andania* eventually returned to service she was on the Liverpool to New York route. *Andania* was involved in an accident when she collided in thick fog with the tanker *British Statesman* in December 1937. The tanker was seriously damaged and there was some damage to the *Andania's* bow. However, speedy repairs were undertaken and only two days were lost from her schedule.

Andania was en route to New York when war was declared on 3 September 1939. On her return to Liverpool she was requisitioned by the Admiralty for war service as an AMC, known to the ordinary seaman by the nickname using the letters AMC as 'Admiralty-Made Coffins'. Converting and fitting out the vessel for war, including arming with eight 6in guns and two anti-aircraft guns, was undertaken by Cammell Lairds in Birkenhead. She was then commissioned HMS *Andania* on 9 November 1939. After completing her trials HMS *Andania* sailed to Greenock to join the Northern Patrol, where the patrols covered the Iceland area for the convoy routes.

It was in the afternoon of 13 June 1940 that HMS *Andania* was spotted by a U-boat, *U-A* (Commander Hans Cohausz) of the 7th Flotilla (Kiel). *U-A* was originally ordered by Turkey to be built by Germaniawerft, Kiel, but with the start of the Second World War she was commissioned into the Kriegsmarine. *U-A* was the most successful of the foreign U-boats, sinking seven ships during her patrols.

To try to avoid submarine attacks, HMS *Andania* was keeping to the established zigzag course. This was not easy for the U-boat shadowing the ship to follow, especially due to poor visibility. When *U-A* tried an attack at 12.17 p.m. on 14 June the three torpedoes she fired did not hit the ship, nor was the trail of the torpedoes seen by the lookouts on board the vessel. This time the U-boat lost HMS *Andania* and was not able to locate her again for twenty-four hours.

On the night of 15/16 June 1940, at 12.29 a.m., HMS *Andania* was eventually hit by one of two torpedoes fired by *U-A* on the starboard aft side. The position was 62.36N, 15.09W, about 230 miles west-north-west of the Faroe Islands. The lookouts had possibly seen the trail of the torpedo or a periscope on the surface because they started to fire the guns where they thought they had identified something suspicious in the water.

HMS *Andania* was in serious trouble because the rudders were out of action and the ship had no steerage. In addition, the main generators were flooded and the water was getting deeper inside the hull, so much so that even with the pumps working at full power the water was still rising. The vessel started to list and to compensate for this the engineers tried moving oil to the opposite side of the ship, hoping that the extra weight would improve the trim.

Although the first torpedo struck HMS *Andania*, the second torpedo missed. *U-A* fired a third torpedo at 1.18 a.m., and the fourth at 1.50 a.m., but both missed their target. At this point the commander of *U-A* appeared to give up his attack, possibly due to using up all his torpedoes or alternatively due to the heavy seas. By this time the situation had become serious and there was no doubt when Captain Bain RN ordered 'abandon ship' as just a matter of hours later HMS *Andania* sank by the stern. All the ship's company were picked up safely by the *Skallagrinur*, an Icelandic trawler, and later were transferred to HMS *Forrester*, which then took them to Scapa Flow.

The author's grandfather, Commodore W.E. Warwick, was one of the officers serving on the *Andania* at the time of the shipwreck. Warwick held a commission in the Royal Naval Reserve and at the outbreak of the Second World War he was mobilised into the navy and appointed to the *Andania* as a sub-lieutenant. Before boarding the lifeboat he changed into his best uniform, which he had recently purchased.

The wreck of *Andania* lies in deep water of at least 2,000m (6,562ft) and is unlikely ever to be found.

🙡 *Andria* (1) 🙣

Andria (1): 1948, 7,242 tons, length 153.4m (503ft), beam 19.81m (65ft), two funnels (forward funnel false), steel construction, three steam turbines geared to single screw at 12 knots. Built by J.L. Thomson & Sons Ltd, Sunderland, in 1948 for the Silver Line as *Silverbriar*. There was originally passenger accommodation for twelve.

Cunard purchased the *Silverbriar* from Silver Line in 1951 and renamed the ship *Andria*. This followed the earlier acquisition of her sister ship *Silverplane* (7,242 tons) in 1951, which was renamed *Alsatia* (2). When Cunard took over the vessels they were both used exclusively for the cargo trade, with *Andria* (1) serving the London–Le Havre–New York route. The redundant luxury passenger cabins were used for the officers' accommodation. The public lounges became the wardrooms and were styled as English pubs; the *Andria's* was decorated with

Andria (1) was purchased from the Silver Line in 1951 and later sold in 1963, at which time the ship was renamed *Union Faith*. (*Warwick Family Collection*)

antique guns, pewter mugs and plates. Needless to say, both ships were very popular with their officers and crew. An unusual feature of the ship was the false forward funnel, which housed the captain's cabin and chart room. One of the early captains of the *Andria* was William 'Bil' Warwick, who commanded the ship from April 1956 to March 1957. Warwick was later master of *Caronia* and all three Queens, eventually becoming commodore of the line, his last command being *QE2*.

In 1963 both vessels were bought by the China Union Lines, Taiwan, with the *Alsatia* being renamed *Union Freedom* and the *Andria* renamed *Union Faith*.

The demise of the *Union Faith* came about on 6 April 1969 when she collided with three oil barges led by *IOC No.7*, which were being towed in tandem down the Mississippi River, New Orleans, by *Warren J. Doucet*. The impact caused the *Union Faith* to burst into flames. A report by the National Transportation Safety Board described the loss:

> The collision occurred slightly upstream from the Greater New Orleans Bridge on the left descending side of the river. I.O.C. No. 7 caught fire on contact and broke loose from the tow. A series of explosions followed almost immediately and the UNION FAITH was engulfed in flames. The barge broke into two sections which drifted down the river ablaze and later sank. Crude oil burned on the river and threatened the moored vessels and the harbour facilities. The UNION FAITH drifted downriver, burning from stem to stern, and sank about 0200 on April 7, 1969. Twenty-five persons aboard the UNION FAITH, including all personnel on the vessel's bridge at the time of the casualty, are missing and presumed dead.

If the burning vessel had drifted downstream on to the New Orleans waterfront the catastrophe would have been even worse, but fortunately the swift actions of the master of the towing vessel *Cappy Bisso* averted major disaster.

The report concluded that:

> … the primary cause of the casualty was the failure of the SS UNION FAITH and the M/V WARREN J. DOUCET to reach an agreement as to the method of passing when in a meeting situation.

Twenty-five members of the *Union Faith*'s crew lost their lives, including Captain Yuen-Lai Fan. There were twenty-six Chinese survivors, of which three received severe burn and smoke injuries.

The *Union Faith* sank in 34m (112ft) of water, but there was only clearance of 17m (55ft) above the wreck. In order to remove the obstruction as quickly as possible the United States Army Corps of Engineers (USACE) elected to bury the ship in the river bed. Work commenced on 17 August 1970, when the ship's superstructure down to the weather deck was removed by divers. Next a long trench 30m (100ft) wide by 15m (50ft) deep was excavated adjacent to the wreck. Finally the earth beneath the vessel was undercut, enabling it to slide into the trench. The work was completed on 31 October 1970. No oil was removed from the wreck because it was believed it would be 'capped' by sediment from the river.

However, twenty-nine years later reports were received of large quantities of oil appearing in the Mississippi River near the wreck. Divers were sent down and confirmed the oil was indeed escaping from a fracture in the hull. Further penetration dives took place deep inside the ship to determine the exact source of the leak. When this was established submersible pumping machinery was installed and an estimated 5,950 gallons of oil was removed. The operation cost $1.1 million and took three months, during which time 200 dives were safely completed.

Asia (1)

Asia (1): 1850, 2,226 tons, length 81.1m (266ft), beam 12.2m (40ft), one funnel, three masts, wood construction, two side-lever engines powering two paddlewheels at 12 knots. Built by Robert Steele & Co., Glasgow, and launched in January 1850. There was accommodation for 130 first-class and 30 second-class passengers.

The *Asia*, along with her sister ship *Africa*, was built for Cunard to meet the increasing demands of the transatlantic mail service. At the time *Asia* was the largest ship that had been built in the Clyde shipyards.

On 18 May 1850 *Asia* left Liverpool for her maiden voyage to Boston via Halifax. After her maiden voyage many of her transatlantic crossings were from Liverpool to New York. In 1867 the *Asia* was sold to Glasgow shipbuilders J. & G. Thomson in part exchange for the new *Samaria* (1). The following year the ship was sold again to Robert Duncan & Co. who removed the engines and converted the *Asia* to sail.

On 2 December 1876 the *Asia* was loading a cargo of jute in Calcutta when a fire broke out on board. The vessel was beached but broke her back and parted midships.

The *Atlantic Conveyor* was requisitioned for the Falklands War in 1982 for transporting equipment. *(Courtesy of James Hutton, RNA area 10)*

Atlantic Conveyor was struck by two Exocet missiles on 25 May 1982 resulting in the loss of twelve lives. *(Eddie Mason – United Towing Company)*

Atlantic Conveyor

Atlantic Conveyor: 1970, 14,950 tons, length 212.1m (696ft), beam 28m (92ft), four turbines powering twin screws, speed 23 knots, was a roll-on, roll-off container ship that was built on the Tyne by Swan Hunter for Cunard in 1970. Along with her sister ship, *Atlantic Causeway*, *Atlantic Conveyor* was requisitioned on 14 April 1982, and took part in transporting equipment to the British Task Force in the Falklands War.

To prepare for *Atlantic Conveyor*'s role in transporting a wide range of stores, the ship had to be modified in Devonport from 16–25 April. Once the work was completed she was loaded with the stores, including five Chinook and six Wessex helicopters, ammunition, materials to construct a land base for the Harriers to relieve pressure on the carriers, and other supplies for the Falklands.

The *Atlantic Conveyor* left England on 25 April 1982, first calling at the Ascension Islands, where she loaded a further eight Fleet Air Arm Sea Harriers (809 Squadron) and six RAF Harrier GR.3 jump jets, and then sailed for the South Atlantic and the Falkland Islands.

Once the *Atlantic Conveyor* arrived in the Total Exclusion Zone on 19 May the Harriers were then flown to HMS *Hermes* and HMS *Invincible*. The *Atlantic Conveyor* remained with the Carrier Battle Group and was tasked to go into the Assault Operations Area on the night of 25–26 May to disembark her helicopters and stores.

On 25 May the *Atlantic Conveyor* was attacked and hit by two Exocet missiles launched by Super Etendard fighter aircraft. The missiles caused massive damage to the vessel, which caught fire and the call to abandon ship was made thirty minutes later. Of the 149 on board, 12 lives were lost, including the master, Captain Ian North, who was posthumously awarded the Distinguished Service Cross (DSC).

Captain North managed to abandon the *Atlantic Conveyor*, but was unable to get to a life raft and is thought to have died from a heart attack from being in the very cold waters of the South Atlantic.

Prince Andrew was piloting a Sea King helicopter and was the first to lift off survivors after the *Atlantic Conveyor* was hit.

On 16 June 2007 a memorial to the *Atlantic Conveyor* was unveiled at Cape Pembroke by Prince Edward. This was the first British merchant vessel lost at sea due to enemy fire since the Second World War.

Ausonia (1)

Ausonia (1): 1909, 7,907 tons, length 137.3m (451ft) long, beam 16.5m (54ft), one funnel, four masts, steel construction, twin-screw powered by six-cylinder turbines, giving a service speed of 12 knots. Built by Swan & Hunter, Wallsend-on-Tyne, and with passenger accommodation for 90 second class and 1,000 third class.

Ausonia (1) served as troopship in the First World War and was torpedoed by *U-62* in May 1918. *(Bert Moody Collection)*

The *Ausonia* was originally built for the Thomson Line and was launched on 18 August 1909 as the *Tortona*. At the start of the First World War the *Ausonia* continued crossing the North Atlantic from August 1914 to July 1915, but at the time was under charter with the Anchor-Donaldson Line, sailing from Glasgow to Moville and New York. Later, in 1915, the *Ausonia* became a troopship in the Mediterranean and also sailed to Indian ports. On her eastbound voyages across the Atlantic she carried Canadian troops to the battlefields in France, as did *Ascania*.

Ausonia was returned to Cunard in 1916.

Ausonia was torpedoed twice by German U-boats. On 11 June 1917 she was torpedoed by *U-55* (Commander Wilhelm Werner) off the coast of Ireland on her transatlantic voyage from Montréal to Avonmouth, but was able to make it to Queenstown. The vessel was repaired and went back into service, but on 30 May 1918 the *Ausonia* was torpedoed by *U-62* (Commander Ernst Hashagen), approximately 620 miles south-west of Fastnet. The submarine surfaced and shelled the ship, causing it to sink. There were no passengers on board, but forty-four members of the crew lost their lives, the remainder of them abandoning ship and travelling 900 miles in lifeboats until 8 June, when they were picked up by HMS *Zennia* and an American destroyer.

Bactria

Bactria: 1928, 2,402 tons, length 89m (292ft), beam 13.7m (45ft), one funnel, steel construction, triple expansion engine, service speed 9 knots. A general purpose cargo vessel built by J. L. Thompson, Sunderland, for the America-Levant Line, of which Cunard owned a controlling interest. The maiden voyage was from

Liverpool to Constantinople on 2 May 1928. On 5 December 1930 ownership was transferred to the Cunard Line.

The *Bactria* was requisitioned by the British Government on 13 April 1940 for use as an ammunition ship and later used for carrying personnel. In August the ship was transferred to the Liner Division operating between the UK and West Africa. After the war the ship was returned to Cunard but sold in 1954 to Cia. Isla Bella, Puerto Rico and renamed *Theo*. In 1958 the ship was sold to Capital S.A., Uruguay, and renamed *Catalina S*. Four years later the vessel was sold to Bahamas Pearl, Bahamas and renamed *Bahamas Pearl* but the same year sold again to National Shipping Trinidad when the name reverted to *Catalina S*.

On 21 December 1962 *Catalina S* was on a voyage from Belize transporting a cargo of timber to West Indies ports when the vessel struck rocks 2 miles west of the San Juan harbour entrance. The ship was declared a constructive total loss.

Balbec

Balbec: 1853, 838 tons, length 63.7m (209ft), beam 9.2m (30ft), clipper bow, one funnel, three masts, iron construction, two-cylinder compound engine powering a single screw at 9 knots, twenty-nine cabins. Built by William Denny & Bros, Dumbarton, in 1852, she entered service in 1853. The *Balbec* was the first Cunard ship to be built specifically for the Mediterranean service, but transferred to the Liverpool to New York service in 1859. In 1873 this ship was fitted with new compound engines by J. Jack, Rollo & Co., Liverpool.

When sailing from Liverpool to Le Havre on 28 March 1884 the ship was holed after striking a submerged object, thought to be another shipwreck off Longships lighthouse, near Land's End. The captain beached the *Balbec* on Nanjizel Beach in Cornwall. The *Balbec* was subsequently written off as a total wreck. All twenty-nine crew and the five passengers were landed safely.

A hydrographic survey in September 2009 reported that the remains of the wreck were in just a few metres of water and mostly buried in sand. The most prominent feature was the boiler and the top of the engine, which could be seen above the seabed.

Beta

Beta: 1873, 1,087 tons, length 71.7m (235ft), beam 8.7m (28ft), one funnel, three masts, steel construction, two-cylindered inverted compound engines powering a single screw at 10 knots. Built as a cargo ship by Aitken & Mansel, Glasgow, launched in November 1873 and registered to William Cunard.

The *Beta* was solely a cargo ship and had no passenger accommodation. After being refitted in 1897 she replaced the *Alpha* on the monthly Halifax–Bermuda–Turks Island service. In 1889 she was sold to the Halifax & West India Steamship Co., Glasgow, under the ownership and management of Pickford & Black, sailing the Halifax–West Indies route.

The *Beta* was wrecked on 22 February 1908, when she ran aground on Grand Turk while sailing from Halifax to the West Indies and carrying general cargo. Supposedly the bell has been recovered from the wreck, but little else is known.

Bosnia

Bosnia: 1928, 2,407 tons, length 89m (292ft), beam 13.7m (45ft), one funnel, two masts, steel construction, three-cylindered triple-expansion engines powering a single screw at 12 knots. Built by Joseph L. Thompson & Sons Ltd, North Sands, Sunderland, and launched in 1928 as a cargo vessel, without passenger accommodation.

Cunard had ordered four cargo vessels to be built in 1928 for their American-Levant Line subsidiary sailing on the Mediterranean service. These were *Bactria*, *Bantria*, *Bosnia* and *Bothnia* (2), and were all launched in that year. However, when Cunard merged with White Star these vessels remained under the management of S. & J. Thompson.

Two days after the start of the Second World War the *Bosnia* was sailing from Licata, Sicily, under the command of Captain Poole. The ship was bound for Manchester and carrying a cargo of sulphur. When approximately 120 miles north-north-west of Cape Ortegal, the *Bosnia* was attacked by gunfire from the *U-47* (Commander Günther Prien) on 5 September 1939 at 8.15 a.m. Shortly after, at 9.38 a.m., she was sunk by a torpedo. One crew member lost his life. The captain and remaining crew of thirty were rescued by the Norwegian tanker *Eidanger* (Captain Johannes Prestus) and taken safely to Lisbon. *Bosnia* was only the second merchant vessel to be lost in the war, the first being *Athenia* of the Anchor Line.

The *Bosnia* is possibly the deepest Cunard wreck, lying in a charted depth in the Bay of Biscay over 4km (2.5 miles) deep. The position is approximately 45°29'N, 09°45'W.

Bothnia (2)

Bothnia (2): 1928, 2,402 tons, length 89.09m (292ft), beam 13.7m (45ft), one funnel, two masts, steel construction, single screw, triple expansion engines and speed 9 knots. General cargo ship built by J.L. Thompson, Sunderland for the America-Levant Line, The ship was launched on 5 April 1928 and made her maiden voyage from Liverpool to Genoa on 30 May 1928. Ownership was transferred to the Cunard Line in December 1930.

The *Bothnia* was requisitioned by the British Government soon after the outbreak of the Second World War and spent most of the war years operating between the UK and West Africa. After the war the ship was stationed in Ceylon and operated on routes to Singapore and India, before being returned to Cunard in July 1946.

In 1955 the *Bothnia* was sold to Vivalet Shipping and Trading Co. S.A.. Panama and renamed *Emily*. The ship was sold again in 1958 to Alexander Sigalas, Athens, and renamed *Capetan Manolis*.

On 24 December 1960 the vessel ran aground 1 mile north of Casablanca on passage from Fedala to Nemours in ballast. The *Bothnia* was refloated on 16 March 1961 but declared a constructive total loss and scrapped at Valencia two months later.

Brest

Brest: 1874, 1,472 tons, length 73.1m (240ft), beam 9.8m (32.2ft), one funnel, three masts, iron construction, two-cylinder compound inverted direct-action engines powering a single screw at 10 knots. Built by Blackwood & Gordon, Port Glasgow, for the Cunard Line and launched in 1873. There was accommodation for 8 first-class and 386 third-class passengers.

Brest and her sister ship *Nantes* undertook the French feeder service, transporting European emigrants from the French ports to join the transatlantic liners sailing from Liverpool. This was because the French Line services to New York were exclusively for French citizens to travel on.

The *Brest* ran into fog while en route for Le Havre and was wrecked off Polberro Point, Cornwall, on 6 September 1879. Of the 134 passengers on board, 5 were drowned. The wreck lies in shallow water very close to the rocks, with a maximum depth of 9m (30ft). What little remains is very flattened, concreted to the rocky seabed and barely recognisable.

Britannia

Britannia: 1840, 1,154 tons, length 63m (207ft), beam 10.4m (34ft), one funnel, three masts, wood construction. Built by Robert Duncan, Greenock, with engines by Robert Napier, Glasgow, propelling two side paddlewheels at a service speed of 9 knots.

Britannia was the first ship of the newly formed North American Royal Mail Steam Packet Co. (Cunard Line) to enter service. She left Liverpool on 4 July 1840 for her maiden voyage to Boston, calling at Halifax and arriving on 17 July. From then on she continued her service from Liverpool to New York and Boston with a call, for some years, in Halifax. Later Queenstown was also added to the route for the mail service and by 1847 the route extended to New York.

By November 1848 *Britannia* had made her last transatlantic voyage and in March 1849 was sold to the German Confederation Navy and sailed from Liverpool to Bremen, where she was renamed *Barbarossa*.

In June 1852 *Barbarossa* was transferred to the Prussian Navy, but only used as an accommodation ship in Danzig and Kiel. However, she was then decommissioned and used for target practice from the torpedo training ship *Zieten*, which was being used to test the effectiveness of newly designed torpedoes. It was on 28 July 1880 that the *Zieten* sank the *Barbarossa* with a torpedo.

It has been generally thought that was the end of the ship, but in fact the wreck was later raised and scrapped in Kiel.

Caria

Caria: 1900, 3,032 tons, length 96.9m (318ft), beam 13.1m (43ft), one funnel, two masts, steel construction, three-cylinder triple-expansion engines powering a single screw at 10 knots. Built for an Antwerp shipping company as a cargo ship by the Tyne Iron SB Co., Newcastle. She was named *Clematis* and launched in 1900. No passenger accommodation.

In 1911 Cunard bought the ship for the Mediterranean routes and renamed her *Caria*. She was travelling from Naples to Alexandria when she was sunk by gunfire on 6 November 1915 by *U-35* (Commander Waldemar Kophamel). The location was 120 miles south-east of Cape Martello, Crete, at 33°14'N, 25°47'E in a depth in excess of 2km.

Carinthia (1)

Carinthia (1): 1895, 5,598 tons, length 135.6m (445ft), beam 14.9m (49ft), one funnel, four masts, steel construction, six-cylinder triple-expansion engines powering twin screws at 13 knots. Built as a cargo ship with no passenger accommodation by London & Glasgow Co., Glasgow, and launched for Cunard in May 1895.

Carinthia made her maiden voyage from Liverpool to Boston on 24 October 1895, and in 1899 the Admiralty chartered the ship for trooping to the Boer War, until July 1900. On 15 May 1900 the *Carinthia* was carrying a cargo of mules from Mexico when she was wrecked off Cape Gravois, Haiti. There was no loss of life, but about 400 mules were believed to have perished. On 21 May 1900 the *New York Times* reported that there was an attempt to refloat the *Carinthia*:

The Hamburg-American steamer *Valencia*, accompanied by the Government steamboat *Ready*, left here to-day for the scene of the wreck of the Cunard Line steamer *Carinthia*, which is ashore at Point Gravois, Haiti. A large quantity of water was taken for the 1,400 mules on the *Carinthia*. Many men and numerous appliances were also carried to assist in floating the steamer. The British cruiser *Proserpine* has also gone to the scene of the wreck.

The salvage vessels found the *Carinthia* stuck fast on a rocky bank and the ship could not be saved. A Liverpool Board of Trade inquiry in July found that the captain George Campbell 'had not navigated with proper care, and his certificate has been suspended for three months'. The captain subsequently tendered his resignation and left Cunard soon after.

Cephalonia

Cephalonia: 1882, 5,517 tons, length 131.2m (430ft), beam 14.2m (46ft), one funnel, three masts, iron construction, two compound engines powering a single screw at 14 knots. Built by Laird Bros, Birkenhead, for Cunard and launched on 20 May 1882. Accommodation was for 200 first-class and 1,500 second-class passengers.

The *Cephalonia* made her maiden voyage on 23 August 1882 and sailed from Liverpool to Boston until September 1899, when she was prepared for trooping in the Boer War. In 1900 *Cephalonia* was sold to an Italian firm and later that year again sold to the Chinese Eastern Railway Co. and renamed *Haylar*. The vessel was scuttled in 1904 at Port Arthur (modern-day Lüshunkou, China) during the Russo-Japanese War.

China

China: 1862, 2,529 tons, length 99.4m (323ft), beam 12.3m (40ft), one funnel, three masts, iron construction, two geared oscillating engines powering a single screw at 12 knots. Built by Robert Napier & Sons, Glasgow, and launched in October 1861. Accommodation for 268 first-class and 771 second-class passengers.

The maiden voyage left Liverpool on 15 March 1862 for New York and the *China* continued on this service until 1865, but then changed to the Liverpool–Halifax–Boston route until 1867, but again returned to its previous route until 1872. In 1879 the *China* was one of several Cunard ships to be chartered as transports for the Zulu War. The next year the vessel was sold to Spanish owners and renamed *Magallanes*. In 1889 the ship was sold to J.D. Bischoff of Bremen, who refitted the vessel as a four-masted sailing barque under the new name *Theodor*. Following another sale in 1898 the ship was sold for the final time in 1901 to A/S Theodor (J. Johanson & Co.), Norway.

On 2 March 1906 the *Theodor* was reported lost with all hands on a voyage from Tampa to Yokohama with a cargo of phosphates.

Columbia

Columbia: 1840, 1,138 tons, length 63m (206ft), beam 9.8m (32ft), one funnel, three masts, paddlewheel steamer, wood construction, two side-lever engines powering paddlewheels at 9 knots, supplied by Robert Napier, Glasgow.

Built for Cunard by Robert Steele & Co., Greenock, and launched in 1840. *Columbia* was built to carry 225 tons of cargo and mail, with accommodation for 115 cabin-class passengers and a crew of eighty-nine. She was one of the original four Cunard Line vessels.

The maiden voyage of the *Columbia* started when she left Liverpool carrying passengers and, importantly, the mail for the British Government on 5 January 1841, bound for Boston, calling at Halifax. In June 1841 *Columbia* took the westbound record from the *Great Western* in ten days, nineteen hours at a speed of almost 10 knots, and also the eastbound record in April 1843, again from the *Great Western*, in nine days, twelve hours, at just over 11 knots. However, *Columbia*'s service was short lived because she only continued on this route until 1843 before her fateful voyage on 2 July 1843.

The *Columbia* had left Boston in thick fog, which was not unusual in that area, but as she sailed along the coastline she met a strong current that started to pull her off course. This was a problem for the captain because the cloud cover was such that he could not use his sextant to 'shoot the sun' to take his bearings. It was later on that day that *Columbia* approached Cape Sable. At the time the ship was sailing at almost her full speed when she struck the Devil's Limb Reef and was grounded. All attempts to free her by the crew failed as she was stuck fast. The eighty-five passengers and crew were all safely rescued by a local boat that came alongside. The mail and most of the passengers' luggage was also taken off. However, all the time the *Columbia* was being battered by the waves until she gradually broke up and sank.

This was the first steamship that Cunard had lost and, not having had the mail contract for long, could have cost the company dearly, especially as they had lost a quarter of their fleet of four ships. This was not to happen for a number of reasons. Firstly, all passengers and crew were saved without loss of life, and secondly, all the mail was saved. Samuel Cunard had also travelled to Cape Sable to attend the wreck personally and saw to it that passengers were looked after and reached their final destinations.

Cape Sable Island is renowned for causing a large number of shipwrecks. In 1860 the *Hungarian* (Allan Line) was lost, along with 205 lives. Directly south of Cape Sable 'Columbia Rock' is marked on the chart of the area. The depths only average a few metres but nothing remains that could be positively identified as part of *Columbia*.

Corsica

Corsica: 1,134 tons, length 68.4m (224ft), beam 9.8m (32ft), one funnel, two masts, iron construction, two-cylinder geared oscillating engines powering a single screw at 10 knots. Built by J. & G. Thomson & Co. for Cunard and launched in 1863 for their Mediterranean service to Italy, Sardinia and Corsica. There was first-class passenger service only.

The *Delta* was sold by Cunard in 1860 and wrecked in Newfoundland in 1899.

After sailing the Mediterranean route until 1867, Cunard sold the *Corsica* to the Royal Mail Steam Packet Co., replacing their vessel *Wye*, which had been lost in a hurricane in the Caribbean. The ship was sold again to another company for trading in the West Indies and was lengthened and fitted with compound engines. *Corsica* was wrecked on 11 October 1881 off Cape Roca, Portugal, on a voyage from London to Bombay, with twenty-one lives lost. The Board of Trade report dated 8 November 1881 concluded:

> The Court, having carefully inquired into the circumstances of the above-mentioned shipping casualty, finds, for the reasons annexed, that the stranding and loss of the said vessel 'Corsica' was due to the master having starboarded his helm for the purpose of laying her on a course for Cape St. Vincent before he was well past Cape Roca, which caused her to strike on to the outer edge of the reef of rocks lying off that point. The master and all the officers having been drowned, the Court is not asked to deal with their certificates, or to make any order as to costs.

☙ Cuba ☙

Cuba: 1864, 2,668 tons, length 103m (338ft), beam 12.8m (42ft), one funnel, three masts, iron construction, two geared oscillating engines powering a single screw at 12 knots. She was built by Tod & McGregor, Glasgow, and had accommodation for 160 cabin-class and 800 third-class passengers.

On 3 December 1864 the *Cuba* left Liverpool on her maiden voyage to New York, calling at Queenstown. The *Cuba* continued on this route until 12 May 1866, when she commenced her first Liverpool to Boston route, calling at Queenstown and Halifax, returning later to the New York route. In 1876 the *Cuba* was sold to David Brown, London, and converted into a four-masted sailing ship. Following a transfer of ownership to Beaconsfield Ship Co in 1883 the ship was given the new name *Earl of Beaconsfield*.

On 8 July 1887 the *Earl of Beaconsfield* sailed from Calcutta with of a crew of thirty-four hands and a cargo of wheat and linseed, bound for Hull. In the early hours of 6 November 1887 the ship was close to her final destination when she ran aground off Aldbrough, Yorkshire, after a night of thick fog. All crew got off safely but the vessel became a total loss.

The distinctive figurehead of the vessel's namesake is on display at Hull Maritime Museum and the bow of the wreck is exposed at low tide.

☙ Cunard Campaigner ☙

Cunard Campaigner: 1972, 15,498 tons, length 175.7m (576ft), beam 22.5m (74ft), steel, six-cylinder Sulzer diesel engines, single screw, 15.5 knots. Bulk carrier launched 23 October 1971 by Astilleros Españoles S.A., Spain for the Cunard Line and managed by Cunard-Brocklebank Bulkers Ltd.

In 1974 the vessel was sold to Great Eastern Shipping, India, and renamed *Jag Shanti* in May the following year. In 1994 ownership of the vessel transferred to Infrastructure Leasing and Finance Services, India.

On 28 May 1994 the *Jag Shanti* was on a voyage from New Mangalore, India, to Eregli, Turkey, with a cargo of iron ore pellets when leaking pipes caused the engine room to be flooded whilst 125 miles off New Mangalore, India.

The following day thirty of the *Jag Shanti*'s forty-five man crew abandoned ship and were rescued by a Great Eastern Shipping vessel, for which Captain Trevor Keelor was later granted a Gallantry at Sea Award. The stricken ship was taken in tow by the tug *Salvanguard* to a position about 25 miles from New Mangalore, India, but foundered at anchor during a storm on 5 June 1994.

☙ Delta ☙

Delta: 1854, 645 tons, length 62.5m (205ft), beam 8.9m (29ft), one funnel, two masts, iron construction, two-cylinder beam-geared engine powering a single screw at 9 knots. Built by Barclay, Curle & Co. for Samuel Cunard and launched in 1854. The *Delta*'s service was on the Halifax–New York–Bermuda route, but she was transferred to new owners in 1875. On 13 September 1899 the *Delta* was wrecked at St Mary's Bay, Newfoundland. This is an area that was prone to shipwrecks, many of which were salvaged by divers using dynamite in the 1960s. To date the wreck of the *Delta* has not knowingly been rediscovered.

✒ *Demerara* ✒

Demerara: 1872, 1,904 tons, length 93.7m (308ft), beam 10.4m (34ft), one funnel, three masts, iron construction, two-cylinder inverted compound engines powering a single screw at 10.5 knots. Built for the British & North American Royal Mail Steam Packet Co. by J. & G. Thomson & Co., Glasgow, and launched in 1872, with accommodation for forty-six first-class passengers.

A new service was started in 1872 from Glasgow to the West Indies for the *Trinidad* (1,900 tons) and *Demerara*, but this was not successful so both ships were transferred to the Mediterranean route. In 1880 the *Demerara* became a cargo ship only, but was lost at sea after leaving Liverpool on 25 December 1887 en route to Gibraltar with the loss of all crew. The total disappearance of the ship was a complete mystery. Although there was known to be bad weather in the Bay of Biscay during the voyage, it was nothing that the *Demerara* had not handled safely before. A detailed inspection of the ship the previous year had found it to be in excellent condition. A Board of Trade inquiry into the loss questioned Thomas Boumphrey, general manager of Cunard:

Mr. Boumphrey further stated that she carried three officers, all with masters' certificates, and that her captain, Mr. William John Lutt, was in all respects a good and trustworthy man, of perfectly sober habits. He also stated that she carried a comfortable cargo, there being nothing of a dangerous character among it, as this would not have been allowed by the rules of the service. He also could form no idea as to the cause of her loss; but he thought it was not probable that she had been overwhelmed by the severity of the sea, but more probable that she had collided with some other ship.

✒ *Emeu* ✒

Emeu: 1854, 1,538 tons, length 81.7m (268ft), beam 11.2m (37ft), one funnel, three masts, iron construction, two geared beam engines powering a single screw at 10 knots. Built by Robert Napier & Sons, Glasgow, for the Australasian Pacific Mail Steam Packet Co. in August 1853, and bought by Cunard to support its own stretched services. This was because many ships in the Cunard fleet had been requisitioned by the Admiralty for war service.

Emeu was used for the Crimean War from 1854–56, and then sailed the Liverpool to New York service, and later from Le Havre to New York, but was stranded on the Nubian coast and later repaired in Bombay. *Emeu* was sold to the P&O Line in 1858 and sold again in 1873, converted to sail and renamed *Winchester*.

The ship was wrecked in the Macassar Strait on 14 July 1880 when on a voyage from Manila to Montréal with a cargo of sugar.

✒ *England* ✒

England: 1964, 8,221 tons, built in 1964 and used for sailings between Esbjerg and Harwich in 1966 and from Esbjerg to Newcastle in 1980 by the DFDS (Det forenede Dampskibs-Selskab – United Steamship Co.), a Danish company formed in Copenhagen in 1866. The main aim of the company was to be a feeder service for emigrants travelling to England and then picking up their emigrant ship. DFDS is still operating services today.

The *England* was purchased by Cunard in 1983 and spent the next two years on a British Government contract transporting construction workers between Cape Town and Port Stanley for the new Falkland Islands airport. After a period being laid up the ship was sold to a Greek concern, renamed *America XIII* and stationed in Jeddah as an accommodation ship for oil refinery workers. In 1987 the vessel was laid-up once more and renamed *Emma*, then *Europa*. After an aborted attempt to convert the ship to a luxury private yacht the vessel was eventually sold for demolition in 2001 and renamed *Europe*. On 3 April 2001 *Europe* sailed from Suez under tow of the Russian salvage tug *Utyos* and encountered a severe storm. The tow was abandoned and the *Europe* foundered in deep water near Aden.

✒ *Franconia* (1) ✒

Franconia (1): 1911, 18,150 tons, length 182.9m (600ft), beam 21.7m (71ft), two funnels, two masts, steel construction, eight-cylinder quadruple-expansion engine powering twin screws at 17 knots, supplied by Wallsend Slipway Co. Ltd. Built by Swan, Hunter & Wigham Richardson, Newcastle, and launched on 23 July 1910, with accommodation for 300 first-class, 350 second-class and 2,200 third-class passengers.

The *Franconia* (1) was torpedoed by *UB-47* during the First World War and sank in deep water 200 miles from Malta. *(Bert Moody Collection)*

Both the *Franconia* and her sister ship the *Laconia* were built to replace the *Ivernia* and *Saxonia* on the Liverpool to Boston service and to cover for the *Lusitania* and *Mauretania* (1) if these were undergoing refit. They were also built to undertake winter cruising to the Mediterranean. The *Franconia's* maiden voyage was from Liverpool to New York, departing on 25 February 1911, calling at Queenstown and Boston. She immediately commenced her first Mediterranean cruise from March to April, calling at Gibraltar, Algiers, Naples and Alexandria before returning to Liverpool.

In February 1915 *Franconia* was requisitioned by the Admiralty to become a troopship and was part of the Dardanelles campaign with the job of transporting wounded soldiers from Gallipoli to Alexandria for treatment.

It was on 4 October 1916 that the *Franconia*, under the command of Captain Miller, was torpedoed by *UB-47* (Commander Wolfgang Steinbauer) 195 miles east by south of Malta, while en route for Salonika, Greece, at position 35°56'N, 18°30'E. Although a troopship, at the time she was not carrying any on the voyage. There were 302 survivors, who were rescued by the hospital ship *Dover Castle* (Union-Castle Line), but there was a loss of twelve crew members. The ship sank in water nearly 4km (2.5 miles) deep. *UB-47* was the same U-boat that later sank the *Ivernia* on 1 January 1917.

Ivernia (1)

Ivernia (1): 1900, 13,800 tons, length 177.4m (582ft), beam 19.8m (65ft), one funnel, four masts, steel construction, eight-cylinder quadruple-expansion engines powering twin screws at 15 knots, supplied by Wallsend Slipway Co. Ltd. Built by Swan & Hunter, Newcastle, and launched on 21 September 1899. She had passenger accommodation for 164 first-class, 200 second-class and 1,600 third-class passengers.

The ships being built at this time by Cunard were part of a new build programme to replace outdated vessels with new ones, complete with plentiful cargo and passenger space and accommodation on the Liverpool to Boston service. The *Saxonia* (1) was also constructed at this time. However, it was not the Liverpool to Boston route that the *Ivernia* sailed on her maiden voyage, but the Liverpool to New York on 14 April 1900. This was because the Admiralty required ships for trooping to the Boer War and *Ivernia* was to take over the service routes of the requisitioned Cunard ships for war service.

By the middle of 1900 *Ivernia* was sailing on her Liverpool to Boston route. Apart from having a serious accident in May 1911 when she was entering Queenstown Harbour in thick fog, where she was holed after hitting a rock, the rest of her career was unblemished. It was shortly after her repairs that *Ivernia* was transferred to the Mediterranean service carrying Italian and Hungarian emigrants from Trieste and Fiume to New York.

From 1915 in the First World War, *Ivernia* became a troop transporter and on 28 December 1916 set sail from Marseilles under the escort of HMS *Rifleman*.

In May 1911 the *Ivernia* (1) ran aground off Queenstown but after being refloated and repaired the ship returned to service the following October. *(Ian Lawler)*

On 1 January 1917 she was attacked by *UB-47* (Commander Wolfgang Steinbauer) 58 miles from Cape Matapan, Greece, and sank in position 35.30'N, 22.53'E with the loss of thirty-six crew and eighty-four troops. The charted position of the wreck places it in water 180m (590ft) deep.

Java

Java: 1865, 2,696 tons, length 102.7m (337ft), beam 13.1m (43ft), one funnel, three masts, two inverted engines powering a single screw at 12 knots. Built by J. & G. Thomson, Glasgow, and launched on 24 June 1865. Accommodation was for 300 first-class and 800 third-class passengers.

The *Java* sailed on her maiden voyage from Liverpool to New York on 21 October 1865 and spent over a decade on the transatlantic route until being sold to G. Palmer, Hampshire, in 1877. After having new compound engines fitted the ship was briefly chartered to various companies, until being sold to the Red Star Line the following year and renamed *Zeeland*. In 1889 the ship was bought by a French company and renamed *Electrique*. Three years later it was purchased by John Herron, Liverpool, who converted the vessel to sail with the new name of *Lord Spencer*.

On 9 April 1895 the *Lord Spencer* sailed from San Francisco bound for Queenstown with a cargo of wheat. Three months later on 13 July the iron-hulled sailing ship *Prince Oscar* collided with an unidentified sailing ship in the South Atlantic, widely believed to be the *Lord Spencer*. Both vessels sank within minutes. The unidentified vessel was lost with all hands, and six lives were lost from the *Prince Oscar*, whose sixteen survivors were found a few days later and landed at New York.

⌖ *Jura* ⌖

Jura: 1854, 2,241 tons, length 95.7m (314ft), beam 11m (36ft), one funnel, three masts, iron construction, two geared beam engines powering a single screw at 11 knots, and built in 1854 by J. & G. Thomson, Glasgow.

At first *Jura* was used as a Crimean War transport ship and did not start commercial service until 1856. Then in March 1857 the ship was chartered to the European & Australian Co. for the Southampton to Alexandria route. Later the ship made transatlantic crossings from Liverpool to New York, calling at Cork. From 1861 the *Jura* started sailing the Liverpool to Montréal route for the Allan Line, who subsequently purchased the vessel. On 3 November 1864 the vessel was shipwrecked at Crosby Point, near Liverpool. The wreck was broken up into sections and removed by February 1865. However, part of the boiler still remains and can be seen on the Crosby foreshore at very low tide.

⌖ *Karnak* ⌖

Karnak: 1853, 1,127 tons, length 6.4m (210ft), beam 9.3m (30ft), one funnel, three masts, iron construction, one-cylinder beam geared engine powering a single screw at 9 knots. Built by William Denny and launched on 22 September 1853. Accommodation was for 40 first-class and 100 second-class passengers.

The *Karnak* first sailed on the Mediterranean route, but later transferred to the New York–Nassau–Havana mail service. In 1854 the ship was chartered by the British Government for transport duties in the Crimean War. On 14 April 1862 the *Karnak* was stranded at Nassau, Bahamas. A few months later the ship was sold at auction, refloated and sailed to New York. The vessel underwent several further changes in ownership and was renamed *Saint Louis* in 1865.

On 7 December 1872 the *Saint Louis* sailed from New Orleans for New York but sprung a leak the following day. At 2 a.m. on 9 December Captain Whitehead ordered everyone to the lifeboats and the ship went down soon after. All hands were picked up the next day by the *Record* and landed at Key West.

⌖ *Laconia* (1) ⌖

Laconia (1): 1912, 18,099 tons, length 182.9m (600ft), beam 21.7m (71.3ft), two funnels, two masts, steel construction, eight-cylinder quadruple-expansion powering twin screws at a service speed of 17 knots, supplied by Wallsend Slipway Co. Ltd. Built in 1911 by Swan, Hunter & Wigham Richardson, Wallsend-on-Tyne, and launched on 27 July 1911. On 12 December 1911 Cunard took over the ship from the builders and she began her service on 20 January 1912, with passenger accommodation for 300 first-class, 350 second-class and 2,200 third-class passengers.

R. M. S. "Laconia" (Cunard Line).

The *Laconia* (1) was torpedoed in the First World War. The wreck was found in deep water in 2009 by the salvage company Odyssey Marine Exploration. (*Bert Moody Collection*)

When the First World War started in 1914 *Laconia* was converted into an AMC and was based at Simonstown in the South Atlantic, from which she patrolled the South Atlantic and Indian Ocean until April 1915. She was then used as a headquarters ship for the operations to capture Tanga and the colony of German East Africa, and after four months was sent back to patrolling the South Atlantic. In September 1916 *Laconia* was decommissioned and returned to Cunard.

On 25 February 1917 the *Laconia* was torpedoed by the German *U-50* (Commander Gerhard Berger) 160 miles north-west by west of Fastnet 52°00'N, 13°40'W, on the return voyage from New York to Liverpool under the command of Captain Irvine. The vessel sank with the loss of six crew and six passengers, two of them being American citizens.

U-50 had been busy on 25 April 1917 because she also sunk two other British ships before the *Laconia*. The first was the steamer *Aries* (3,071 tons), sunk 190 miles north-west by west of Fastnet (51°55'N, 14°30'W) while en route from Melilla to Glasgow with a cargo of iron ore. There were no casualties, but the master was taken prisoner. Then *U-50* attacked and sunk the steamer *Huntsman* (7,460 tons) 180 miles north-west by west of Fastnet (52°04'N, 12°02'W) while en route from Liverpool to Calcutta carrying general cargo, and then it was the *Laconia* at 160 miles NW by W of Fastnet. So in a distance of 30 miles *U-50* had sunk three vessels. The probable fate of *U-50* was that she was sunk by a mine off Terschelling, one of the West Frisian Islands, around 31 August 1917 with the loss all forty-four crew.

When the *Laconia* left New York on 17 February 1917 bound for England the influential *Chicago Tribune* writer Floyd Gibbons was one of the passengers. It was his account that started the change in American opinion of the war in Europe, and helped prompt their subsequent declaration of war against Germany shortly after.

The wreck of the *Laconia* was found in March 2009, 160 miles off the coast of Ireland by Odyssey Marine Exploration from Tampa, Florida. When it was announced that the wreck of the *Laconia* was located and claimed by Odyssey it was opposed by Britain, who 'claims it is the legitimate owner of the wrecks because, under a wartime insurance scheme, it paid the owners of the vessels when they sank, in effect making the remains the property of the taxpayer'.

Odyssey Marine Exploration, an American treasure-hunting company, claimed ownership of the wreck due its valuable cargo of bullion. They have now been appointed 'custodian' of the wreck and its contents, which includes 852 bars of silver and 132 boxes of silver coins with an estimated worth of £3 million.

⚓ *Laconia* (2) ⚓

Laconia (2): 1922, 19,680 tons, length 183.3m (601ft), beam 22.5m (74ft), one funnel, two masts, steel construction, steam turbine direct-acting engines powering twin screws at 16 knots. Built by Swan, Hunter & Wigham Richardson, Wallsend-on-Tyne, and launched on 9 April 1921, with accommodation for 350 first-class, 350 second-class and 1,500 third-class passengers.

The maiden voyage departed from Southampton on 25 May 1922 for New York, calling at Queenstown (Cobh). After sailing from Liverpool to New York in June 1922 she transferred to sailing from Hamburg to New York, calling at Southampton and Cherbourg for four voyages, and in January 1923 she undertook the first world cruise, returning to the Liverpool to New York service. In 1928 the *Laconia* was refitted for cabin-, tourist- and third-class passengers, but in 1934 she was involved in a collision in thick fog with the freighter *Pan Royal* off the coast of the United States. Both vessels were seriously damaged, but able to continue under their own steam. The *Laconia* returned to New York for repairs and in 1935 was back in service. She was converted to an AMC in 1939 and joined the British 3rd Battle Group in Halifax, later becoming a troopship in 1941.

The *Laconia* was en route from Suez to Canada when she was hit by two torpedoes fired by *U-156* (Commander Werner Hartenstein) at 10.07 p.m. on 12 September 1942, and sank just over an hour later. At the time the *Laconia* was unescorted, but of the 2,741 on board, the ship's master, Captain Rudolf Sharp, 97 crew members, 133 passengers, 33 Polish guards and 1,394 Italian prisoners were lost. There were 1,083 survivors.

When the captain of *U-156* realised who the passengers were he ordered immediate rescue operations, and raised the Red Cross flag to indicate that they had survivors from the sinking boat on board. However, a US Army B-24 Liberator bomber from its base on Ascension Island arrived and flew over *U-156*, which was surfaced with its deck crowded with survivors. The bomber pilot radioed its base for orders and was told to attack the U-boat. *U-156* was forced to submerge and leave the survivors in the water, and it was left to the Vichy French warships to arrive eventually and rescue them.

This incident led to what became known as the 'Laconia Order' by Admiral Dönitz, where U-boat captains were ordered that from then on they were not to rescue survivors from torpedoed ships.

The wreck lies in the Atlantic Ocean at a depth of over 4km (2.5 miles).

Laconia (2) suffered the same fate as her predecessor when the ship was torpedoed by *U-156* in the Second World War. *(Bert Moody Collection)*

🖎 *Laurentic* 🖎

Laurentic: 1927, 18,724 tons, length 176.2m (578ft), beam 22m (75ft), two funnels, two masts, steel construction, eight-cylinder triple-expansion engines combined with steam turbines powering triple screws at 16 knots. Built for White Star Line by Harland & Wolff, Belfast, and launched on 16 June 1927. There was accommodation for 594 cabin-class, 406 tourist-class and 500 third-class passengers.

The *Laurentic* made her maiden voyage from Liverpool to New York on 12 November 1927, and had the distinction of being the last triple-expansion, coal-fired major Atlantic liner. In April 1928 *Laurentic* started to sail on the Liverpool to Québec and Montréal route and became part of the newly formed Cunard White Star Line in 1934, continuing on the same route. In 1935 she collided with the *Napier Star* of the Blue Star Line in the Irish Sea, when six crew members were killed. Despite undergoing repairs, the ship faced an uncertain future and was laid up until September 1936 when she transported troops to Palestine. She was then laid up in Falmouth until the start of the Second World War.

In September 1939 *Laurentic* was required for the war effort and became an AMC, HMS *Laurentic* (F 51). On 3 November 1940 HMS *Laurentic*, commanded by Captain Eric Vivian RN, was torpedoed by *U-99* (Commander Otto Kretschmer) while going to the assistance of a ship already torpedoed by *U-99*, but was herself hit in the engine room. Later a second torpedo hit the ship but did not explode, although the third torpedo went straight through the hole made by the first torpedo. This became a very difficult time for all the ships rescuing men in the water, and they found themselves being attacked by *U-99*. In the early hours of the morning *U-99* again fired a torpedo at a range of 250m from HMS *Laurentic*, hitting her in the stern and causing stored depth charges to explode. This was the end for the ship and she sank by the stern with a loss of forty-nine seamen. There were 368 survivors, including the captain.

Prior to the merger with Cunard, White Star had owned another ship called *Laurentic*, which was completed in 1909. The earlier *Laurentic* is a popular dive off the north coast of Ireland but the wreck of the 1927 vessel has yet to be found.

🖎 *Lebanon* 🖎

Lebanon: 1855, 1,383 tons, length 77m (253ft), beam 9.2m (31ft) one funnel, three masts, iron construction, single screw, two-cylindered geared oscillating engine and speed 10 knots. Built by J. & G. Thomson, Govan, and launched 22 November 1854 as *Aerolith* for Robert Miles Sloman, Hamburg. The ship was acquired by Cunard Line prior to completion and renamed *Lebanon*. The maiden voyage sailed from Liverpool to Constantinople in February 1855 and the *Lebanon*'s first sailing from Liverpool to New York was made in July the same year.

The *Lebanon* was chartered by the British Government in 1857 as an Indian Mutiny troopship.

In May 1859 *Lebanon* was sold to the Spanish Government, converted to a troopship and renamed *General Álava*.

On 12 November 1863 the *General Álava* was on a voyage from Cádiz to Havana with 805 troops and ammunition when a fire broke out in the coal bunkers. The vessel put into Santa Cruz de La Palma, Tenerife, but in an attempt to flood the bunkers the ship was sunk. All the troops were safely landed by HMS *Speedwell*.

In October 1980 the wreck of the *General Álava* was positively identified off the beach at Bajamar in a depth of 10m (33ft) by a local diver and a few small artefacts were preserved in the Naval Museum. In the 1990s the wreck site was entirely buried as a result of construction work in the city of Santa Cruz de La Palma.

🖎 *Lotharingia* 🖎

Lotharingia: 1923, 1,256 tons, length 61m (200ft), beam 11.6m (38ft), one funnel, one mast, steel construction, two three-cylinder triple expansion engines powering twin screws at 12 knots. Built by William Hamilton & Co., Glasgow and launched on 8 March 1923. *Lotharingia* was a specially built passenger tender with a capacity for 750 people.

In 1933 *Lotharingia* was sold to La Société Cherbourgeoise de Remorquage et de Sauvetage, Cherbourg, France and renamed *Alexis De Tocqueville*. In 1939 the ship was requisitioned by the French Navy (pendant X 26) and employed as a minelayer.

In June 1940 the ship was scuttled at Brest but refloated by the Germans, who re-commissioned the ship as *Pelikan* (FB 20) for use as an anti-aircraft battery. On 25 August 1944 the vessel was sunk a second time during an Allied air raid. After the war the wreck was raised for scrap.

🖎 *Lycia* (1) 🖎

Lycia (1): 1896, 2,715 tons, length 93.9m (308ft), beam 13.2m (43.3ft), one funnel, two masts, steel construction, three-cylinder triple-expansion engines powering a single screw at 10 knots. Built by Sir Raylton Dixon & Co., Middlesbrough, as the *Oceano* for the Plate Steamship Co. Ltd (Gellatly, Hankey & Co.) and launched as a cargo ship on 28 July 1896.

The *Oceano* was acquired by Cunard for their Mediterranean cargo service in 1909 and renamed *Lycia*. She continued on this service, but while on her voyage from Genoa and Bougie carrying general cargo to Liverpool, calling at Swansea, *Lycia* met her fate. The *Lycia*, under the command of Captain T.A. Chesters, was torpedoed and sunk on 11 February 1917 by *UC-65*

(Commander Otto Steinbrinck) 20 miles north-east by north off South Bishop lighthouse at position 52°12'N, 05°27'W. Her crew took to the lifeboats and were quickly picked up by two minesweepers and the *Ireland Moor*, then landed safely at Holyhead.

An eyewitness account was given of the attack in Captain Sir Edgar T. Britten's *A Million Ocean Miles* (1936):

> It was at 8.30 a.m. on February 11th, 1917, and about twenty miles nor'west of South Bishop's Light, that the submarine was sighted, and by the time Captain Chesters had picked her up on the starboard beam his vessel had already been hit by a shot from the U-boat. The *Lycia*'s course was at once altered so as to bring the submarine astern, and Captain Chesters himself opened fire, at about 3000 yards range. His gun, which was of Russian make and very light in calibre, was one of the first type supplied by the Admiralty to merchant vessels, at a time when there was a great shortage of ordnance owing to the needs of the Army and Navy. This gun misfired several times during the fight, and soon the Third Officer, Third Engineer and Steersman were badly wounded by the accurate shooting of the submarine. In the unequal duel the *Lycia*'s funnel, starboard boats, forward cabins, chart-room, officers' and engineers' quarters were soon wrecked and in flames. At last, being unable to steer the ship under the continuous force and accuracy of the enemy's shells, Captain Chesters was forced reluctantly to abandon his vessel. Issuing orders to cease fire and stop the engines, as soon as the ship had sufficiently lost way, the crew were safely embarked in the port boat, with the exception of the Captain, Chief Officer, Third Engineer, the Gunner, and one of the boys, who succeeded in scrambling into the starboard boat which was dragging alongside.
>
> When the lifeboats cleared the ship the submarine ceased firing, submerged and reappeared alongside Captain Chesters' boat. The submarine commander then ordered Captain Chesters to board the U-boat, which he did, and he was at once asked why he had fired his gun without flying his ensign. Captain Chesters explained that this had not been possible as before he could fire his gun he had to remove the flagstaff aft. The German accepted this explanation and Captain Chesters, who had been treated with every courtesy, was allowed to return to the lifeboat. The submarine then ordered the lifeboat alongside again, and placing three German sailors in the boat, together with eight bombs, they rowed back to the *Lycia*, and there the Germans hung the bombs on each side of the rigging besides in the engine-room. The ship's papers, the breech block of her gun, her telescope and three live shells were lowered into the boat, after which the bomb safety-pins were removed, and the bombs placed below the water line. The U-boat sailors were then rowed back to the submarine, and before they were safely aboard the bombs began to explode. Shortly afterwards the *Lycia* sank, stern first, and the submarine went in chase of another vessel that appeared on the horizon. The *Lycia*'s lifeboats were picked up that same evening by two mine-sweepers, and the S.S. *Ireland Moor*, the crew being treated with the utmost hospitality and safely landed at Holyhead. Their conduct had been worthy, to use Captain Chesters' own words in praise of his men, 'of all the best traditions of British seamen'.

Sources differ regarding the exact location of the wreck. Some believe that the *Lycia* lies 6 nautical miles off the Pembrokeshire coast in a depth of around 50m (164ft). If the wreck can be located then this would be well within diving range.

⚓ *Media* (2) ⚓

Media (2): 1963, 5,586 tons, length 127.7m (419ft), beam 18.3m (60ft) was a cargo ship powered by a seven-cylinder Sulzer diesel engine driving a single screw at 17 knots. Built by John Readhead & Sons Ltd, South Shields, and launched on 20 June 1963. The maiden voyage left Liverpool on 18 October 1963 for New York.

Media was sold in June 1971 to the Western Australian Coastal Shipping Commission, Fremantle and renamed *Beroona*, operating on the coastal route from Fremantle to Darwin.

In 1978 the vessel was sold to Seaforth Investment Trust Inc, Piraeus, Greece, and renamed *Palm Trader*.

On 13 October 1983, while on a voyage to Bombay with a cargo of beans the *Palm Trader* caught fire at Bandar Abbas, Iran, causing serious damage to the engine room and accommodation area. The vessel was later declared a constructive total loss and laid up off Bandar Abbas. It was reported in July 1987 that the vessel had capsized at Larak Island, south of Bandar Abbas.

⚓ *Melita* ⚓

Melita: 1853, 1,060 tons, length 71m (233ft), beam 8.8m (29ft), one funnel, two masts, iron construction, two geared oscillating engines provided by MacNab & Clark, Greenock, powering a single screw at 9 knots. Built by Alexander Denny, Dumbarton, and launched in 1853 for the Cunard Mediterranean service.

The *Melita* commenced the Liverpool to Montréal service calling at Québec when she was chartered by the Allan Line in June 1860. Her first transatlantic voyage for Cunard was from Liverpool to New York in September 1860. However, in 1861 the *Melita* was taken by William Denny in part payment for the building of the *Sidon*, and then she was sold on to S. & S. Isaac in 1862 for the Liverpool to Philadelphia route.

It was on 5 September 1868 that she was destroyed by fire while at sea on a voyage from Boston to Liverpool. All her passengers and crew were safely rescued by the sailing ships *Jacob A. Stamler* and *Monequash*.

⤝ *Nantes* ⤜

Nantes: 1873, 1,473 tons, 72.62m (238.3ft), beam 9.81m (32.2ft), one funnel, three masts, iron construction, two-cylindered compound inverted direct-action engines powering a single screw at 10 knots. Built by Blackwood & Gordon, Port Glasgow, and launched in 1873. She had accommodation for 8 first-class and 386 third-class passengers.

The *Nantes* and her sister ship *Brest* were both built for the Liverpool to the French Channel ports service, acting as an emigrant feeder ship to connect with the transatlantic mail steamers.

The *Nantes* was lost on 6 November 1888 when she sank after colliding with the sailing ship *Theodore Ruger* 36 miles south-east of the Lizard while sailing from Liverpool to Le Havre. Three of the crew were fortunate to jump on the sailing ship, but the rest of the crew stayed on board. However, suddenly the next morning she sank without warning, dragging the crew down with her, with only one surviving.

Queen Elizabeth was sold and renamed *Seawise University*. During conversion work in 1971 several fires broke out simultaneously in different parts of the ship. (*John A. Hudson*)

⌦ *Niagara* ⌫

Niagara: 1848, 1,824 tons, length 76.5m (251ft), beam 11.6m (38ft), one funnel, three masts, wood construction, two side-lever engines by Robert Napier, Glasgow, powering two paddlewheels at 10 knots. Built by Robert Steele & Co., Glasgow, and fitted with accommodation for 140 first-class passengers.

To meet the requirements of the mail contract and also to build vessels that could be used for war service, Cunard built the *America*, *Niagara*, *Europa* and *Canada*. The *Niagara* was launched on 28 July 1847 and left Liverpool on her maiden voyage to Halifax and Boston the following year. In 1854 the *Niagara* was requisitioned for Crimean War transport. In 1886 she was sailing from Liverpool to Le Havre, but was then sold and had her engines removed. On 6 June 1875 the *Niagara* was wrecked near South Stack, Anglesey, in shallow water. According to the UK Hydrographic Office the bell has been recovered.

⌦ *Queen Elizabeth* ⌫

Queen Elizabeth: 1940, 83,673 tons, length 314.24m (1,031ft), beam 35.96m (118ft); built by John Brown & Co., Clydebank. Her accommodation was for 823 first-class, 662 cabin-class, 798 tourist-class passengers and 1,318 officers and crew. For her maiden voyage she sailed secretly to New York on 3 March 1940. *Queen Elizabeth* was used as a troopship during the war and her first commercial voyage was not until 16 October 1946, when she sailed from Southampton to New York.

Later, due to the gradual drop in passenger numbers through increased use of aircraft for a speedier means of travel, a decision was made to undertake cruises from New York to the Bahamas. In 1965 the *Queen Elizabeth* had air conditioning installed, was fully redecorated and had an outdoor swimming pool added, which would appeal to the passengers on cruises. This work was finally completed in the spring of 1966, but a seamen's strike in 1966 caused a serious drain on Cunard's financial resources, and it was in 1967 that Cunard announced that the *Queen Mary* was to be withdrawn from service, followed by *Queen Elizabeth* in the autumn of 1968.

The *Queen Elizabeth* made her final Atlantic crossing on 5 November 1968, later being bought by some Philadelphia businessmen, sailed to Port Everglades and opened to the public in February 1969. This was not to be a success due to losing money and the local authorities deemed it a fire hazard. In 1970 she was bought by C.Y. Tung of Hong Kong and it was planned for her to become a floating university. She was renamed *Seawise University*, then sailed for Hong Kong in February 1971. However, due to machinery problems she did not arrive until July, when work began to refit her for her new role.

On 9 January 1972 *Seawise University* was anchored in Hong Kong's Victoria Harbour when a series of fires broke out simultaneously shortly before noon. Normally around 2,000 workmen would have been aboard but most had gone

Some of the 2,000 workmen who were on board can be seen gathering on the bow of the doomed *Queen Elizabeth* as the flames take hold. Fortunately there were no fatalities. *(John A. Hudson)*

The *Queen Elizabeth* is settled on the seabed and the steel hull plating, at least an inch thick in parts, has buckled in due to the intense heat. *(John A. Hudson)*

ashore for lunch, leaving about 600 people and a further group of 60 visitors attending a special luncheon on board. Fortunately the majority of people escaped without injury, despite the rapidly spreading fire. Fireboats eventually arrived but failed to contain the blaze, and by the next day the ship had burned out and keeled over. The vast amount of water that was sprayed on the *Seawise University* by the fireboats had caused the vessel to capsize.

John Hudson was on a small boat cruising the harbour when he witnessed the event first-hand: 'What caught our attention from a distance across the water was smoke coming from the ship's portholes; not just one or two portholes but from almost all of them from stem to stern on one side.' Over a three-hour period he saw how the fire 'turned into a raging inferno in the upper superstructure generating huge volumes of smoke'.

It was generally believed that the fire was an act of arson due to the fact that at least three fires broke out simultaneously. This was confirmed by the court of inquiry in Hong Kong, which concluded that the fires were 'deliberate acts on the part of a person or persons unknown'. It was a very sad end to what was once Cunard's flagship and one of their greatest liners.

⫷ *Russia* ⫸

Russia: 1867, 2,960 tons, length 109.1m (350ft), beam 13.1m (42ft), one funnel, three masts, iron construction, two inverted engines powering a single screw at 13 knots. Built by J. & G. Thomson, Glasgow, and launched on 20 March 1867, with accommodation for 235 first-class passengers. *Russia* had the distinction of being the last Cunard ship to have a clipper bow. On 15 June 1867 *Russia* made her maiden voyage from Liverpool to New York and became very popular with her passengers because of her luxury and her speed.

The *Russia* was sold in 1879 to the Red Star Line and was lengthened to 132m (433ft), adding an extra mast, fitting a compound engine and increasing the passenger accommodation to 120 first-class and 1,500 third-class passengers. This raised the tonnage to 4,752 tons. She was renamed *Waesland*, sailing on the Antwerp to New York from 1880–95, until chartered by the American Line on the Philadelphia to Liverpool route. On 5 March 1902 she was involved in a collision with the *Harmonides* in thick fog, off the coast of Anglesey while under command of Captain Apfield. The *Harmonides* was badly damaged but was eventually able to make port in Liverpool. However, the *Waesland* was in a very bad way so the passengers and crew took to the lifeboats, the ship sinking a few hours later. Sadly, two of the *Waesland* passengers died during the impact: a man from Texas and a young girl called Emmett.

There has been a report of an unidentified wreck being found in the Irish Sea at a depth of 50m (164ft). It is some distance from the last reported *Waesland* position but since it has been referred to by divers as 'the pointy bow' wreck it is a strong candidate for being the final resting place of the *Russia*.

Russia was sold by Cunard in 1879 and subsequently renamed *Waesland*. The ship was lost after a collision in fog somewhere off the coast of Anglesey in 1902. *(Courtesy of Paul D. Edwards)*

Samaria (3)

Samaria (3): 1965, 5,837 tons, length 133m (436ft), beam 18.2m (60ft), powered by a six-cylinder, two-stroke cycle single-acting engine with a speed of 17.5 knots. Built by Cammell Laird, Birkenhead and launched on 22 October 1964. Registered in Liverpool under the ownership of North Western Line (Mersey) Ltd and initially chartered to Cunard Line until their acquisition of the vessel in December 1969. However the *Samaria* was sold just a few weeks later to Charente Steamship Co who renamed the ship *Scholar*.

In January 1979 the ship was laid up at Manchester and sold to Brora Shipping Corporation, Liberia, renamed *Steel Trader* and placed under the Greek flag.

At the start of the Iran–Iraq War the *Steel Trader* was trapped in the Shatt-el-Arab waterway at Khorramshahr along with ninety other vessels on 23 September 1980. This was an important waterway for Iraq since it was the only outlet to the Persian Gulf. The shipping lanes were seriously affected by the constant Iran attacks, and on 5 October 1980 *Steel Trader* was seriously damaged by gunfire and abandoned by her crew. The ship was later declared a war loss and is thought to have been towed by Iraqi forces to Basra, where the ship was reportedly lying in a sunken condition until at least 1993.

Siberia

Siberia: 1867, 2,498 tons, length 97.5m (320ft), beam 11.9m (39.2ft), one funnel, two masts, iron construction, two inverted engines powering a single screw at 12 knots. Built by J. & G. Thomson, Glasgow, originally as *Sumatra*, but the name was changed so as not to conflict with another vessel of the same name prior to launch on 2 July 1867. There was accommodation for 100 first-class and 800 third-class passengers.

The *Siberia* made her maiden voyage on 24 September 1867 from Liverpool to New York, calling at Queenstown. By February 1871 *Siberia* started calling at Boston as well as New York, but this changed shortly after to just Boston. It was on 5 September 1878 that the *Siberia* made her last voyage on this route, before being sold to the shipbuilders J. & G. Thomson in 1880 as a contribution towards the cost of building the *Catalonia* (1881, 4,841 tons). The *Siberia* was then sold again in 1880 to the Marquis de Campo, Cádiz, who renamed her *Manila*. The vessel was wrecked on 11 May 1882 at San Juan, Puerto Rico.

Sidon

Sidon: 1861, 1,782 tons, length 84m (275.6ft), beam 11m (36.2ft), one funnel, two masts, iron construction, geared oscillating engines powering a single screw at 10 knots. Built by William Denny & Bros, Dumbarton, for the Cunard Mediterranean service and launched on 20 August 1861. There was accommodation for 69 first-class and 550 third-class passengers.

The *Sidon* made her first transatlantic crossing on 19 May 1863 from Liverpool to New York, calling at Queenstown, and continued this service until 1867. In 1873 the ship was fitted with compound engines by J. Jack, Rollo & Co., Liverpool.

The *Sidon* was carrying fourteen passengers and a crew of forty-three when on the very stormy night of 27 October 1885 she was wrecked on rocks in heavy seas near Malpica, Spain, with a loss of five crew and four passengers. The master was Captain Peter Whealan, who had been with Cunard for seventeen years, but this was his first voyage in command of *Sidon*. He was absolved of any blame by the Board of Trade inquiry in December 1885, which concluded:

The Court, having carefully inquired into the circumstances attending the above-mentioned shipping casualty, finds, for the reasons stated in the annex hereto, that the said ship was stranded owing to a strong set of current which carried her far to the eastward of their assumed position, and to the neglect of the 2nd and 3rd officers in not duly reporting lights and change of weather to the master, for which default the Court suspended their certificates for four months.

Slavonia

Slavonia: 1903, 8,831 tons (1904 10,606 tons), length 155.4m (510ft), beam 18.1m (59ft), one funnel, two masts, steel construction, six-cylinder triple-expansion engines (Wallsend Slipway Co. Ltd) powering twin screws at 13 knots. Built by

Slavonia ran aground near the Azores in 1909 and was the first ship to use the new international SOS distress call. *(Rich Turnwald Collection)*

Sir J. Laing & Sons, Sunderland, for the British India Line as the *Yamuna* and launched on 15 November 1902. The accommodation was for 71 first-class, 74 second-class and 1,954 third-class passengers.

The *Yamuna* was built for the London and Calcutta service, sometimes calling at Malayan and Burmese ports. However, the ship proved unsuitable for this service because there was a need to serve some ports for which it was too big. The vessel was then purchased by Cunard for the Italy to New York service carrying Hungarian emigrants. The *Slavonia* made her first voyage for Cunard from Sunderland to Trieste on 17 March 1904, and continued on the Fiume to New York route, calling at Trieste and Palermo, and this was a very successful service in carrying many emigrants to America.

On the 3 June 1909 *Slavonia* left New York for Trieste, but ran into fog on 9 June near the Azores, running aground on 10 June, 2 miles west of Flores Island. After sending an SOS the Hamburg–America *Batavia* and North German Lloyd *Prinzess Irene* arrived to help rescue the passengers and crew. This was the first time the new international distress signal was used for an emergency at sea.

Detailed information was reported in the *New York Times* on 12 June 1909 about the grounding of the *Slavonia*, under the headline: 'Slavonia on Reef Passengers Saved':

The big Cunarder *Slavonia*, built in 1903 and one of the crack passenger carriers running out of this port to the Mediterranean, is ashore on the reef off the south-west end of Flores island, one of the Azores group. Her 410 passengers have been rescued and taken on board passing steamships, and there is of every probability that the steamer will be a total loss. These facts were contained in a short cable message received yesterday from Captain F. von Letten Peterson, commanding the North German Lloyd liner *Prinzess Irene* bound from here to Naples and Genoa.

The message from Capt. Peterson announcing the wreck of the *Slavonia* was received at the local office of the line at three o'clock yesterday afternoon. It was dated from Velas, in the Azores, June 11. The message reads: 'Have taken on board the *Prinzess Irene* the 110 cabin passengers from the *Slavonia* which was stranded at the south-west of Flores Island. The 300 steerage passengers of the vessel had been taken on board the *Batavia* of the Hamburg Line. The *Slavonia* will probably be a total loss.'

It appeared that the *Slavonia* was following the course of the *Batavia*, which had left the same day, and as both ships maintained the same speed they would have been still fairly close together when they arrived in the vicinity of the Azores. It was the *Batavia* that was the first ship to respond to the *Slavonia*'s signals for help. At about the same time the *Prinzess Irene*, which sailed from New York on 5 June, also bound for the Mediterranean on the same course, arrived to assist in the rescue of passengers.

The newspaper suggested a theory regarding *Slavonia*'s close proximity to the dangerous reef:

Steamers heading a direct course from New York to Gibraltar on the Great Circle track should pass sixty miles north of the north end of Flores. In some cases however, it is customary for skippers to run in close to Flores Island, the most western of the Azores group in order to correct their chronometers.

It was alleged in at least one contemporary account that Captain Arthur Dunning steamed closer in to the islands in order to comply with requests from passengers to get a better view. Regardless of whether this was true, the Board of Trade inquiry found him to blame for poor judgement. Captain Dunning had been with Cunard since 1894 but resigned a few months after the incident took place.

A considerable quantity of the *Slavonia*'s cargo was salvaged at the time of loss but the vessel itself could not be saved. The remains of the *Slavonia* lie in a depth range of 5–15m (16–49ft) off the coast of Lajedo, Flores Island. In 2015 the Government of the Azores created the 'Underwater Archaeological Park of Slavonia' in order to preserve the archaeological heritage of the site and protect the diverse marine life in the vicinity.

Stromboli

Stromboli: 1856, 724 tons, length 60.5m (198ft), beam 8.8m (29ft), one funnel, three masts, iron construction, one-cylinder vertical direct-acting engine powering a single screw at 9 knots. Built by J. & G. Thomson, Glasgow, as the *James Brown* and launched on 25 March 1856.

The *Stromboli* was built for the Liverpool–Mediterranean service, but also served on the Liverpool–Le Havre feeder service. The ship was later fitted out with new boilers and a compound engine. The *Stromboli* was wrecked on Maeneere Rock, off the Lizard Point, on 20 March 1878 while en route from Liverpool to Le Havre. The ship was carrying a general cargo of 600 bags of flour, sugar, wines and silk. All the thirty-two crew and sixteen passengers were saved. The ship broke in two during the night and sank in just a few feet of water. The *Stromboli* was salvaged soon after the loss and all that now remains is a boiler and some hull plating.

Transylvania

Transylvania: 1914, 14,315 tons, length 167.1m (548ft), beam 20.29m (66.6ft), two funnels, two masts, steel construction, engines were two steam turbine, single reduction powering twin screws at 16 knots. Built by Scott's Shipbuilding & Engineering Co. Ltd, Greenock, and launched on 23 May 1914. There was accommodation for 263 first-class, 260 second-class, and 1,858 third-class passengers.

When the *Transylvania* was built she was planned for a joint operation by Cunard and the Anchor Line sailing the Mediterranean to New York route. Her maiden voyage was on 7 November 1914 from Liverpool to New York, and in February 1915 the ship was taken over by the Anchor Line. In May 1915 *Transylvania* was requisitioned by the Admiralty for war service as a trooper and fitted out to carry 3,600 troops.

Trooping continued from 1915 until 4 May 1917, when the *Transylvania* was en route from Marseille to Alexandra and was torpedoed by *U-63* (Commander Otto Schultze) and sank 2.5 miles south of Cape Vado in the Gulf of Genoa with a loss of 414 men. In October 2011 the wreck of the Transylvania was located by Guido Gay of the Italian company Gaymarine 3 miles off Bergeggi island in a depth of 630m (2,067ft) using the ROV *Plutopalla*. The ship was found to be in two parts about 100m (328ft) apart with the upper structures collapsed.

Trinidad

Trinidad: 1872, 1,900 tons, length 93.7m (307ft), beam 10.4m (34ft), one funnel, two masts, iron construction, two-cylinder inverted compound engines powering a single screw at 10.5 knots. Built by J. & G. Thomson & Co., Glasgow, for a new service from Glasgow to the West Indies and was launched in 1872. There was accommodation for forty-six first-class passengers.

The *Trinidad* inaugurated the new Cunard service from Glasgow to the West Indies in 1873, along with the *Demerara*, and from 1880 served on various Cunard cargo routes. She was sold in 1898 to German owners, but sank in the China Sea in August of the same year.

Tripoli

Tripoli: 1863, 2,061 tons, length 89.2m (292ft), beam 11.6m (38ft), one funnel, two masts, iron construction, two geared oscillating engines powering a single screw at 11 knots. Built by J. & G. Thomson, Glasgow, and launched for the Cunard Mediterranean service on 15 August 1863. There was accommodation for 50 first-class and 650 third-class passengers.

The *Tripoli* made her first transatlantic crossing for Cunard on 19 August 1865 from Liverpool to New York, calling at Halifax. Many of her voyages from 1886–1872 were on the Liverpool to New York route, calling at Queenstown, and also including calls at Boston.

The *Tripoli* met her fate when she was wrecked on Tuskar Rocks, St George's Channel, on 17 May 1872. The vessel was travelling at full speed in thick fog with 2 pilots and 328 passengers on board, but there was no loss of life. The wreck is broken up in shallow water of a few metres' depth.

Ultonia

Ultonia: 1898, 8,056 tons, length 152.4m (500ft), beam 17.5m (57ft), one funnel, four masts, steel construction, six-cylinder triple-expansion engines powering twin screws at 13 knots. Built by Swan & Hunter Ltd, Newcastle, for Cunard, and launched on 4 June 1898.

The *Ultonia* was built as a cargo ship with no passenger accommodation and sailed at first to Boston, but by 1899 the vessel was converted to carry 675 third-class passengers and began its passenger service from Liverpool to Boston on 9 February 1899. In 1904 further conversion took place when more passenger accommodation was added to service the emigrant trade. This included 120 second-class passengers and 2,100 third-class passengers, increasing the gross tonnage to 10,402 tons.

The *Ultonia* embarked on her maiden voyage for her increased passenger trade from Trieste to New York, calling at Fiume and Naples, on 29 April 1904. This service continued with a brief change to Southampton to Montréal before returning to the Mediterranean to New York service.

In the First World War *Ultonia* became a troopship for a time before returning to Cunard, when on 27 June 1917 she was sunk by *U-53* (Commander Hans Rose) with the loss of one life, 190 miles south-west of Fastnet, while sailing from New York to London carrying general cargo. The wreck is likely to be in deep water in excess of 3km (1.8 miles) down.

The cargo ship *Ultonia* was built in 1898 and sunk by *U-53* in 1917. *(Bert Moody Collection)*

Valacia (1)

Valacia (1): 1910, 6,526 tons, length 140.2m (460ft), beam 17.4m (57ft), steam triple-expansion engine powering a single screw at 11 knots. Built by Russell & Co., Port Glasgow, for Andrew Weir & Co. as *Luceric* and launched in 1910. The ship was sold to Cunard in 1916 when she was renamed *Valacia*, serving as a cargo ship on the London–Glasgow–New York route.

On 30 March 1917 the *Valacia*, under the command of Captain J.F. Simpson, left London for New York. At 5.30 p.m. the next evening, while in the English Channel and 5 miles from the Eddystone lighthouse, the *Valacia* was attacked by a torpedo fired from *U-59* (Commander Wilhelm von Fircks), which struck the port side filling her No.6 hold, engine room and stoke hold with water. When several British destroyers arrived on the scene attempts were made by one of them to take the disabled *Valacia* in tow. However, she proved too heavy and tugs were sent for to tow her to Plymouth Harbour, which was successfully undertaken. The *Valacia* was then put into dock for repairs. She returned to service and was eventually bought by a Genoa shipping company and renamed *Ernani* in 1931.

In 1940 she was seized by the Germans at Las Palmas and thought to have been renamed *Sleipner II*. However, on 29 June 1941 *U-103* (Commander Viktor Schütze) torpedoed the *Ernani* 450 miles west of Las Palmas while en route from Las Palmas to Bordeaux. She sank within twenty-one minutes by the stern. After the sinking, the U-boat commander questioned the survivors who said that they were from the Italian steamer *Ernani* en route from Las Palmas to Horta. The U-boat commander did not believe this because the course of the ship did not match the route the survivors had described.

In the event *U-103* had sunk the *Ernani* by mistake. She was a blockade runner that had been disguised as the Dutch steam merchant *Enggano*. It was not the fault of the U-boat commander because he had not been informed that one of their own ships was in the area. The wreck is in deep water.

Valeria

Valeria: 1913, 5,865 tons, length 129m (423ft), beam 17m (56ft), three-cylinder triple-expansion engines powering a single screw at 12 knots. Built as a cargo ship by Russell & Co., Port Glasgow, for the Barrie Line and named *Den of Airlie* (3). She was launched in 1913 and purchased by Cunard from Charles Barrie, Dundee, in 1916 and renamed *Valeria*.

In June 1917 the *Valeria* was attacked by a submarine and an account of this encounter was given by Sir Edgar T. Britten in his book *A Million Ocean Miles*:

The *Valeria*, under the command of Captain W. Stewart, when homeward bound from New York on June 20 1917, came in contact with a submarine under the most surprising circumstances. About 3 o'clock in the afternoon both Captain Stewart, who was on the port side of the bridge, and the Second Officer who was on the starboard side, felt the ship quiver as if she had struck some obstacle. The Captain immediately crossed over to the starboard side, and was amazed to see an enemy submarine just under the waves, almost touching his ship. The working of her motors was distinctly audible.

For a moment the *Valeria*'s gun crew were completely taken aback at this unexpected appearance of a U-boat at such close quarters. Captain Stewart, however, gave prompt orders to fire, and the gunners depressing the gun as far as possible fired a shell at literally point blank range.

Immediately a volume of vapour shot up from the U-boat, together with fountain-like spouts of water. A second shot was fired into her, but missed, but a third shot struck fair and square on her conning tower, and she sank like a stone. It is believed that the *Valeria*, when she first came in contact with the submarine, probably broke her periscope. Captain Stewart's first impulse was to stop in order to pick up any survivors from the U-boat, but in view of the fact that German submarines were at that time hunting in couples he thought it wiser to continue his voyage, and brought his ship safely back to Liverpool.

For this successful action, both Captain Stewart and his crew received special awards from the Admiralty, the Cunard Company, and other Associations.

It is thought that the U-boat was *U-99*, which only took part in one patrol from 7 June 1917 to 7 July 1917, when she was sunk with the loss of all hands by a British submarine HMS *J-2*, commanded by Lt V.M. Cooper RN in the North Sea.

The *Valeria* was not so fortunate on 21 March 1918, when she was sailing inbound from New York and caught fire. The vessel was beached on Taylor's Bank at the mouth of the River Mersey. There were no casualties, but the ship was a total loss.

Vandalia (1)

Vandalia (1): 1912, 7,333 tons, length 129.5m (425ft), beam 17.1m (56ft), triple-expansion engine, single screw. Built for Nitrate Producers' Steamship Co. Ltd (Lawther, Latta & Co.), London, as *Anglo-Californian* by Short Bros Ltd, Sunderland, and launched in 1912.

The *Anglo-Californian* was damaged by gunfire from *U-39* (Commander Walter Forstmann) on 4 July 1915 on a voyage from Québec to Avonmouth. The vessel made for Queenstown and in 1916 was bought by Cunard and renamed *Vandalia*.

On 9 June 1918 the *Vandalia*, commanded by Captain J.A. Wolfe, was torpedoed and sunk in St George's Channel by *U-96* (Commander Heinrich Jess) 18 miles west-north-west of The Smalls, at position 51°44'N, 06°10'W, while in convoy on a voyage from Liverpool to Montréal in ballast and escorted by six American destroyers. The vessel sank within two hours with no loss of life. A hydrographic survey by HMS *Bulldog* in 1980 reported a wreck in the given position at a general depth of 106m (348ft).

Vardulia (1)

Vardulia (1): 1917, 5,691 tons, length 128.9m (423ft), beam 17m (56ft), steel construction, steam triple-expansion engine powering a single screw at 11 knots. Built by Russell & Co., Port Glasgow, and launched as the *Verdun* in 1917. Purchased by Cunard in 1919 and renamed *Vardulia* for the London to New York cargo service. She was sold to Donaldson Bros, Glasgow, in 1929 under the same name.

The ship was lost with Captain William Paterson and all hands on the North Atlantic on 19 October 1935 while en route to St John, New Brunswick. An SOS message was sent out at 6.48 a.m. GMT stating: '58°00N. 18°30W, steering S. 22 E. Wanting immediate assistance. Have taken dangerous list.' This was followed a few minutes later by a final message at 6.55 a.m.: 'Now abandoning ship.' The loss of the ship, which was known to be in sound condition with good officers and crew, was a complete mystery. The Board of Trade inquiry conjectured that the loss could have been caused by shifting coal or cargo, compounded by force-9 gales that were reported by other vessels in the area.

Vasconia (1)

Vasconia (1): 1918, 5,680 tons, length 129m (422ft), beam 17.1m (56ft), steel construction, single screw, service speed 12 knots. Built as the cargo vessel *Valverda* by Russell & Co., Port Glasgow, and launched in 1918 for Gow, Harrison & Co., London. Purchased by Cunard in 1919 and renamed *Vasconia*. The ship was sold to Japan in 1927 and renamed *Shiraha Maru*.

On 14 January 1943 the US submarine *Searaven* (*SS-196*), commanded by Lt Cdr H. Cassedy, attacked a Japanese convoy and sank *Shiraha Maru* in deep water north-west of Palau in the Pacific.

Vennonia

Vennonia: 1918, 5,225 tons, length 121.9m (400ft), beam 15.38m (52ft), triple-expansion steam engine powering a single screw at 11 knots. Built by Caledon Shipbuilding & Engineering Co., Dundee, for the British Government First World War shipping controller, managed by Ben Line and named *War Carp*. The vessel was launched in 1918.

She was sold to Cunard Line in 1919 and renamed *Vennonia* for the London to New York service, then sold to S. & J. Thompson and renamed *River Hudson* in 1924 for Mediterranean to New York service. She was sold once more to the

Vennonia was sold by Cunard in 1924 and owned by two further companies. The ship ended her days as *Zeffiro* for the Corrado Line when she was mined in 1941 near Tunisia. *(Bert Moody Collection)*

Corrado Line in 1931 and renamed *Zeffiro*. On 20 May 1941 she struck a mine and sank near Cape Bon, Tunisia. The depth of water in the reported position averages 100m (328ft).

Venusia

Venusia: 1918, 5,222 tons, length 121.9m (400ft), beam 15.8m (52ft), triple-expansion steam engine powering a single screw at 11 knots. Built by Harland & Wolff Ltd, Belfast, in 1918 for the British Government First World War shipping controller, managed by G. Heyn & Sons and named *War Snake*.

The vessel was sold to Cunard in 1919 and renamed *Venusia* for the London to New York cargo service. In 1923 she was sold to S. & J. Thompson and renamed *River Delaware* for the Mediterranean to New York service. The ship was again sold in 1931 to the Corrado Line and renamed *Rino-Corrado*.

The *Rino-Corrado* was sunk on 9 November 1941 by British naval gunfire in the Ionian Sea in very deep water at 37°08'N 18°09'E.

Verentia

Verentia: 1918, 5,185 tons, length 122.2m (401ft), beam 15.8m (52ft), triple-expansion steam engine powering a single screw at 11 knots. Built by Harland & Wolff Ltd, Belfast, as *War Lemur*, a cargo ship for the British Government First World

War shipping controller, managed by T. Dunlop & Son and launched in May 1918. In 1919 she was sold to Cunard and renamed *Verentia* for the London to New York service.

In 1926 *Verentia* was sold to Andrew Weir & Co. and renamed *Foreric*, and then again in 1927 when she was sold to Buenos Ayres Great Southern Railway Co., London, and renamed *Galvan*. The sales were to continue when the *Galvan* was acquired by Kaye, Son & Co. Ltd and in 1937 sold to Pedder and Mylchreest Ltd, London, to Nisshin Kaiun Shokai Ltd, Japan, and again resold to Chang Shu Chang, Tsingtao, China, and renamed *Pei Tai*. In 1938 the ship was sold for the final time to Kitagawa Sangyo Kaiun, Osaka and renamed *Hokutai Maru*.

The *Hokutai Maru* was operating as a Japanese Army cargo ship when she was attacked and bombed by TF 58 aircraft from a US aircraft carrier on 30 March 1944, off Babeithuap in the Palau Islands. The *Hokutai Maru* was hit along with submarine chaser *Ch-35*, net-layer *Shosei Maru* and tanker No.2 *Hishi Maru* at position 07°30'N, 134°30'E.

Veria

Veria: 1899, 3,229 tons, length 100.7m (330ft), beam 13.8m (45ft), one funnel, two masts, triple-expansion engine powering a single screw at 10.5 knots. Built for Cunard as a cargo ship with no passenger accommodation by Armstrong, Whitworth & Co. Ltd, Newcastle, and launched on 15 November 1898.

The *Veria* and her sister ship *Brescia* both sailed on the Cunard Mediterranean cargo routes. The *Veria* was captured on 7 December 1915 by *U-39* (Commander Walter Forstmann) 24 miles north-west by west of Alexandria (31°30'N, 29°28'E) while sailing from Patras to Alexandria in ballast. This was the result of a cunning trap set by the U-boat, whose commander had sunk the Greek vessel *L.G. Goulandris* on 6 December while en route from Alexandra to Hull. The next day the *Veria* found two lifeboats with crew from the *L.G. Goulandris* and stopped to pick them up. *U-39* had been waiting below the surface and immediately surfaced to attack the *Veria*.

Captain Thomson ordered his crew to man the lifeboats, but even while they were doing that the submarine continued firing her shells, destroying the chart house and the bridge, just as the boats were leaving the vessel's side. The submarine approached, demanding the ship's papers, but Captain Thomson had already destroyed all confidential documents, leaving just the ship's register for the German commander. The Germans then attached four bombs to the hull of *Veria* and scuttled the ship in 800m (2,625ft) of water. Captain Thomson and his crew made for Alexandria in the lifeboats and arrived the next morning. There was no loss of life, but the captain and chief engineer were taken prisoner.

Vinovia

Vinovia: 1906, 5,503 tons, length 127.5m (418ft), beam 161.6m (54ft), four-cylinder quadruple-expansion engines driving a single screw. A general cargo vessel built by Short Bros Ltd of Sunderland as the *Anglo-Bolivian* for Lawther, Latta & Co., London, in 1906. The ship was bought by Cunard in 1916 and renamed *Vinovia*.

On 19 December 1917 the *Vinovia* was sailing from New York to London with general cargo when she lost sight of the convoy she was in and was badly damaged by severe weather conditions. At 3.30 p.m. she was attacked, torpedoed and sunk by *U-105* (Commander Friedrich Strackerjan) 8 miles south of Wolf Rock at position 49°56'N, 05°33'W. Some crew were picked up by patrol vessels, but there was a loss of nine lives.

Captain Sir Edgar T. Britten, in his book *A Million Ocean Miles*, praises the actions of the Cunard captain when he writes:

High as was the standard set by and expected of my gallant comrades of the Cunard, there were few instances, during the war of greater coolness and bravery than that of the *Vinovia*'s skipper, Captain Stephen Gronow, when she was torpedoed in the English Channel on December 19th, 1917. She was then on her way to New York with a Chinese crew, and it was at half-past three in the afternoon that the torpedo struck her on the starboard side. As the *Vinovia* did not at first appear to be sinking, Captain Gronow ordered his engines full speed ahead, and made a gallant endeavour to reach the land.

At 4 p.m., half an hour later, a small tug came on the scene and made fast to the disabled vessel, after some of her Chinese crew had left the ship in one of the lifeboats. A patrol boat then arrived and came alongside, when the remainder of the crew jumped aboard her. For the next three hours Captain Gronow, the only man left in the sinking vessel, steered her by means of the hand gear. Three hours later, at seven in the evening, a drifter approached when the Chief Engineer returned on board to assist his Captain in making a rope fast between the two vessels, and then returned to the patrol boat.

It was now quite dark, but still alone on board Captain Gronow stuck to his forlorn hope, continued to steer her and attend to the ropes. By half-past seven, as he noticed that she appeared to be making no headway, he groped his way forward by means of the rails, and found the fo'c'sle deck submerged four feet beneath the water. He also discovered that the tug had slipped the wire, and had disappeared. Clawing his way back aft to the steering gear, he was struck by a falling piece of wreckage from aloft and knocked unconscious. He lay thus for some time, but on recovering he made his way to the bridge and donned a life-belt. There he remained until, at eight o'clock, five miles from land and in pitch darkness, the *Vinovia* literally sank, beneath his feet, and he was hurled into the sea. He succeeded, however, in supporting himself on some wreckage, to which as it happened the ship's bell was attached, and it was this little fact that in the end proved his salvation. Attracted by the ringing of the bell, a small patrol boat the next morning decided to investigate the wreckage, and there the brave Officer was found lying unconscious. Unfortunately, his gallant efforts proved unavailing, as the *Vinovia* with her valuable cargo was totally lost. Still, Captain Gronow had provided yet another illustrious example for his successors at sea, and happily survived to receive from the Cunard Directors a handsome, inscribed silver vase, together with a certificate, and a silver medal and monetary gift from Lloyds.

Captain Gronow had also been master of the *Ascania*, *Volodia*, *Saxonia*, *Valacia* and *Vardulia*, and an officer on the *Aquitania*.

The wreck of the *Vinovia* lies in a depth of 61m (200ft) and was heavily salvaged for her cargo of copper, brass and steel by Risdon Beazley in 1975. The remains of the ship are now heavily dispersed but the bow section stands as the highest point 5m (16ft) above the seabed.

Virgilia

Virgilia: 1918, 5,697 tons, length 128.9m (423ft), beam 17.1m (56ft), steam triple-expansion engine powering a single screw at 11 knots. Built by Russell & Co., Port Glasgow, as a cargo ship for Cunard Line in 1918 and named *Virgilia*.

In 1925 the ship was sold to James Chambers & Co., Liverpool, and renamed *Corby Castle*. She was sold again to Japan in 1928 and renamed *Tatsuha Maru*. On 17 February 1944 *Tatsuha Maru* was sailing in Convoy No. 3206 when she was bombed by US planes as part of Operation Hailstone. The ship sank 75 miles west of Chuuk in the Pacific at 7°46'N, 150°27'E.

Volodia

Volodia: 1913, 5,689 tons, length 129.1m (424ft), beam 17.1m (56ft), three-cylinder triple-expansion engine, speed 12 knots. Built in 1913 by Russell & Co., Port Glasgow, as *Den of Ogil* for the Barrie Shipping Co. Ltd, Dundee, and sold to Cunard in 1916, who renamed her *Volodia*.

On 21 August 1917 *Volodia*, under the command of Captain Wolfe, was torpedoed and sunk by *U-93* (Commander Helmut Gerlach) 285 miles of Ushant at position 46°30'N, 11°30'W, while on a voyage from Montréal to London.

There had been no warning and the torpedo hit the *Volodia* in the engine room, killing some of the crew. Three lifeboats were launched and Captain Wolfe, the second officer and surviving crew got away. The lifeboats were followed by *U-93* and the U-boat commander caught up with the second officer's lifeboat and asked for the captain. The second officer, covering for Captain Wolfe, told the submarine commander that he thought that the captain had gone down with the ship. After being taken on board and further questioned he was later released back to the lifeboat.

Captain Wolfe again took charge and set the course they would sail, but they ran into a gale and suffered extreme weather conditions. They survived and three days later were rescued by a destroyer 30 miles from the Lizard, after sailing 300 miles across the Atlantic. There was a loss of ten lives. The charted position of the loss puts the wreck in water 4.5km (2.8 miles) deep.

Appendix A

~ DIVING INFORMATION ~

THE REFERENCE INFORMATION contained in this section is intended for divers who are interested in diving the wrecks for themselves. No attempt has been made to classify the dives into any kind of experience level as this is too subjective, especially given the diversity of the wrecks, geographical location and diving conditions. Divers are therefore strongly encouraged to contact local dive operators and clubs for further advice. There are also specialised diver books and publications that cover many of the areas and wrecks, a selection of which can be found listed in the bibliography.

For the latest information on these wrecks, links to websites and details of any new discoveries please refer to the companion website, www.linerwrecks.com.

Alaunia

Location:	Sussex, England
Position:	50°41.086'N 000°27.186'E
Depth:	36m (118ft)
Tides:	Slack water only
Visibility:	Poor to average
Dive Boats:	www.dive125.co.uk, www.sussexshipwrecks.co.uk

Andania

Location:	Rathlin Island, Northern Ireland
Position:	55°18.917'N 005°58.583'W
Depth:	112m (367ft)
Tides:	Slack water only
Visibility:	Poor
Dive Boats:	Specialised technical dive

Ascania

Location:	Petites, Newfoundland
Position:	47°36.719'N 58°38.472'W
Depth:	15m (49ft)
Tides:	Any time, beware of strong swells
Visibility:	Average
Dive Boats:	www.oceanquestadventures.com

Aurania

Location:	Mull, Scotland
Position:	56°36.138'N 006°19.443'W
Depth:	26m (85ft)
Tides:	Slack water, beware of heavy swells
Visibility:	Average to good
Dive Boats:	www.lochalinedivecentre.co.uk, www.lochaline-boats.co.uk

Campania

Location:	Burntisland, Firth of Forth, Scotland
Position:	56°02.406'N 003°13.511'W
Depth:	30m (98ft)
Tides:	Slack water only, neaps preferred
Visibility:	Generally very poor (but best on a Wednesday)
Dive Boats:	Dive Bunker (www.divebunker.co.uk). All diving services inc. boats, gas (inc. nitrox) and equipment rental
Notes:	The wreck is a designated Historic Marine Protected Area (2011).

⇌ *Carinthia* ⇋

Location: North-west Ireland, 30m offshore
Position: 55°14.850'N 009°17.982'W
Depth: 117m (384ft)
Tides: Any
Visibility: Excellent
Dive Boats: www.rosguill.com

⇌ *Caronia (Caribia)* ⇋

Location: Apra Harbor, Guam
Position: Harbour entrance, off inside tip of Glass Breakwater
Depth: 5–50m (16–160ft)
Tides: None
Visibility: Excellent
Dive Boats: www.mdaguam.com, www.gtds.com, Blue Planet (Will Naden, hotshark@teleguam.net)
Notes: There is hardly anything left to see of the wreck (see text)

⇌ *Carpathia* ⇋

Location: Atlantic
Position: 49°30.030'N 010°43.040'W
Depth: 158m (518ft)
Notes: Specialised technical dive. The wreck is owned by RMS Titanic Inc.

⇌ *Curlew* ⇋

Location: Bermuda
Position: Outer north reef, just west of *Cristobal Colon*
Depth: 10m (33ft)
Tides: Any time
Visibility: Excellent
Dive Boats: www.trianglediving.com
Notes: The local dive boats seldom visit the *Curlew*

⇌ *Feltria* ⇋

Location: 8m south-east Mine Head, Southern Ireland
Position: 51°57.737'N 007°18.715'W
Depth: 66m (217ft)
Tides: Slack water
Visibility: Poor
Dive Boats: www.dungarvanbaycharterboats.com

⇌ *Flavia* ⇋

Location: North-west Ireland, 25 miles offshore
Position: 55°18.828'N 008°59.488'W
Depth: 108m (354ft)
Tides: Any
Visibility: Excellent
Dive Boats: www.rosguill.com

⇌ *Folia* ⇋

Location: Southern Ireland
Position: 51°52.879'N 007°40.630'W
Depth: 38m (125ft)
Tides: Slack water
Visibility: Average
Dive Boats: See *Feltria*

⇌ *Lancastria* ⇋

Location: St Nazaire, France
Position: 47°09.049'N 002°20.389'W
Depth: 26m (85ft)
Notes: The wreck of the *Lancastria* is a war grave and all diving is prohibited

⌦ *Lusitania* ⌫

Location:	Southern Ireland
Position:	51°24.745'N 008°32.869'W
Depth:	93m (305ft)
Tides:	Slack water only
Visibility:	Poor to average
Notes:	All diving requires permission from the wreck's owner and the Irish authorities

⌦ *Malta* ⌫

Location:	Cape Cornwall, England
Position:	50°08.158'N 005°42.202'W
Depth:	15m (49ft)
Tides:	Strong Atlantic swells
Visibility:	Good, but wreck obscured by kelp in summer months
Dive Boats:	Land's End Diving

⌦ *Oregon* ⌫

Location:	15 miles south-south-west of Moriches Inlet, Long Island, USA
Position:	40°30.823'N 072°50.406'W
Depth:	40m (131ft)
Tides:	Any time, but can experience strong currents
Visibility:	Variable
Dive Boats:	See the Long Island Divers Association (www.lidaonline.com)

⌦ *Scotia* ⌫

Location:	Guam
Position:	Just off outside tip of Glass Breakwater, Apra Harbor
Depth:	12m (39ft)
Tides:	Strong tides can run in the area
Visibility:	Excellent
Dive Boats:	See *Caronia*
Notes:	Wreck was covered in sand in 2011

⌦ *Thracia* ⌫

Location:	Quiberon, France
Position:	47°30.809'N 003°17.406'W
Depth:	30m (98ft)
Tides:	Not known
Visibility:	Good
Dive Boats:	Not known

Appendix B

～ MAPS ～

Diveable Cunard Line Shipwrecks Around the World

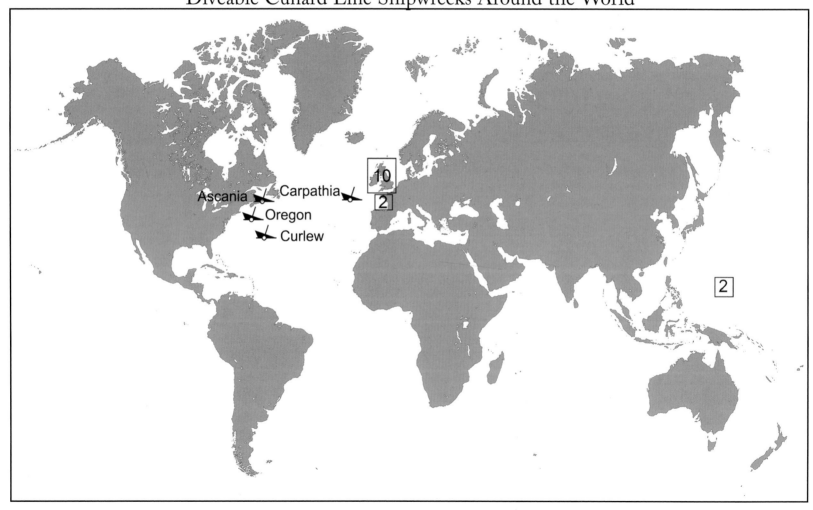

Cunard Shipwrecks of the British Isles

1. *Carinthia*
2. *Flavia*
3. *Andania*
4. *Lusitania*
5. *Folia*
6. *Feltria*
7. *Aurania* (2)
8. *Campania*
9. *Malta*
10. *Alaunia*

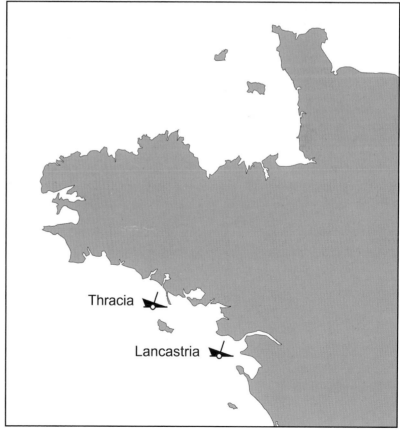

Cunard Shipwrecks of France

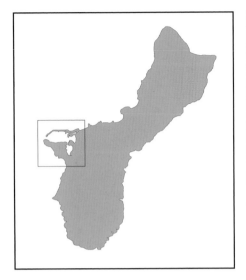

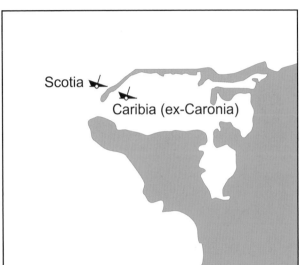

Cunard Shipwrecks of Guam

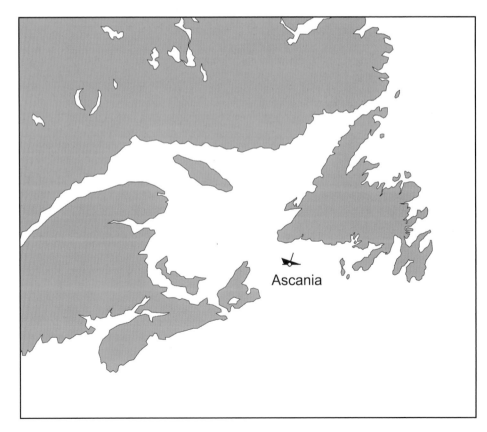

Cunard Shipwrecks of Newfoundland

Appendix C

~ CUNARD LINE FLEET ~

WHILE EVERY EFFORT has been made to ensure this list is as accurate as possible, it remains the subject of ongoing research. The authors welcome any corrections or additional information, especially on the remaining few vessels whose final fate is unknown.

The fleet list does not include the large number of ships that were managed by Cunard Line in the First and Second World Wars, or any vessels that were chartered by the company.

SHIP	BUILT	FATE	NOTE
Abyssinia	1870	Wrecked (Fire)	
Acadia	1840	Scrapped	
Africa	1850	Scrapped	
Alaunia (1)	1913	Mined (*UC-16*)	
Alaunia (2)	1925	Scrapped	
Alaunia (3)	1960	Scrapped	
Alaunia (4)	1973	Scrapped	
Albania (1)	1900	Scrapped	
Albania (2)	1920	Bombed	
Aleppo	1865	Scrapped	
Algeria	1870	Scrapped	
Alpha	1863	Wrecked	Halifax–Bermuda service
Alps	1852	Scrapped	

SHIP	BUILT	FATE	NOTE
Alsatia (1)	1923	Scrapped	
Alsatia (2)	1948	Scrapped	
Alsatia (3)	1972	Scrapped	
America	1848	Scrapped	
Andania (1)	1913	Torpedoed (*U-46*)	
Andania (2)	1922	Torpedoed (*U-A*)	
Andania (3)	1960	Scrapped	
Andania (4)	1972	Scrapped	
Andes	1852	Scrapped	
Andria (1)	1948	Wrecked (Fire)	
Andria (2)	1973	Scrapped	
Antonia	1922	Scrapped	
Aquitania	1914	Scrapped	
Arabia (1)	1852	Scrapped	
Arabia (2)	1852	Scrapped	
Arabia (3)	1947	Scrapped	
Ascania (1)	1911	Wrecked	
Ascania (2)	1925	Scrapped	
Asia (1)	1850	Wrecked (Fire)	
Asia (2)	1947	Scrapped	

SHIP	BUILT	FATE	NOTE
Assyria	1950	Scrapped	
Atlantic Causeway	1969	Scrapped	ACL
Atlantic Conveyor (1)	1970	Bombed	ACL
Atlantic Conveyor (2)	1985	In service	ACL
Atlantic Star	1967	Scrapped	ACL
Atlas	1860	Scrapped	
Aurania (1)	1883	Scrapped	
Aurania (2)	1917	Torpedoed (*UB-67*)	
Aurania (3)	1924	Scrapped	
Ausonia (1)	1909	Torpedoed (*U-62*)	
Ausonia (2)	1922	Scrapped	
Australasian	1857	Scrapped	
Bactria	1928	Wrecked	
Balbec	1853	Wrecked	
Bantria	1928	Scrapped	
Batavia	1870	Scrapped	
Berengaria	1913	Scrapped	
Beta	1873	Wrecked	Halifax–Bermuda service
Bosnia	1928	Torpedoed (*U-47*)	
Bothnia (1)	1874	Scrapped	
Bothnia (2)	1928	Wrecked/Scrapped	
Brescia (1)	1903	Scrapped	
Brescia (2)	1945	Scrapped	
Brest	1874	Wrecked	
Britannia	1840	Torpedoed/ Scrapped	
Britannic	1930	Scrapped	ex White Star
British Queen	1849	Scrapped	
Caledonia	1840	Scrapped	
Cambria	1845	Scrapped	
Campania	1893	Wrecked	
Canada	1848	Scrapped	
Caria	1900	Shelled (*U-35*)	
Carinthia (1)	1895	Wrecked	
Carinthia (2)	1925	Torpedoed (*U-46*)	
Carinthia (3)	1956	Scrapped	
Carinthia (4)	1973	Scrapped	
Carmania (1)	1905	Scrapped	
Carmania (3)	1972	Scrapped	
Caronia (1)	1905	Scrapped	
Caronia (2)	1948	Wrecked	
Caronia (3)	1973	Static	
Carpathia	1903	Torpedoed (*U-55*)	
Catalonia	1881	Scrapped	
Cephalonia	1882	Scuttled	
Cherbourg	1875	Scrapped	
China	1862	Lost	
Columbia	1840	Wrecked	
Corsica	1863	Wrecked	
Crown Dynasty	1993	In service	
Crown Jewel	1992	In service	
Crown Monarch	1990	In service	
Cuba	1864	Wrecked	
Cunard Adventurer	1971	Scrapped	
Cunard Ambassador	1972	Scrapped	
Cunard Calamanda	1973	Scrapped	Cunard-Brocklebank
Cunard Campaigner	1972	Wrecked	Cunard-Brocklebank
Cunard Caraval	1971	Scrapped	Cunard-Brocklebank
Cunard Carrier	1973	Scrapped	Cunard-Brocklebank

Cunard Carronade	1972	Scrapped	Cunard-Brocklebank
Cunard Cavalier	1973	Scrapped	Cunard-Brocklebank
Cunard Champion	1973	Scrapped	Cunard-Brocklebank
Cunard Chieftain	1973	Scrapped	Cunard-Brocklebank
Cunard Countess	1976	Scrapped	
Cunard Princess	1977	In Service	
Curlew	1853	Wrecked	Halifax–Bermuda service
Cypria	1898	Scrapped	
Damascus	1856	Scrapped	
Delta	1854	Wrecked	Halifax–Bermuda service
Demerara	1872	Wrecked	
Emeu	1854	Wrecked	
Emily	1827	Condemned	Halifax–Bermuda service
England	1964	Wrecked	
Etna	1855	Scrapped	
Etruria	1885	Scrapped	
Europa	1848	Scrapped	
Falcon	1848	Wrecked	Halifax–Bermuda service
Feltria	1891	Torpedoed (UC-48)	
Flavia	1902	Torpedoed (U-107)	
Folia	1907	Torpedoed (U-53)	
Franconia (1)	1911	Torpedoed (UB-47)	
Franconia (2)	1923	Scrapped	
Gallia	1879	Scrapped	
Georgic	1932	Scrapped	ex White Star
Hecla	1860	Scrapped	
Hibernia	1843	Scrapped	
Homeric	1922	Scrapped	ex White Star
Ivernia (1)	1900	Torpedoed (UB-47)	
Ivernia (2)	1955	Scrapped	
Ivernia (3)	1964	Scrapped	
Jackal	1853	Scrapped	
Java	1865	Lost	
Jura	1854	Wrecked	
Karnak	1853	Wrecked	
Kedar	1860	Scrapped	
Kestrel	1849	Wrecked	Halifax–Bermuda service
Laconia (1)	1912	Torpedoed (U-50)	
Laconia (2)	1922	Torpedoed (U-156)	
Lady Ogle	1827	Wrecked	Halifax–Bermuda service
Lancastria	1922	Bombed	
Laurentic	1927	Torpedoed (U-99)	ex White Star
Lebanon	1855	Wrecked (Fire)	
Levantine	1846	Unknown	Halifax–Bermuda service
Lotharingia	1923	Bombed	
Lucania	1893	Scrapped	
Lusitania	1907	Torpedoed (U-20)	
Lycia (1)	1896	Torpedoed (UC-65)	
Lycia (2)	1954	Scrapped	
Majestic	1914	Scrapped	ex White Star
Malta	1865	Wrecked	
Marathon	1860	Scrapped	

SHIP	BUILT	FATE	NOTE
Margaret (1)	1824	Wrecked	Halifax–Bermuda service
Margaret (2)	1835	Scrapped	
Mauretania (1)	1907	Scrapped	
Mauretania (2)	1939	Scrapped	
Media (1)	1947	Scrapped	
Media (2)	1963	Wrecked	
Melita	1853	Wrecked (Fire)	
Merlin	1850	Wrecked	Halifax–Bermuda service
Morocco	1861	Scrapped	
Nantes	1873	Wrecked	
Niagara	1848	Wrecked	
Olympic	1911	Scrapped	ex White Star
Olympus	1860	Scrapped	
Oregon	1883	Wrecked	
Ospray	1848	Wrecked	Halifax–Bermuda service
Otter	1880	Scrapped	
Palestine	1858	Scrapped	
Palmyra	1866	Scrapped	
Pannonia	1904	Scrapped	
Parthia (1)	1870	Scrapped	
Parthia (2)	1948	Scrapped	
Parthia (3)	1963	Scrapped	
Pavia (1)	1897	Scrapped	
Pavia (2)	1953	Scrapped	
Pavonia	1882	Scrapped	
Persia	1856	Scrapped	
Phrygia (1)	1900	Scrapped	

SHIP	BUILT	FATE	NOTE
Phrygia (2)	1955	Scrapped	
Queen Elizabeth (1)	1940	Wrecked (Fire)	
Queen Elizabeth (2)	2010	In service	
Queen Elizabeth 2	1969	Static	
Queen Mary	1936	Static	
Queen Mary 2	2003	In service	
Queen Victoria	2007	In service	
Royal George	1907	Scrapped	
Royal Viking Sun	1988	In service	
Russia	1867	Wrecked	
Sagafjord	1965	Scrapped	
Samaria (1)	1868	Scrapped	
Samaria (2)	1922	Scrapped	
Samaria (3)	1965	Wrecked	
Samaria (4)	1973	Scrapped	
Saragossa	1874	Scrapped	
Satellite (1)	1848	Scrapped	
Satellite (2)	1896	Scrapped	
Saxonia (1)	1900	Scrapped	
Saxonia (2)	1954	Scrapped	
Saxonia (3)	1964	Scrapped	
Saxonia (4)	1972	Scrapped	
Scotia (1)	1862	Wrecked	
Scotia (2)	1966	Scrapped	
Scythia (1)	1875	Scrapped	
Scythia (2)	1921	Scrapped	
Scythia (3)	1964	Scrapped	
Scythia (4)	1972	Scrapped	
Sea Goddess I	1984	In service	
Sea Goddess II	1985	In service	

SHIP	BUILT	FATE	NOTE
Servia (1)	1881	Scrapped	
Servia (2)	1972	Scrapped	
Siberia	1867	Wrecked	
Sidon	1861	Wrecked	
Skirmisher	1884	Scrapped	
Slavonia	1903	Wrecked	
Stromboli	1856	Wrecked	
Susan	1823	Wrecked	Halifax–Bermuda service
Sylvania (1)	1895	Scrapped	
Sylvania (2)	1957	Scrapped	
Tarifa	1865	Scrapped	
Taurus	1853	Hulked	
Teneriffe	1853	Unknown	
Thracia	1898	Torpedoed (*UC-69*)	
Transylvania	1914	Torpedoed (*U-63*)	
Trinidad	1872	Wrecked	
Tripoli	1863	Wrecked	
Tyria	1897	Scrapped	
Ultonia	1898	Torpedoed (*U-53*)	
Umbria	1884	Scrapped	

SHIP	BUILT	FATE	NOTE
Unicorn	1836	Unknown	
Valacia (1)	1910	Torpedoed (*U-103*)	
Valacia (2)	1943	Scrapped	
Valeria	1913	Wrecked (Fire)	
Vandalia (1)	1912	Torpedoed (*U-96*)	
Vandalia (2)	1943	Scrapped	
Vardulia (1)	1917	Wrecked	
Vardulia (2)	1944	Scrapped	
Vasconia (1)	1918	Torpedoed (*SS-196*)	
Vasconia (2)	1944	Scrapped	
Vellavia	1918	Scrapped	
Velocity	1812	Unknown	Halifax–Bermuda service
Vennonia	1918	Mined	
Venusia	1918	Bombed	
Verbania	1918	Scrapped	
Verentia	1918	Bombed	
Veria	1899	Torpeoded (*U-39*)	
Vindelia	1918	Scrapped	
Vinovia	1906	Torpedoed (*U-105*)	
Virgilia	1918	Bombed	
Vitellia	1918	Scrapped	
Volodia	1913	Torpedoed (*U-93*)	

GLOSSARY

AMC Armed Merchant Cruiser. A merchant ship equipped with guns, usually for defensive purposes.

Argon A gas used for inflating a *drysuit*, chosen for its thermal insulation properties.

Barquentine A sailing vessel with three or more masts, with a square-rigged foremast and fore-and-aft-rigged main, mizzen and any other masts.

BCD Buoyancy Compensation Device.

Bends See *decompression sickness*.

Bottom time The duration of elapsed time from leaving the surface to begin a dive until starting the ascent.

Dead reckoning A form of navigation based on course and speed.

Decompression The time spent by a diver in the water during the ascent phase to allow any absorbed gas to be safely removed from the body.

Decompression sickness A sometimes fatal disorder characterised by joint pain and paralysis, breathing difficulty and collapse that is caused by the release of gas bubbles, usually nitrogen, from the tissues following a too-rapid ascent from depth.

Dive profile A graphical representation of the depth-time relationship during a dive.

Dive tables A tabulation of decompression schedules, based on time and maximum depth.

DPV Diver Propulsion Vehicle. A form of small underwater battery-powered scooter.

Droit A legal title, claim or due. Used by the British Receiver of Wreck along with a unique reference number for a declared artefact recovered from a shipwreck.

Drysuit A suit worn by a diver that does not allow any water entry. Worn with thermal undergarments.

GPS Global Positioning System. An accurate means of electronic navigation based on satellite positions.

Hard-hat diver Common term for a commercial diver, due to the use of a metal diving helmet.

Hawser A heavy line used for towing and mooring.

Hedgehog mine A form of anti-submarine depth charge launched automatically from a device known as a hedgehog.

Hypoxic A breathing gas containing less than 21 per cent oxygen.

Jon line A rope used by a diver to attach to a *shot line* for more comfortable *decompression* in a strong current.

Lift bag An inflatable bag that is filled with gas (typically air) at depth to raise heavy items.

Magnetometer A form of underwater metal detector towed behind a boat to detect wrecks.

Manifold A pipe for connecting one or more dive cylinders together, typically with an isolation valve in the centre.

Mixed gas A breathing mixture other than air consisting of one or more inert gasses, typically including helium.

Nitrogen narcosis Narcotic effect induced by breathing air under pressure. Most notable at depths beyond 30m (98ft).

Nitrox Oxygen-enriched air. Used to reduce decompression time on shallow dives or increase safety factor.

Normoxic A breathing gas having the same proportion of oxygen as air, i.e. 21 per cent.

One-atmosphere diving suit One-person metal suit with articulated arms and legs, designed to operate at one atmosphere, regardless of external pressure.

Open-circuit A form of *scuba* diving equipment where gas is breathed from a cylinder and expired into the water.

Oxygen toxicity Oxygen breathed at partial pressures higher than about 1.6 atmospheres that occurs at a depth of 66m (218ft) for a diver breathing air becomes toxic and can lead to sudden convulsions and unconsciousness.

Partial pressure The part of the total pressure of gases in a mixture contributed by a particular gas; since air is composed of about 21 per cent oxygen, at sea level (one atmosphere of pressure), the partial pressure of oxygen is 0.21, while at a depth of 10m (33ft) (two atmospheres) the partial pressure of oxygen is 0.42.

Pelagic A free-swimming or floating organism of the open sea, often meaning shark.

Port The left side of a boat or vessel.

Rebreather A form of *scuba* equipment where expired gas is recycled, removing excess carbon dioxide and replenishing oxygen.

Reef A ridge or chain of rocks, sand or coral occurring in or causing a shallow area.

ROV Remote Operated Vehicle. An unmanned robot used for underwater survey work. Typically used for exploring wrecks that are too deep for scuba divers.

Rigid Inflatable Boat A small open boat with a fibreglass hull and inflatable rubber sides.

Screw Propeller.

Scrubber Part of a *rebreather*, responsible for removing carbon dioxide from expired gas.

Scuba Breathing equipment used by recreational divers, originally from 'SCUBA', Self Contained Underwater Breathing Apparatus.

Shot line A rope from the surface down to the wreck, often attached to an anchor or heavy lead weight. Often 'tied-in' to the wreck by the first diver on the wreck.

Side-scan sonar A type of sonar system to create underwater images of the seabed, useful in locating shipwrecks.

Slack water A period when the tidal flow is at the weakest, normally occurring when the tide turns.

Starboard The right side of a boat or vessel.

Steering quadrant The mechanism by which the rudder post is actually pivoted. Called a quadrant because it is close to one-quarter of a circle in shape.

Stem The forward part of a vessel (bow), an upright into which the side timbers or plates are joined.

SMB Surface Marker Buoy. An inflatable bag deployed by a diver from depth to mark his location to the surface cover. Essential when performing drift *decompression*. Often different colour SMBs (e.g. yellow) can be used to signal an emergency such as 'out of gas'.

Swell A large and fairly smooth wave.

Thermocline A thin but distinct layer in in the sea in which temperature changes more rapidly with depth than it does in the layers above or below.

Trimix A gas mixture made of helium, oxygen and nitrogen. Used for deep dives to offset *nitrogen narcosis*.

Visibility (aka 'viz') An estimate of the horizontal distance that a diver can see underwater.

— BIBLIOGRAPHY —

Books

Baird, Bob. *Shipwrecks of the Forth and Tay*, Whittles, 2009

Ballard, Robert D. *Exploring the Lusitania*, Weidenfield & Nicholson, 1995

———. *Lusitania*, Haynes Publishing, 2009

———. *The Discovery of the Titanic*, Madison Press Books, 1989

Berg, Daniel & Denise. *Bermuda Shipwrecks*, ebook

Berg, Daniel. *Wreck Valley III*, ebook

Bond, Geoffrey. *Lancastria*, Oldbourne Books Co. Ltd, 1959

Bonsor, N.R.P. *North Atlantic Seaway*, T. Stephenson & Sons Ltd, 1955

Bourke, Edward, J. *Shipwrecks on the Irish Coast 1105–1993*, E.J. Bourke, 1994

Braynard, Frank O. & Miller, William H. *Fifty Famous Liners 1*, Patrick Stephens Ltd, 1982

———. *Fifty Famous Liners 2*, Patrick Stephens Ltd, 1985

———. *Fifty Famous Liners 3*, Patrick Stephens Ltd, 1987

Britten, Sir Edgar T. *A Million Ocean Miles*, Hutchinson & Co. Ltd, 1936

Butler, Daniel Allen. *The Age of Cunard*, Lighthouse Press, 2003

———. *The Other Side of the Night*, Casemate, 2009

Carter, Clive. *Cornish Shipwrecks: The North Coast*, Pan, 1978

Cartwright, Roger & Harvey, Clive. *Cruise Britannia*, The History Press, 2004

Clark, Mike. *Wrecks and Reefs of Southeast Scotland* , Whittles Publishing, 2010

Cornford, Leslie Cope. *The Merchant Seaman in War*, Doran, 1918

Cowan, Rex. *Castaway & Wrecked*, Duckworth, 1978

Dawson, Philip. *The Liner*, Retrospective & Renaissance, Conway, 2007

De Kerbrech, Richard P. and Williams, David. *Cunard White Star Liners of the 1930s*, Conway, 1988

Delgado, James P. *Adventures of a Sea Hunter*, Douglas & McIntyre, 2004

Dodman, Frank E. *Ships of the Cunard Line*, Adlard Coles, 1955

Duff, Douglas V. *May the Winds Blow*, Hollis & Carter, 1948

———. *On Swallowing the Anchor*, John Long, 1954

Dwyer, Terry. *The Wreck Hunter*, Pottersfield Press, 2004

Eaton, John P. & Haas, Charles A. *Falling Star-Misadventures of White Star Line Ships*, W.W. Norton & Co., 1990

Fenby, Jonathan. *The Sinking of the Lancastria*, Simon & Schuster, 2005

Fox, Stephen. *Transatlantic: Samuel Cunard, Isambard Brunel and the Great Atlantic Liners*, Perennial, 2004

Galbraith, Russell. *Destiny's Daughter: The Tragedy of RMS Queen Elizabeth*, Mainstream, 1988

Gentile, Gary. *Shipwrecks of New York*, Gary Gentile Productions, 1996

———. *The Lusitania Controversies Book 1*, Gary Gentile Productions, 1998

———. *The Lusitania Controversies Book 2*, Gary Gentile Productions, 1999

Grattidge, Harry, Capt. *Captain of the Queens*, E.P. Dutton, New York, 1956

Great Britain, Admiralty. *British Vessels Lost at Sea 1914–18*, Stephens, 1977

———. *British Vessels Lost at Sea 1939–45*, Stephens, 1976

Grohman, Adam. *Claimed by the Sea*, UHRS, 2008

Grossmith, Frederick. *The Sinking of the Laconia*, Paul Watkins, Stamford, 1994

Hanauer, Eric. *Diving Micronesia*, Aqua Quest, 2001

Haws, Duncan. *Merchant Fleets in Profile 2*, P. Stephens, 1979

Hocking, C. *Dictionary of Disasters at Sea During the Age of Steam*, Naval & Military Press Ltd, 1994

Humble, Richard. *Aircraft Carriers The Illustrated History*, Winchmore Publishing Services Ltd, 1982

Hutchings, David F. *QE2*, Kingfisher Railway Production, 1988

———. *RMS Queen Mary*, Kingfisher Railway Production, 1986

Hurd, Archibald. *A Merchant Fleet at War*, Cassell and Co. Ltd, 1920

Isherwood, John H. *Cunard Portraits*, World Ship Society, 1990

Johnson, Howard. *The Cunard Story*, Whittet Books, 1987

Kassmann, Herb. *Oregon Greyhound of the Atlantic*, Old Walrus Productions, 1993

Keatts, Henry C. *Guide to Shipwreck Diving: New York and New Jersey*, Pisces Books, 1992

Kludas, Arnold. *Great Passenger Ships of the World*, Patrick Stephens Ltd, 1976

Langley, John G. *Steam Lion: A Biography of Samuel Cunard*, Nimbus, 2006

Larn, Richard & Bridget. *Shipwreck Index of British Isles Vol 1*, Lloyd's Register, 1995

————. *Shipwreck Index of Ireland*, Lloyd's Register, 2002

Larn, Richard & Carter, Clive. *Cornish Shipwrecks of the South Coast*, Pan, 1969

Macdonald, Rod. *Dive England's Greatest Wrecks*, Mainstream Publishing, 2003

McCart, Neil. *Atlantic Liners of the Cunard Line*, Patrick Stephens Ltd, 1990

McDonald, Kendall. *Dive Sussex*, Underwater World Publications, 1999

Miller, William H. & Brian Hawley, *RMS Caronia: Cunard's Green Goddess*, The History Press, 2011

Miller, William H. *The First Great Ocean Liners*, Dover Publications, 1984

————. *Under the Red Ensign*, The History Press, 2008

————. *Doomed Ships, Great Ocean Liner Disasters*, Dover, 2006

Moir, Peter & Ian Crawford. *Argyll Shipwrecks*, Moir-Crawford, 1994

Newall, Peter. *Cunard Line a Fleet History*, Ships in Focus Publications, 2012

O'Sullivan, Patrick. *The Lusitania: Unravelling the Mysteries*, Sheridan House, 1998

Ridley, Gordon. *Dive Scotland Volume III: The Northern Isles and East Coast*, Underwater World Publications, 1995

Rosenthal, David. *Scuba Diving the Wrecks and Shores of Long Island, NY*, The Wharves Project, 2008

Roussel, Mike. *Southampton Maritime City Ocean Liners to Cruise Ships*, Derby Books, 2010

————. *The Story of Southampton Docks*, Breedon Books, 2009

Sauder, Eric. *RMS Lusitania: The Ship & Her Record*, The History Press, 2005

Sheard, Bradley. *Lost Voyages: Two Centuries of Shipwrecks in the Approaches to New York*, Aqua Press, 1997

Vautier, Clarence. *The Coast of Newfoundland: The Southwest Corner*, Flanker Press, 2002

Warren, Mark D. *Campania & Lucania*, Patrick Stephens Ltd, 1993

Warwick, Ronald W. *QE2: The Cunard Line Flagship Queen Elizabeth 2*, W.W. Norton & Co., 1999

Williams, David. *Wartime Disasters at Sea*, Patrick Stephens Ltd, 1997

Wills, Elspeth. *The Fleet 1840–2008, Cunard*, The Open Agency, 2004 (2007 updated)

Magazines

Dive (UK)

Dive New Zealand

Diver (UK)

Sport Diver

Websites

www.linerwrecks.com

www.cunard.co.uk

www.lelancastria.com

www.norwayheritage.com

www.nytimes.com

www.plimsoll.org

www.theshipslist.com

www.uboat.net

www.wrecksite.eu

Other Sources

150 years of Cunard 1840–1990, official souvenir history of the Cunard line

Barron, David. Northern Shipwrecks Database

Collins, Louis W. 'Samuel Cunard – Citizen of Halifax', paper presented to the East Hants Historical Society, September 1968

Edwards, Paul D. 'Scotia', *Nautical Research Journal*, autumn 2002

HMT Lancastria Association Newsletter, February 2000

Hutchings, David F. 'Maiden Voyage of the RMS Carpathia', *Journal of the British Titanic Society*, No.3, 2002

Nissen, William. 'Last Seen in the Bermuda Triangle', paper presented at the Chicago Literary Club, 29 November 2004

Prothero, Captain W. 'Sinking of the Carpathia', *The Titanic Commutator*, Vol.22, No.1, first quarter, May 1998–July 1998

'Sir Samuel Cunard 1861–1870', *Dictionary of Canadian Biography Online*, Volume IX

Smy, W.A. 'Loyalist Cunards', *Loyalist Gazette*, autumn 1997

Stevenson, Rich. RMS Carpathia 2001, dive report from the Inspiration List

Strong, Dianne. 'In Memoriam 1948–1974 S.S. Cariba', Coral Reef Marine Center Inc., November 1974

~ INDEX ~

(Page numbers in *italics* denote illustrations)

Also published by the History Press

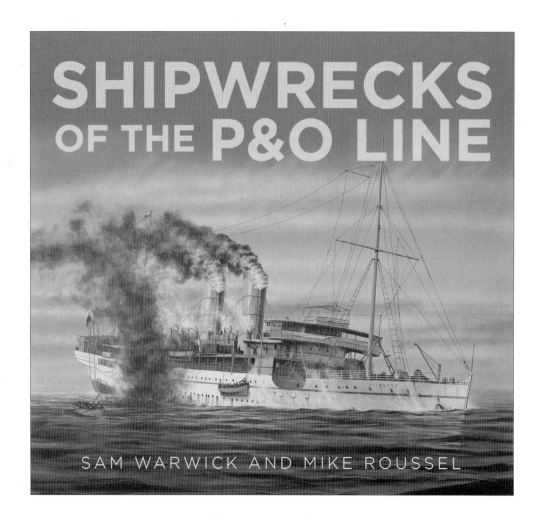

SHIPWRECKS
OF THE P&O LINE

SAM WARWICK AND MIKE ROUSSEL

The destination for history
www.thehistorypress.co.uk